I0803139

IMAGES
of America

DIXIE HIGHWAY IN INDIANA

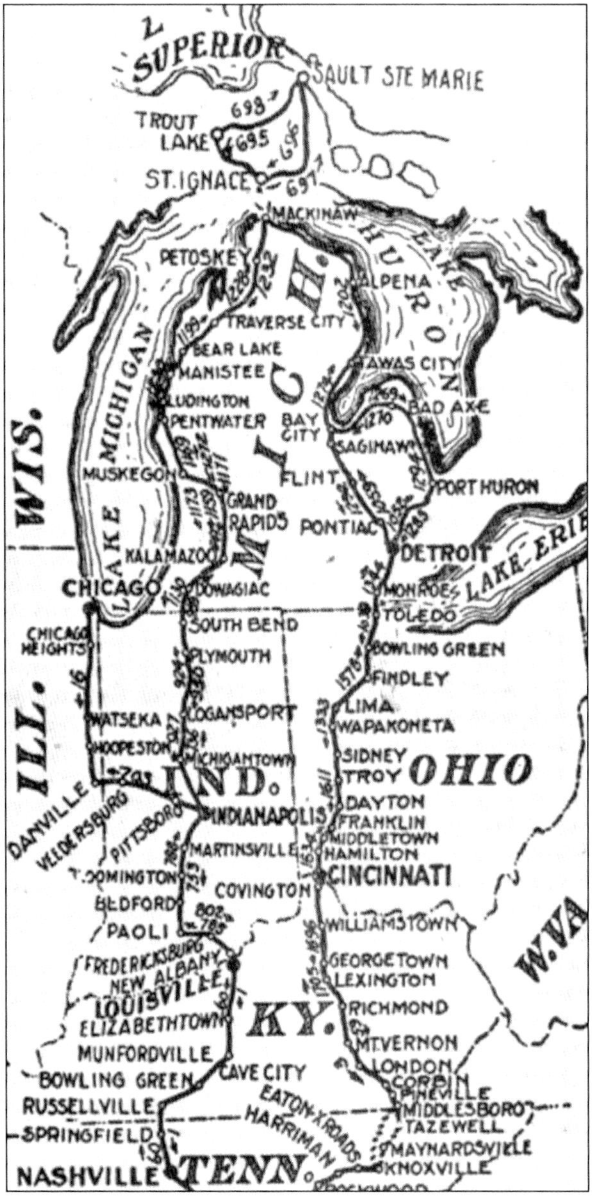

This map of the Dixie Highway was published in the *Scarborough's Official Tour Book* in 1921. Carl G. Fisher conceived the highway as the first north-south transcontinental automobile route. From the Soo Locks at Sault Ste Marie to Miami Beach, the route promoted tourist accommodations, recreational opportunities, and most importantly, warm wintertime vacations for Northerners and cool summer vacations for Southerners. (Courtesy Russell Rein.)

On the Cover: In the 1930s, the Dixiana Café and Service Station was a one-stop hub south of La Paz on the Dixie Highway where travelers purchased Texaco gasoline, rented a cabin for the night, or ate in the café. The building is still a residence but was moved behind Mac's Market and Grocery at 2083 US Highway 31. According to a local resident: "This was the Dixiana Café and Texaco Gas Station. It was run by Foster Albert and his wife, Elaine. They later sold to Paul and Salena Albert." (Courtesy Marshall County Historical Museum.)

IMAGES
of America

DIXIE HIGHWAY IN INDIANA

Russell S. Rein and Jan Shupert-Arick

ARCADIA
PUBLISHING

ISBN 978-0-7385-8367-9

Published by Arcadia Publishing
Charleston, South Carolina

Printed in the United States of America

Library of Congress Control Number: 2010931935

For all general information, please contact Arcadia Publishing:
Telephone 843-853-2070
Fax 843-853-0044
E-mail sales@arcadiapublishing.com
For customer service and orders:
Toll-Free 1-888-313-2665

Visit us on the Internet at www.arcadiapublishing.com

This book is dedicated to Carl G. Fisher, whose vision inspired America's first transcontinental automobile highways.

Contents

ACKNOWLEDGMENTS

This book was inspired by the authors' involvement with the Lincoln Highway Association and historic research for the association's 2009 national conference, which was held in South Bend, Indiana. The authors worked to complete conference materials relating to Carl G. Fisher and the beginnings of the Lincoln Highway and the Dixie Highway. In the process, the authors visited a number of archives that provided invaluable assistance.

We would like to thank the following people: Kathleen Dow at the University of Michigan's Special Collections Library, which holds the official Lincoln Highway Association archive and many materials on the Dixie Highway; Dennis Horvath for his vast knowledge of Indiana automotive history; Jim Grey, Dixie Highway researcher and explorer; Brandy Ison at Shapiro's Deli in Indianapolis; Todd Zeiger, executive director of the Northern Regional Office of Indiana Landmarks; Tim Ashley, news reporter and photographer; Mike Kelly; Kurt Garner; Linda McIver and Charles and Karen Pace for the private tour of the Bedford area; staff at the Marshall County Historical Museum; the Plymouth Parks and Recreation Department; Randy Elliott at the History Center in Fort Wayne, Indiana; the Center for History; Andrew Beckman of the Studebaker National Museum; Fred Sachtleben and Monte Gillespie, board members of the Indiana Lincoln Highway Association who shared their knowledge of antique automobiles; Jim Wright, author of *The Dixie Highway In Illinois*, for his encouragement and research assistance; Deborah Lawrence at Marian University in Indianapolis for providing assistance with the history of Millionaire Row, once the location of the Fisher and Allison estates; LaDonna Weber for providing photographs from the Argos area; and Harley Sheets, a notable postcard dealer and collector in Indiana.

A special thanks to Bill Arick for his unwavering commitment in assisting with travel details, research, and editing. Coauthor Jan Shupert-Arick extends a sincere and heartfelt thank-you to Russell Rein for serving as coauthor, for providing access to his extensive Dixie Highway collection, and for his unwavering devotion to Carl G. Fisher's "other road."

INTRODUCTION

The Dixie Highway was the north-to-south transcontinental automobile highway inspired by Hoosier Carl G. Fisher. At a time when society was changing and growing rapidly, the road opened up the South for Northerners and provided a road to Northern resorts for Southerners. The impact was significant both economically and culturally. The Dixie was, in some ways, a symbolic celebration that would work to unify the nation 50 years after the Civil War had ended.

The Dixie Highway corridor was marked from its most northern point at Sault Ste Marie, Michigan, to Miami Beach, Florida. A dogleg route from Chicago to Indianapolis was created, and parallel routes ran from Mackinaw along both of Michigan's shorelines. The main routes through the heart of the Midwest traversed Indiana, Ohio, Kentucky, and Tennessee. Travelers followed painted poles marked with red and white rectangles and the letters *DH* in the center. Early markers included a symbol that represented a bale of cotton.

Unlike the Lincoln Highway, no official guidebook with driving directions was ever published for the Dixie Highway. The best surviving source for specific driving instructions is a series of tour books published by the Scarborough Motor Guide Company of Indianapolis, Indiana. *Scarborough's Official Tour Book* was published for early automobile clubs and only covered the eastern half of the United States in various regional volumes.

Starting in 1916 and continuing through 1924, the Midwest volume *of Scarborough's Official Tour Book* carried a special *Dixie Highway Supplement* with light-blue pages. The 1916 guide for Indiana, Ohio, Michigan, Illinois, Wisconsin, and the Wolverine Auto Club (Michigan) was a huge, 1,140-page volume filled with maps, city-by-city driving instructions, and advertisements targeted to tourists. The *Dixie Highway Supplement* covered the Southern Dixie Highway routes from Kentucky to Florida. The Midwest Dixie Highway routes appeared in the regular parts of the volume.

Communities and states understood the importance of a location on the designated route. Because the Dixie Highway Association did not want to get involved in local political battles, it agreed to include new sections at the requests of various communities. Through political pressure, the Dixie grew to be a very complicated set of parallel routes, scenic routes, loops, connectors, and feeders. Travelers that filtered into the Hoosier state drove from Sault Ste Marie, Michigan, and Chicago, Illinois. In Indiana, the Dixie Highway route is current State Roads 25, 29, 37, and 933, and US Routes 31, 150, and 421. The dogleg from Chicago to Danville ran east into western Indiana along what became US Highway 136 and ran through Crawfordsville and Speedway City, entering the heart of Indianapolis at Sixteenth and Meridian Streets.

From South Bend to Indianapolis, the Dixie Highway followed the path of the historic Michigan Road that was built in the 1830s. The Michigan Road had been laid out at a width of 100 feet, making it the widest portion of the Dixie Highway along the entire route. Towns along this portion of the route included small, agricultural centers and several larger communities that served as county seats. Whether large or small, the Dixie was an economic boost and served farmers by providing an improved way to deliver goods to the marketplace.

In 1925, the Indiana Dixie Highway Association was chaired by M.E. Noblet of Indianapolis. Several vice-chairmen were appointed, including J.H. Trimble, Sen. Samuel M. Ralston, and Frank Wampler, all of Indianapolis; Carl G. Fisher of Miami; Hon. Thomas Taggart of French Lick; and E. W. Steinhart of Fort Wayne. Vice-chairman Taggart had influenced the Dixie Highway Commission in selecting the route through southern Indiana. The road from Indianapolis to New Albany skirted Taggart's internationally known French Lick Springs Hotel and mineral spa 10 miles west of Paoli. (The Dixie Highway Commission had held one of its early meetings at the French Lick Hotel and decided not to follow the more improved route that ran from Indianapolis to Madison.)

In 1926, the construction of the Dixie Highway was completed, the federal interstate highway system was established, and named highways were numbered. In much of the South, the Dixie became US Route 41, while the Dixie route sections in Kentucky, Ohio, and Michigan were numbered as US Routes 25 and 31.

The route of the Dixie continued to be significant for automotive travel long after the numbered highways replaced the red and white DH signs. Until the superhighway interstate system was completed in the 1960s and early 1970s, at least some portions of the old Dixie route continued to function as an integral part of the American commercial and recreational landscape. In 1977, the last portion of Interstate 75 was completed, connecting Sault Ste Marie, Michigan, with Tampa, Florida, and the era of the Dixie Highway as a key national transportation route ended.

Today, many people have heard of the Dixie Highway as parts of the road continue to carry the Dixie name. Most people, however, think the road named Dixieway is just a local road, not realizing it is part of the nation's second transcontinental automobile road and a road that greatly impacted the nation in the early 20th century. Retracing the path of the Dixie Highway today is a challenge. In Indiana, only three known sections of the road still carry the name. Near the Michigan-Indiana state line in Roseland and South Bend, several sections of the road are still named Dixie Way North and South. South of Indianapolis in the Bedford area, the road is designated the Dixie Highway.

This volume, *The Dixie Highway in Indiana,* was inspired by a deep appreciation of a Hoosier named Carl G. Fisher. Fisher inspired the creation of the Dixie and Lincoln Highways at a time when automobiles were known as machines, and the nation's roads and bridges were not capable of carrying automobile traffic.

Fisher was well connected within the automotive world, and he dreamed of what could be for automobile owners and the growing automotive industry. His unwavering genius and unending energy would change the world. The southern terminus of the Dixie Highway was Miami Beach; Fisher literally pulled it from the bottom of the bay. The phenomenon of winter migration from the North to Florida began in earnest with the Dixie Highway and has continued since.

Fisher was successful in undertaking emerging automobile-related businesses and building them into state-of-the-art enterprises. From a bicycle shop, an automobile dealership, the Prest-O-Lite Auto Lamp Company, the Indianapolis Motor Speedway, and the Lincoln and Dixie Highways, Fisher's work symbolizes the achievement of Indiana's automobile- and road-building industries. Following the success of the Indianapolis Motor Speedway, Carl G. Fisher began to focus on the creation of a transcontinental highway system in response to the poor condition of the nation's roads. He began by organizing and inspiring the Lincoln Highway and then the Dixie Highway. Through huge private efforts and the formation of the Lincoln Highway Association, Fisher pieced together an effective campaign and received backing from Henry Bourne Joy, the president of the Packard Motor Car Company, and from Frank Seiberling, president of Goodyear Tire and Rubber Company. Between 1913 and 1925, the Lincoln and Dixie Highways were hugely successful. Their success inspired local, state, and the federal governments to take responsibility for good roads, improved bridges, and the growth of tourism industries.

The involvement of Indiana automobile companies and the Packard Motor Car Company in Detroit assisted Fisher in his road projects. To promote support for good roads, Fisher along with automobile racers and manufacturers, set off across the nation on automobile tours. The tours mapped routes, tested vehicles, and promoted the routes to communities along the way. Caught in a rainstorm late one night, Fisher and his companions came to a fork in the road. Fisher saw a sign on a pole above the road and climbed the pole to read a sign posted high above the road. The message on the sign—"Chew Battle Ax Plug"—offered no assistance and reinforced his belief that automobile owners deserved improved travel conditions. Thus, his vision for coast-to-coast travel was born.

On September 10, 1912, Fisher and James A. Allison organized a dinner party at Das Deutsches Haus, or the German House, in Indianapolis (now known as the Athenaeum). At this meeting, Fisher unveiled his plan for a highway spanning the country from New York City to California. The Indianapolis newspapers covered the dinner meeting and included a photograph of the automobile leaders in attendance. Frank Seiberling, president of Goodyear, immediately pledged $300,000 and took on a leadership role in the Lincoln Highway Association, serving as a board member or officer until the association completed its work and closed its doors in 1928. Henry Joy, president of Packard Motor Car Company, pledged $150,000 for the proposed roadway. Joy also became a leader in the coast-to-coast highway cause and was the person who suggested the road be named in honor of Abraham Lincoln as living memorial to the martyred president.

As work progressed on completing America's first transcontinental highway, Fisher had turned his sights to other projects, in particular, the improvement of the jungle of swamps known as Miami Beach. Southern Florida, as Fisher envisioned the state, could be the perfect vacation spot for Midwestern automobile executives and their families tired of frigid winter weather. But to get vacationers to his resort, Fisher, nicknamed the "Father of the Lincoln Highway," had to use his promotional talents once again to nurture the birth of another highway. On December 4, 1914, he wrote to Indiana governor Samuel Ralston suggesting that a highway be built from Chicago to Miami. Ralston believed in good roads and supported Fisher's proposal. Ralston hosted fellow governors from Illinois, Ohio, Kentucky, Tennessee, and Georgia for a meeting about the highway, which was held in Chattanooga, Tennessee, on April 3, 1915.

The governors agreed and pledged support of the road by appointing two persons from each state to be directors of the association along with seven other directors, including Carl G. Fisher. In a promotional bid for the road, Fisher lead 15 cars from Indianapolis to Miami on a Dixie Highway path-finding tour similar to his earlier Lincoln Highway tour. A lasting tribute must be made to William S. Gilbreath, Carl G. Fisher's partner in the Dixie Highway idea. Gilbreath, the secretary of the Hoosier Auto Club in Indianapolis, had also participated in the 1913 cross-country Hoosier Auto Tour. A famous photograph of Gilbreath at the end of tour in San Francisco with his hands in the air holding a pennant became known as "The Spirit of the Lincoln Highway." A stature in bronze was made based on this photograph and was placed in the downtown Detriot AAA office (see page 92). At Fisher's request, Gilbreath was named field secretary of the Dixie Highway Association and began promoting the route. From the ceremony in Martinsville, Indiana, that marked the opening of the road on September 15, 1915, to the disbanding of the Dixie Highway Association in 1927, the communities that were touched by the road were greatly impacted. The increase in tourist traffic demanded more hotels, tourist cabins, tourist camps, cafés, and service stations. Local businesses, such as the Dixiana Café in La Paz, Indiana, sprouted up to meet the needs of the new transcontinental automobile travelers. In the process, the nation was forever changed by the vision of a Hoosier named Carl G. Fisher.

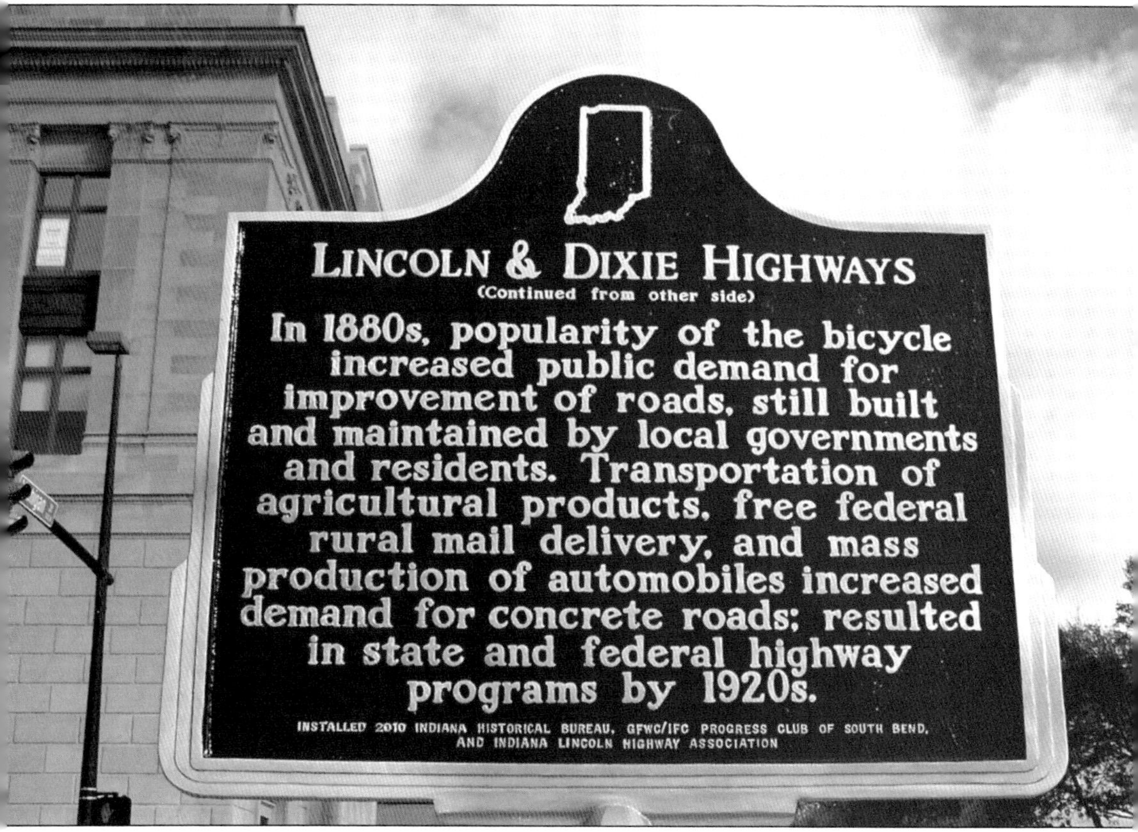

This Dixie Highway-Lincoln Highway historic marker located across the street from the American Trust Bank Building was dedicated in South Bend, Indiana, on October 2, 2010. The marker was placed at the intersection of the original Lincoln Highway and Dixie Highway routes by the Indiana Historical Bureau, the GFWC/IFC Progress Club of South Bend, and the Indiana Lincoln Highway Association. The crossing today marks the intersection of Michigan Street (the Dixie Highway/Michigan Road) and Washington Street. (Courtesy Tim Ashley.)

One

South Bend
Transcontinental Crossroads

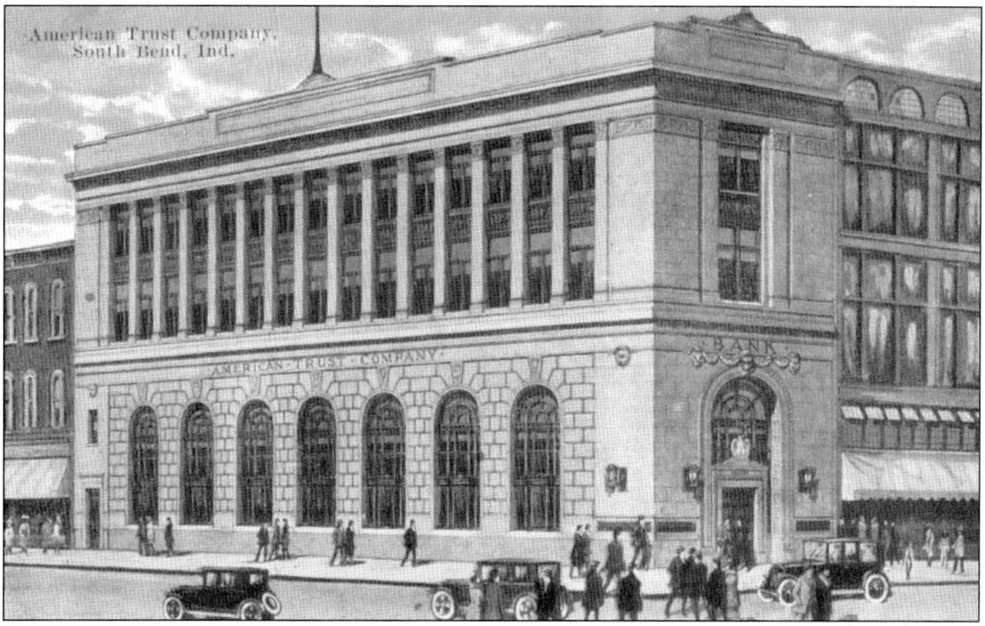

The American Trust Bank began business in 1904 at the northwest corner of Michigan and Washington Streets in South Bend. This four-story limestone building was constructed in 1922–1923. The main level featured a detailed high ceiling, tall palisade windows, 21 teller windows, and marble surfaces. A large, four-sided clock was added at the corner of the intersection in 1913, but it was removed and later restored for placement in the atrium of the First Source Bank Building in the adjoining block. A new clock has been placed on the street outside the original building, which is now known the American Trust Place. (Courtesy Jan Shupert-Arick.)

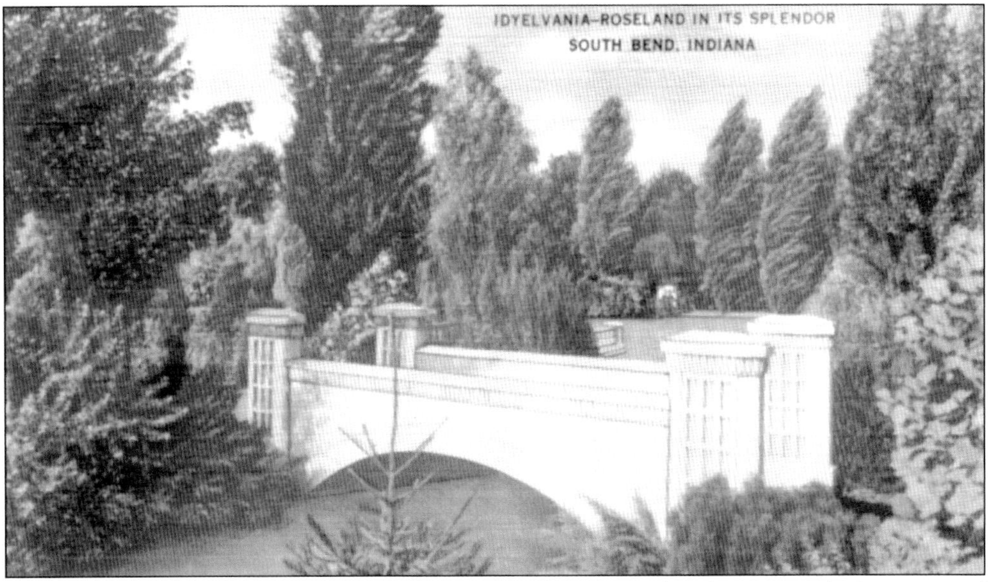

Idyelvania was a picturesque tourist attraction located in Roseland, Indiana, near the University of Notre Dame. This corridor extends from the Indiana-Michigan state line to South Bend. Roseland is an unincorporated village with a main street named Dixie Way North. Many small businesses and motels once lined this section of the road. Today, the area serves as a major commercial hotel-motel district. This section has been designated State Road 933 and carried traffic from the old US Routes 31 and 33. (Courtesy Center for History.)

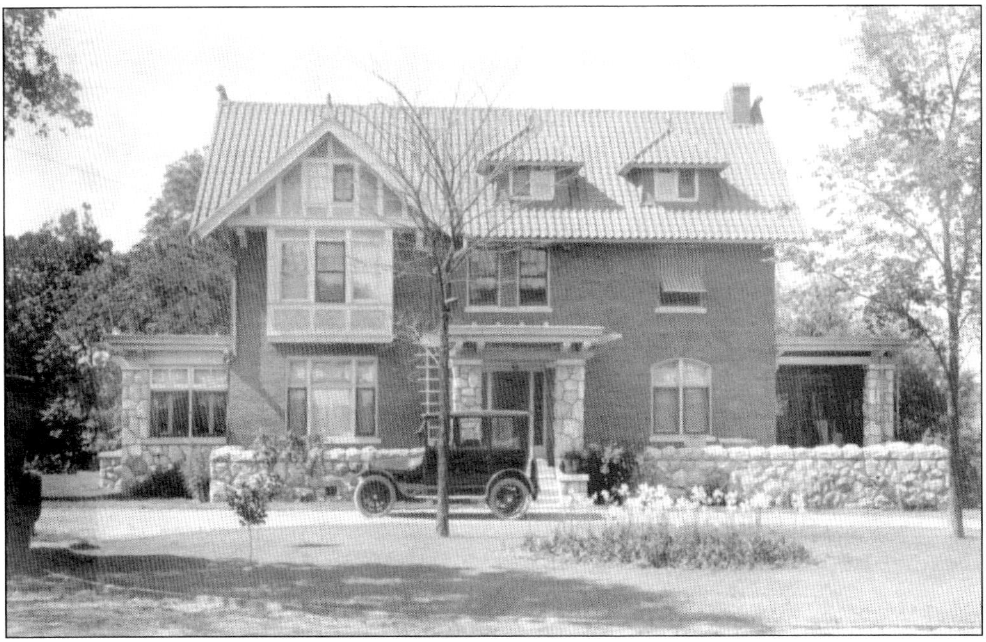

This photograph captures the feeling of the Roseland area when it was filled with beautiful private homes on long lots. This home stood near the intersection of Cleveland Road and Michigan Street (Dixie Highway/US Route 31 north of South Bend and Notre Dame). Many large homes were demolished during the road expansion and when more commercial buildings were erected to serve a growing population. (Courtesy Center for History.)

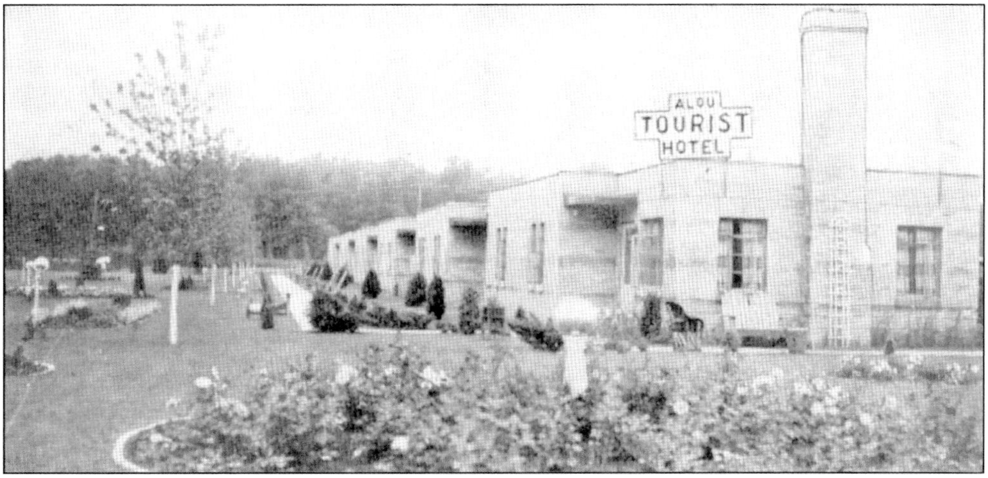

The Alou Tourist Hotel, built in the 1930s, and later the Dixie Village Motel were two of the many motels built along Dixie Way North between Niles, Michigan, and South Bend. The Alou boasted flower and rose gardens complete with gazing balls. The Alou's open lawn areas provided relaxing spaces for travelers, who could also enjoy the wooden lawn furniture placed around the grounds. The Dixie Villa (below) was a larger complex of buildings with a shared central lawn space. Painted white posts and neon signs attracted tourists to stop for the night. (Both, courtesy Russell Rein.)

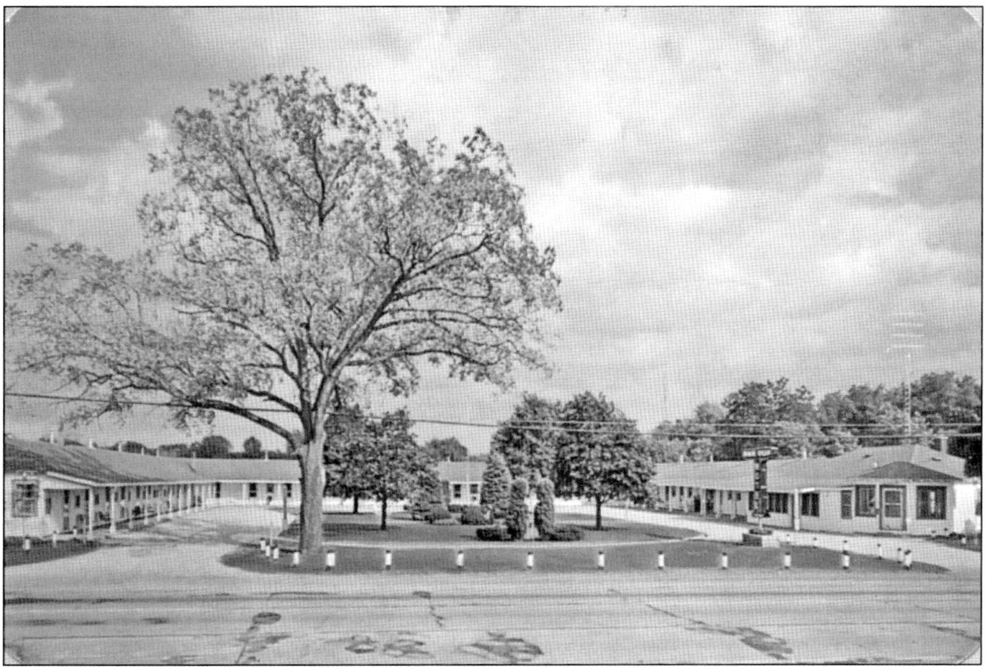

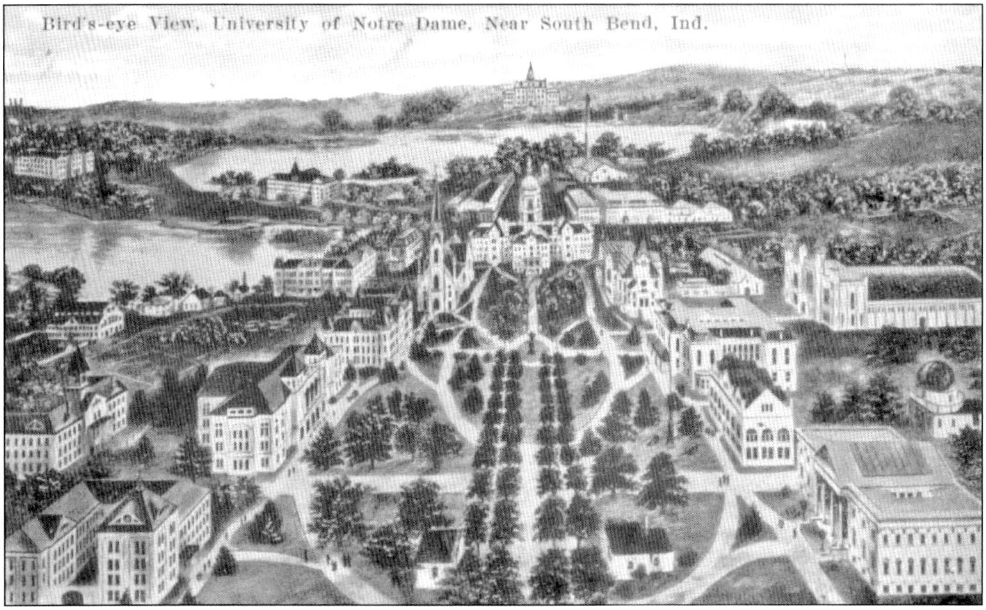

The University of Notre Dame was founded in 1842 by Fr. Edward Sorin, who became the school's first president. The university first enrolled women undergraduates in 1972. Today, Notre Dame's female students make up 47 percent of enrollment. St. Mary's College was established for female students when Notre Dame was an all-boys' school. The famous Golden Dome of Notre Dame's Main Building is a centerpiece of the campus. Today, it serves primarily as administration offices, although it still contains classrooms. The building was erected in 1879, the same year the previous structure was destroyed by fire. At one time it was a hub where students learned, ate meals, and resided. The Golden Dome was added in 1882 and was regilded in 2005. The gilding process uses about a fist-full of gold leaf to cover the entire structure. Atop the Golden Dome, a 19-foot-tall, 4,000-pound statue of Mary, the Mother of God, Notre Dame (meaning "Our Lady"), brings the Main Building to a height of 187 feet. (Both, courtesy Center for History.)

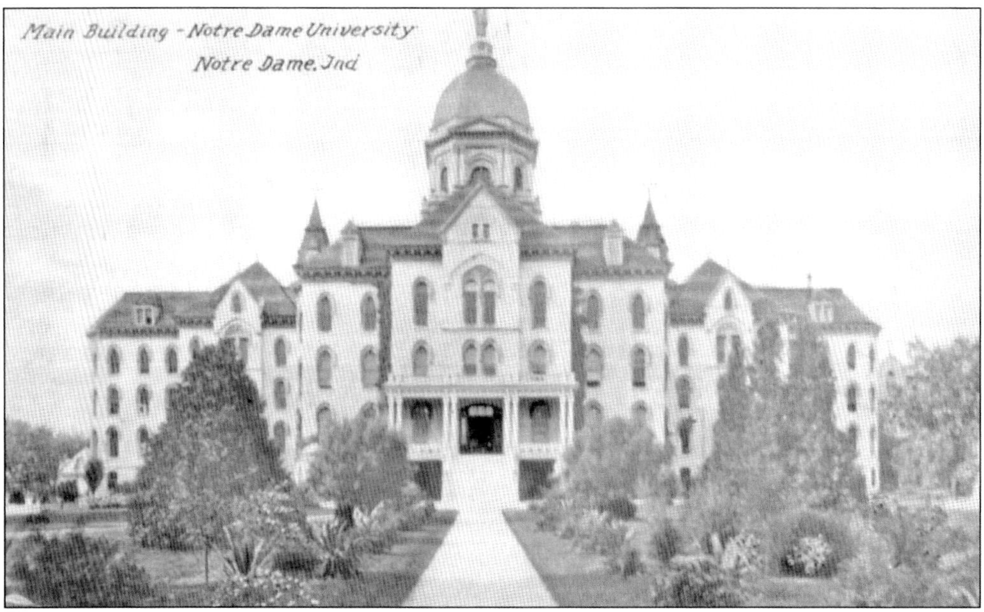

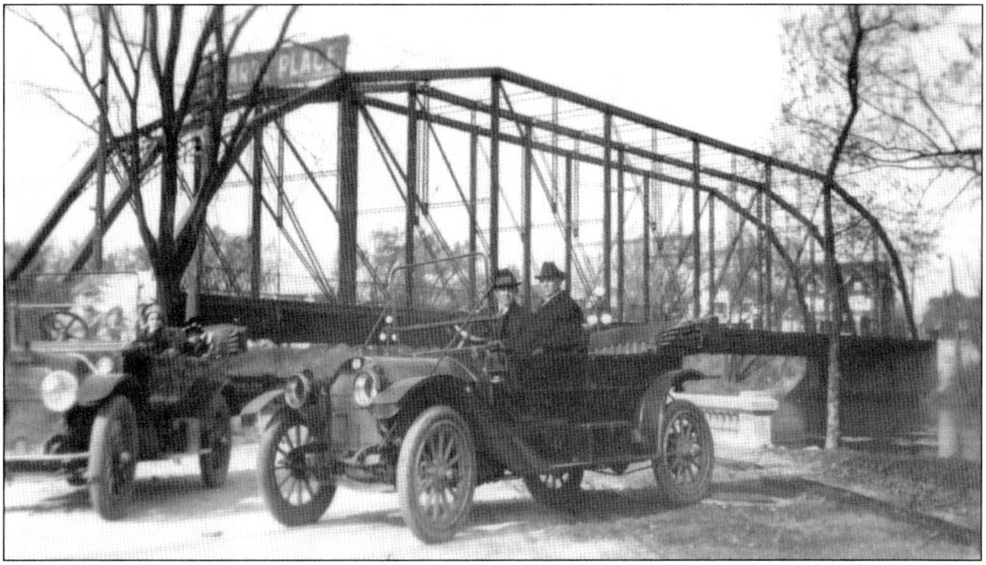

Early automobile owners pause on the southeast side of the metal truss bridge built in the late 19th century to provide a northern gateway to downtown along Leeper Park. The bridge span reads "Navarre Place," which was the neighborhood named for Pierre Navarre, South Bend's first settler and a fur trader. Navarre's cabin still stands in Leeper Park today. (Courtesy Center for History.)

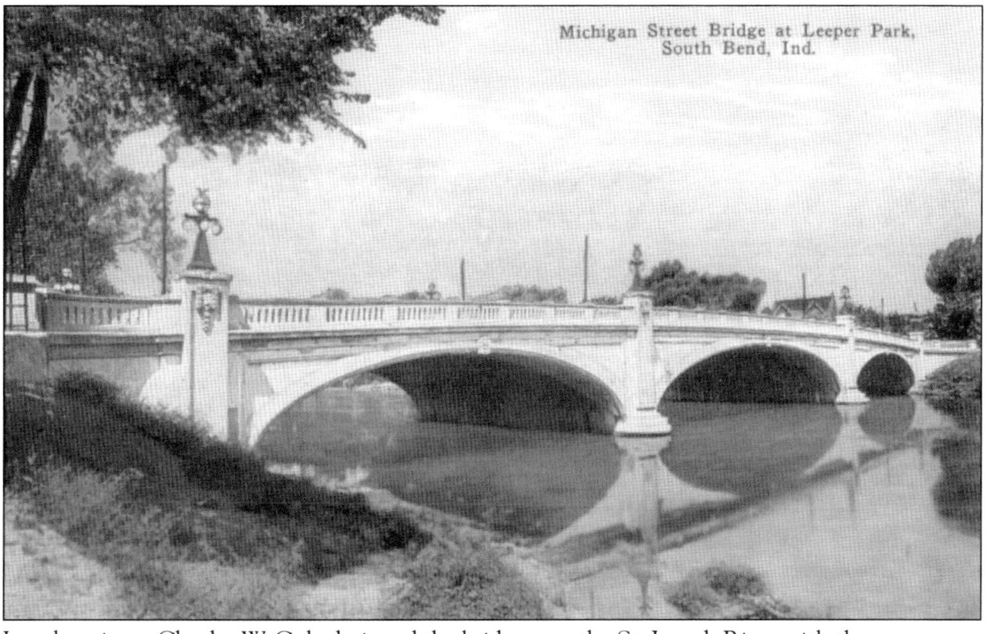

Local engineer Charles W. Cole designed the bridge over the St. Joseph River with three concrete spans that stretched nearly 300 feet from bank to bank. The bridge was built in 1914 by Kuert Contracting Company of Indianapolis, Indiana, at a cost of $93,663. The rails and bridge details were made of limestone from Bedford, Indiana. The ornate pier-towers were topped with lamp posts manufactured by the Cutter Light Company of South Bend. In the era of the automobile, street lighting became a symbol of civic pride and local prosperity. The Michigan Street Bridge has been restored and continues to serve as a South Bend landmark. (Courtesy Center for History.)

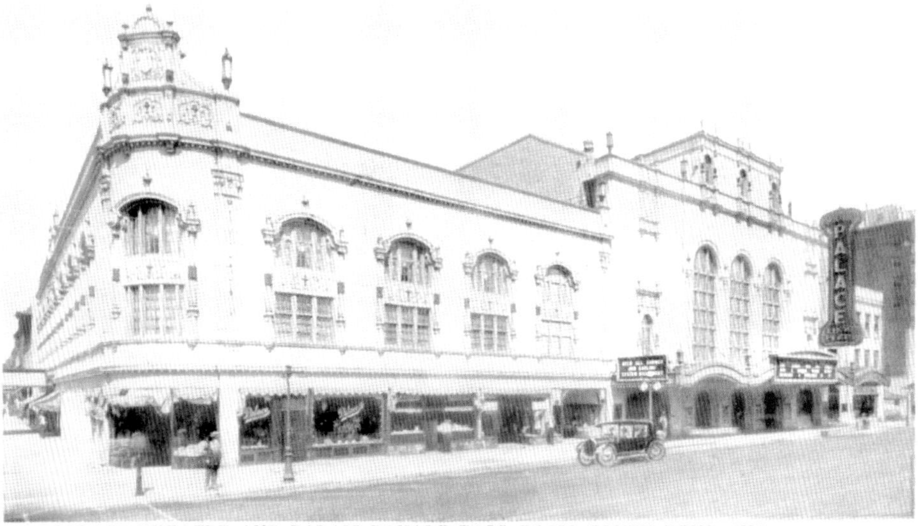

4726—PALACE THEATRE AND PALAIS ROYALE BALL ROOM, SOUTH BEND, IND.

The Palais Royale, known later as the Palace Theatre, was built in 1921 as a vaudeville house and part of the Orpheum theater chain. Vaudeville shows ran continuously with a new act every 10 minutes. Patrons could purchase admission for 22¢ and enjoy the day's new acts as they made their way on and off the stage. Architect J.S. Aroner from Chicago envisioned the theater as a little palace. The Palace hosted the world premiere of *Knute Rockne: All American*, starring Ronald Regan, Rudy Vallée, Bob Hope, and Kate Smith, in 1940. In 1959, the board of the Palace Theatre voted for demolition. The theater was saved from the wrecking ball by Mrs. E.M. Morris, who purchased the Palace and sold the building to the city for $1. In recognition of her efforts, the theater was officially renamed the Morris Civic Auditorium. Michigan Street in South Bend carried the Dixie Highway. (Both, courtesy Center for History.)

Michigan Street looking North from Colfax Avenue, South Bend, Ind.

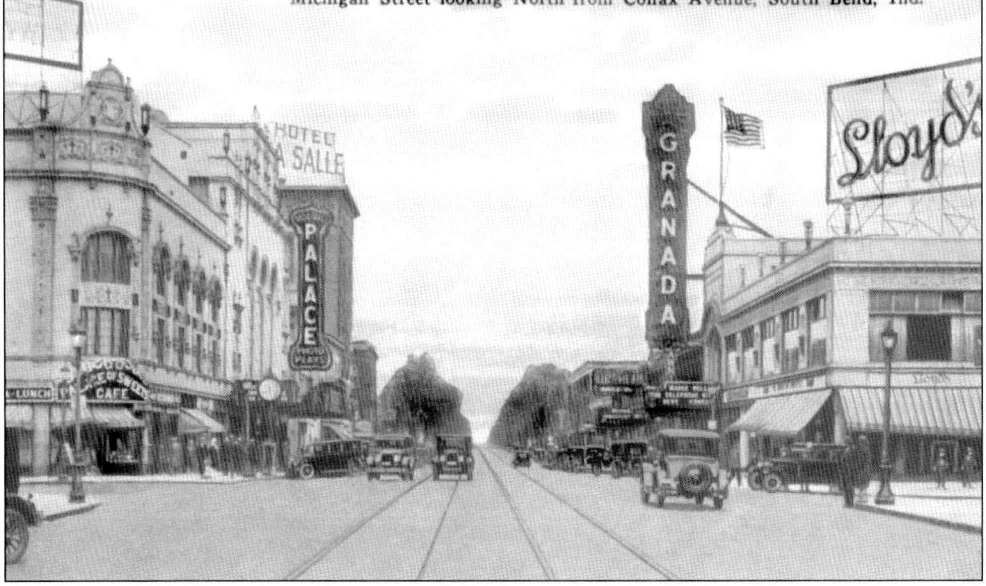

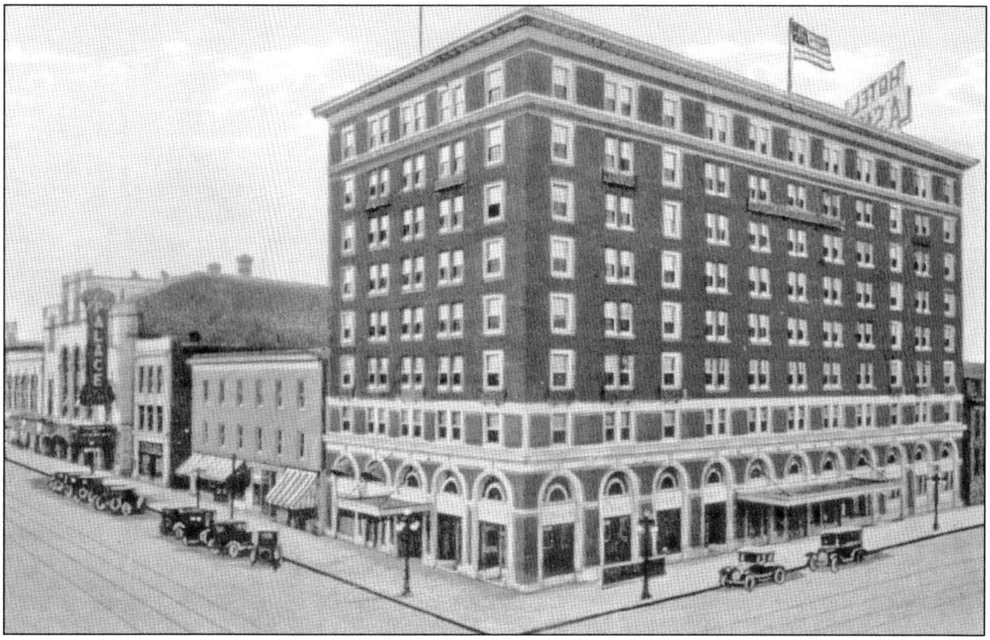

Built in 1921 at 237 North Michigan Street, the LaSalle Hotel stood at the terminus of the South Shore Electric Interurban, which ran between Randolph Street in Chicago and South Bend. The LaSalle became a hub for travelers arriving in South Bend. Serving the nation as the last interurban, the electric commuter trains of the Chicago South Shore & South Bend Railroad still run between South Bend and Chicago, but the eastern terminus has been relocated to the South Bend Regional Airport. (Courtesy Center for History.)

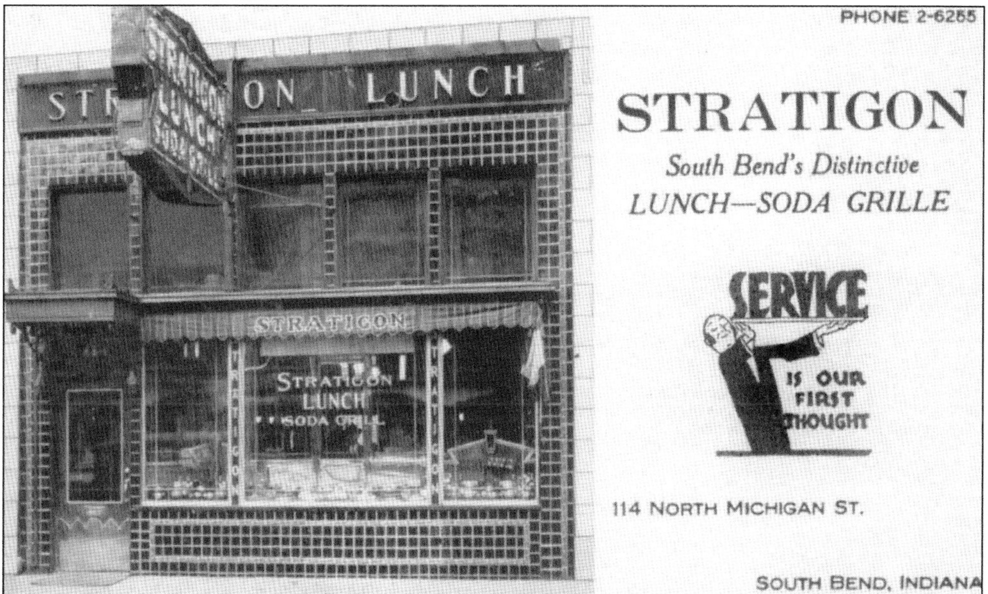

The Stratigon Restaurant was located between the LaSalle Hotel and the Morris Civic Auditorium and was famous for its lunch selection, soda fountain, and grill. It provided a much-needed service to touring artists, hotel guests, train and automobile travelers, and the locals. (Courtesy Center for History.)

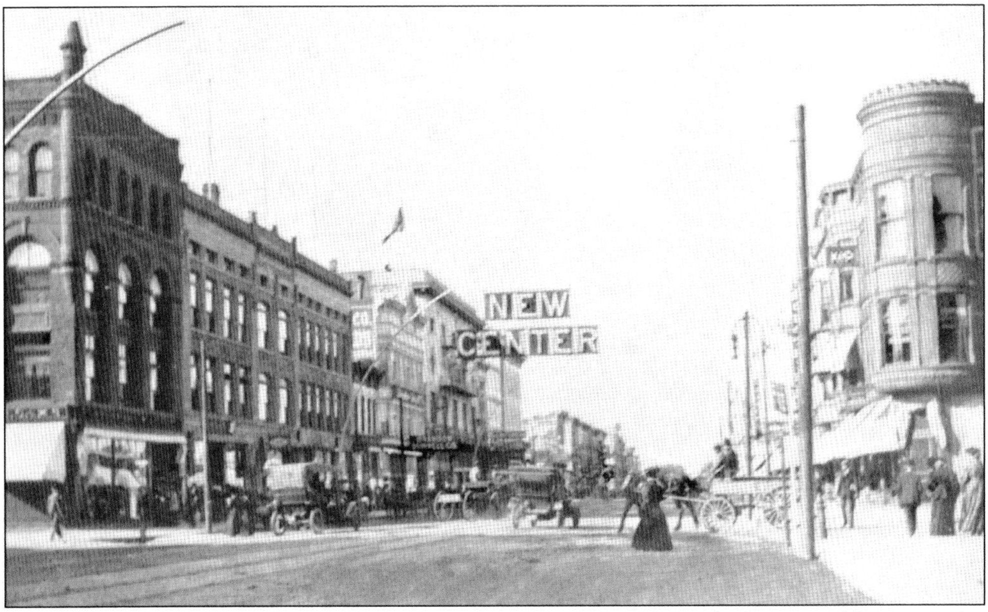

This image of downtown South Bend captures the transition from the horse and buggy to the automobile. The New Center of the city was celebrated with electric lights. (Courtesy Center for History.)

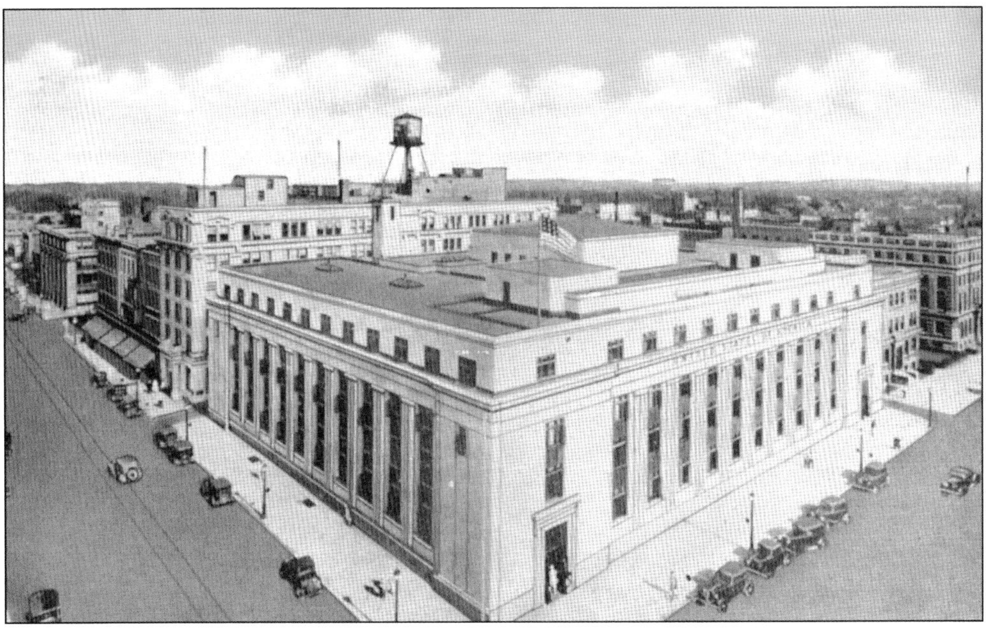

The four-story Federal Building at Jefferson and Lafayette Streets was built of limestone. It originally served as the South Bend Post Office, but is now the Federal District Court Building and home of the FBI. (Courtesy Jan Shupert-Arick.)

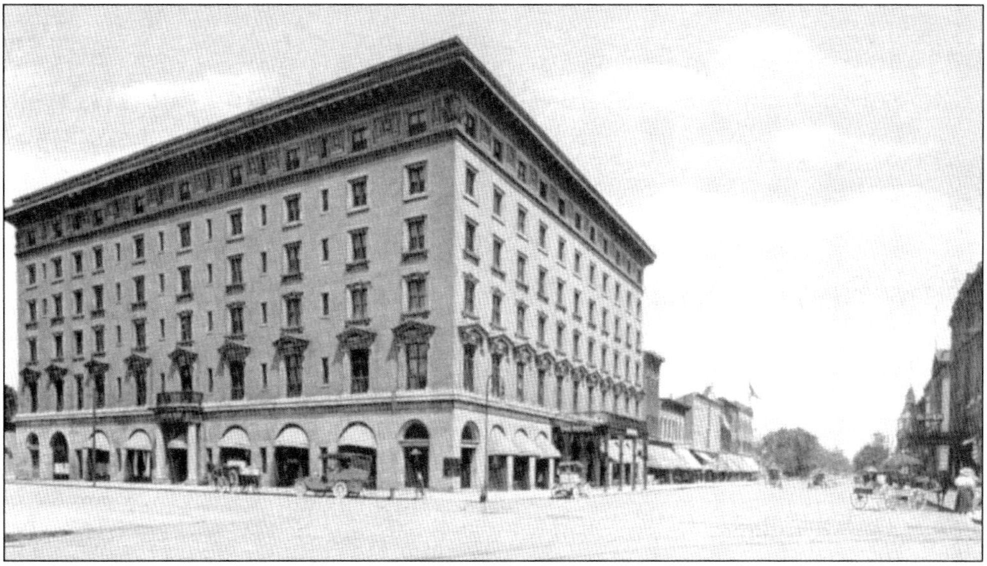

The Oliver Company became the world's largest plow manufacturer and attracted businessmen to South Bend, which, at the time, lacked adequate hotel space. James Oliver built the Oliver Hotel at Main and Washington Streets to impress travelers with 136 rooms and an elaborate lobby decorated with fine furniture and painted murals. The hotel opened on December 20, 1899, and 2,000 guests attended its gala. Local advertisements lauded the Oliver as one of the finest hotels in the United States. On the lower level was a haberdashery and an automobile garage where tourists could safely park their cars overnight. The hotel served as the Control Station, offering services similar to AAA today for travelers on the Lincoln Highway from 1915 to 1926. The hotel eventually became the Pick-Oliver Hotel and fell into decline. It was razed during the 1970s. (Above, courtesy Russell Rein; below, courtesy Center for History.)

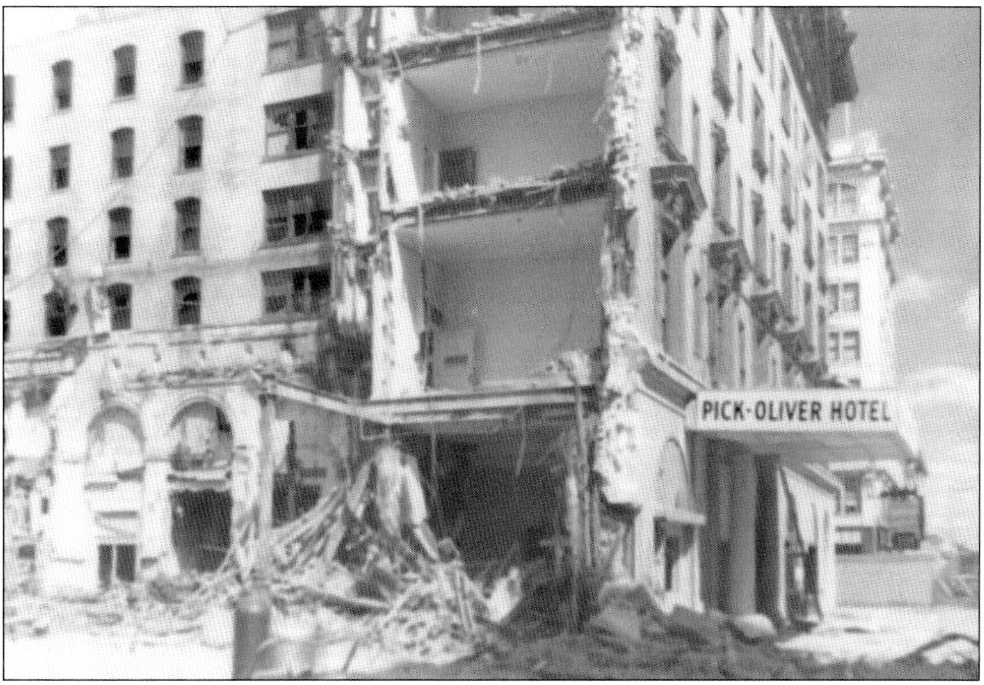

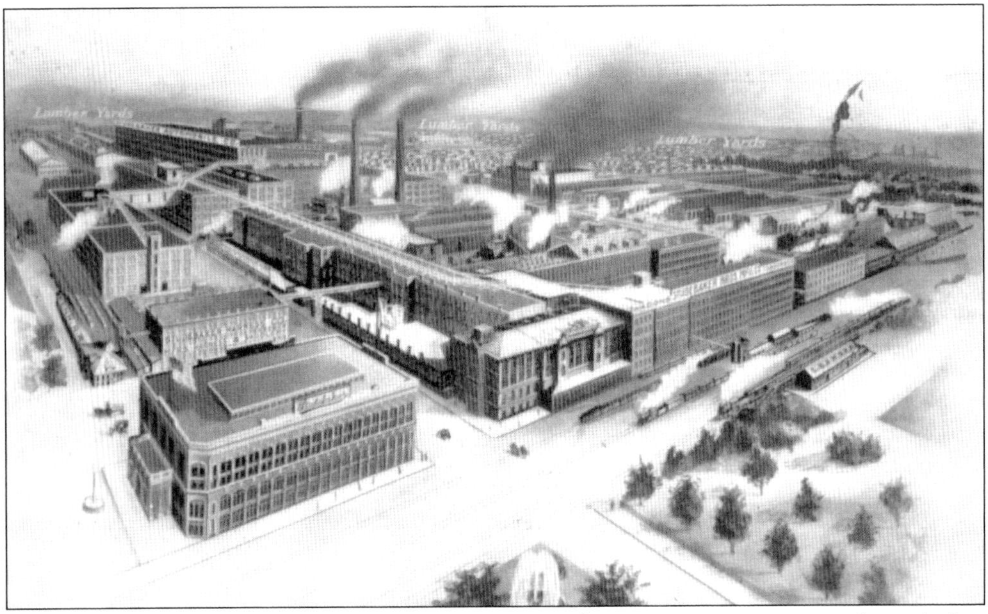

This aerial view shows the Studebaker factory's massive layout; it was to grow even larger before it closed in 1963. When Main Street became one-way, the Dixie Highway passed through the Studebaker factory area with automobile manufacturing buildings on both sides. The Studebaker brothers had supported the Lincoln Highway project and provided cars for transcontinental highway path-finding adventures. (Courtesy Jan Shupert-Arick.)

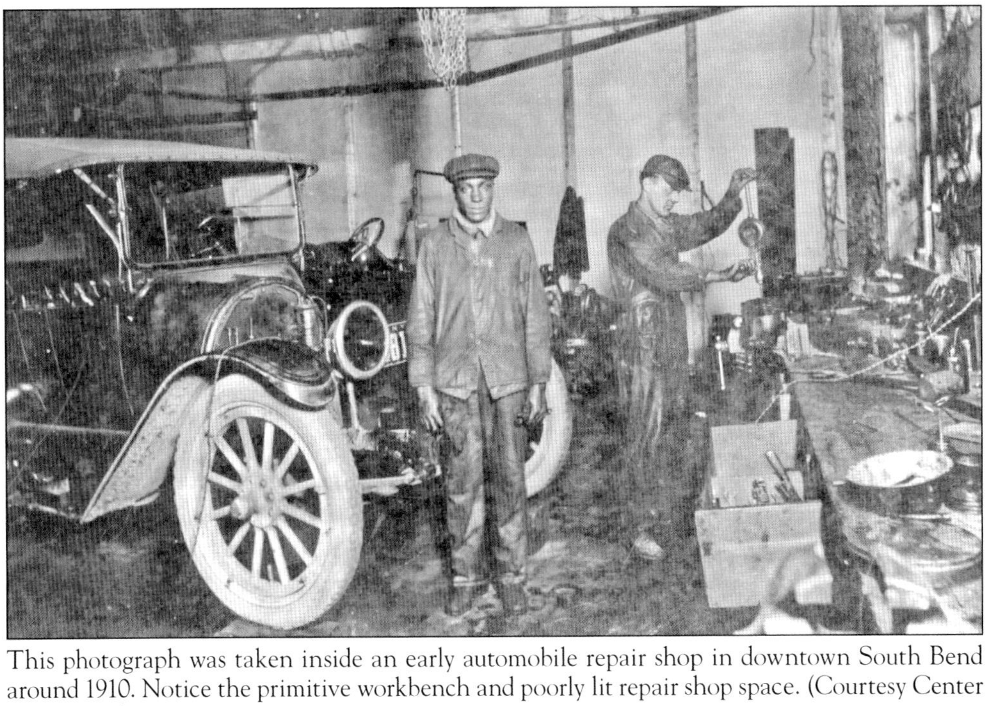

This photograph was taken inside an early automobile repair shop in downtown South Bend around 1910. Notice the primitive workbench and poorly lit repair shop space. (Courtesy Center for History.)

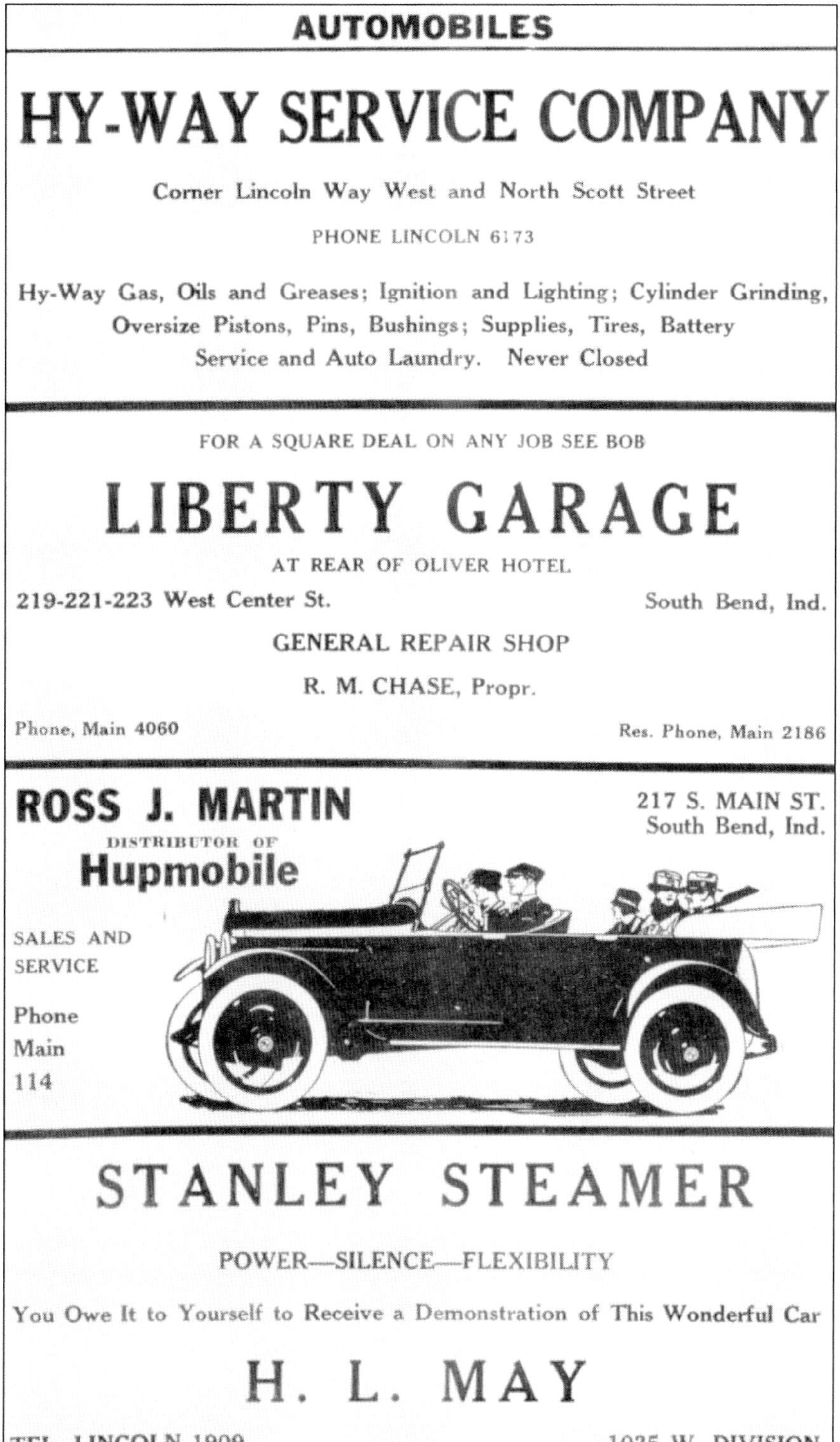

South Bend advertisement shows businesses in the area that catered to automobile owners. (Courtesy Center for History.)

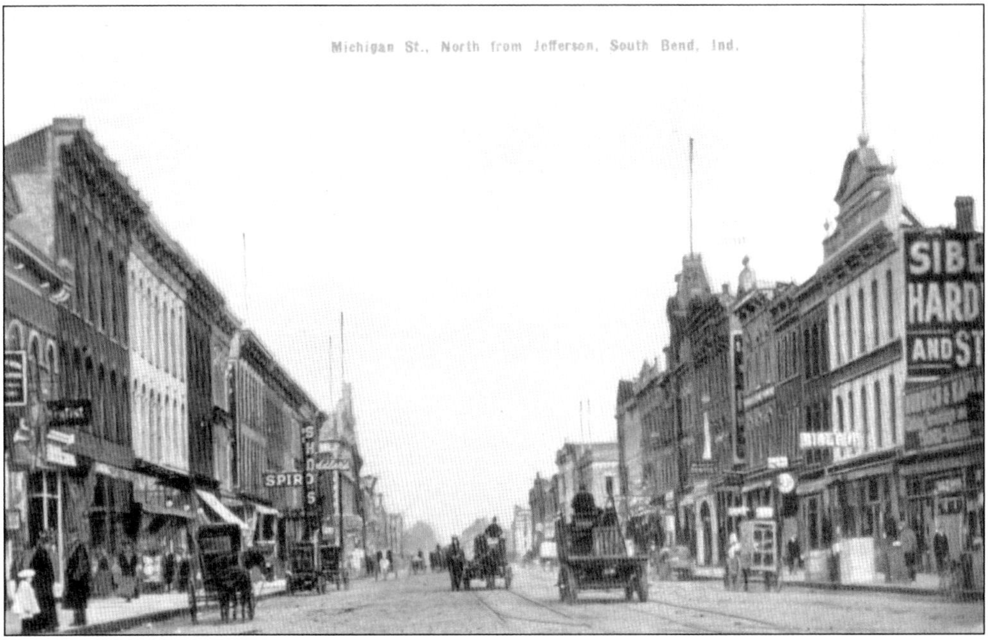

In this view of Michigan Street looking north from Jefferson Street, Spiro's Store, Robertson's Department Store, and S.S. Kresge's Department Store and Soda Fountain are on the left. The State Theater is on the east side, and Planter's Peanut Shoppe was just down the road at Wayne and Michigan Streets. This area was a popular place to be on Saturday nights in the 1930s and 1940s. (Courtesy Center for History.)

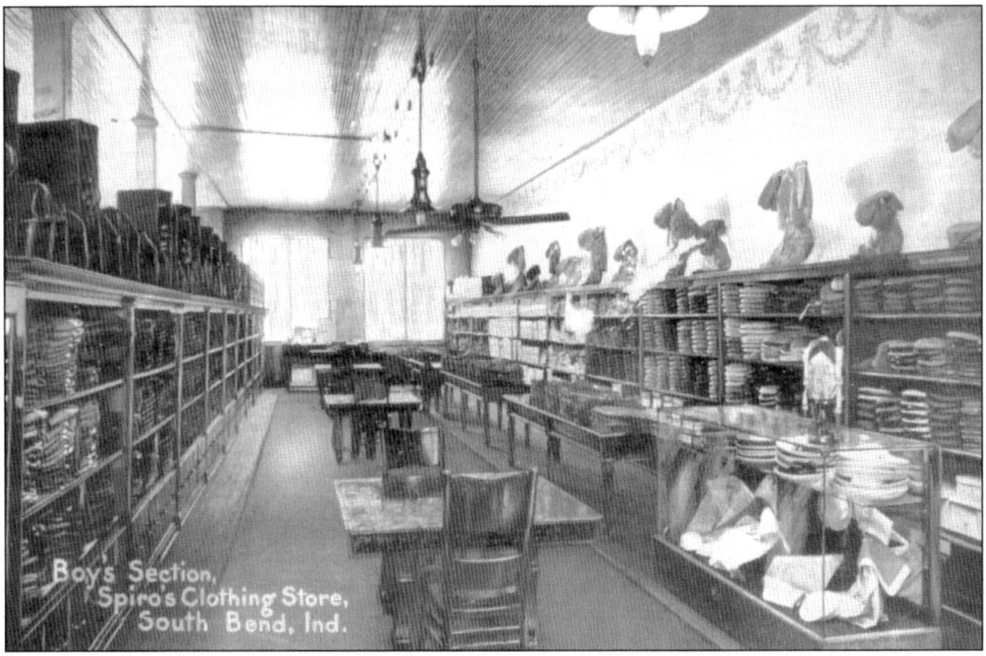

This is a rare interior photograph taken in the boys' department of Spiro's Clothing Store. The Spiro family's success led to their generous support in building the South Bend Public Library at the corner of Wayne and Lafayette Streets. (Courtesy Center for History.)

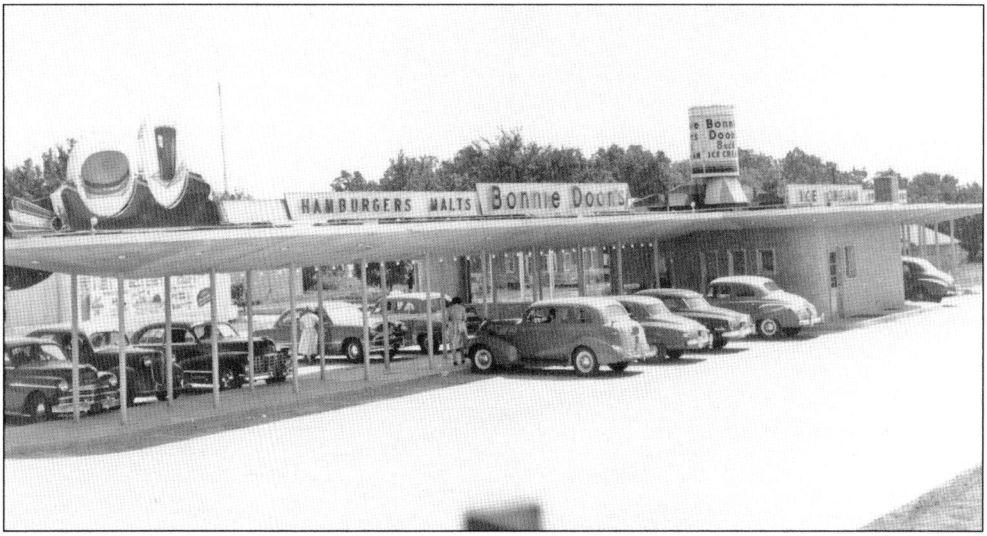

Bonnie Doon's Drive-Ins were popular hangout spots for teenagers and adults alike. The Muldoon family produced ice cream products sold at their drive-ins in South Bend and Mishawaka. The drive-ins were located on Lincolnway East and West and on North and South Michigan Street (the Dixie Highway/US Route 31). (Courtesy Center for History.)

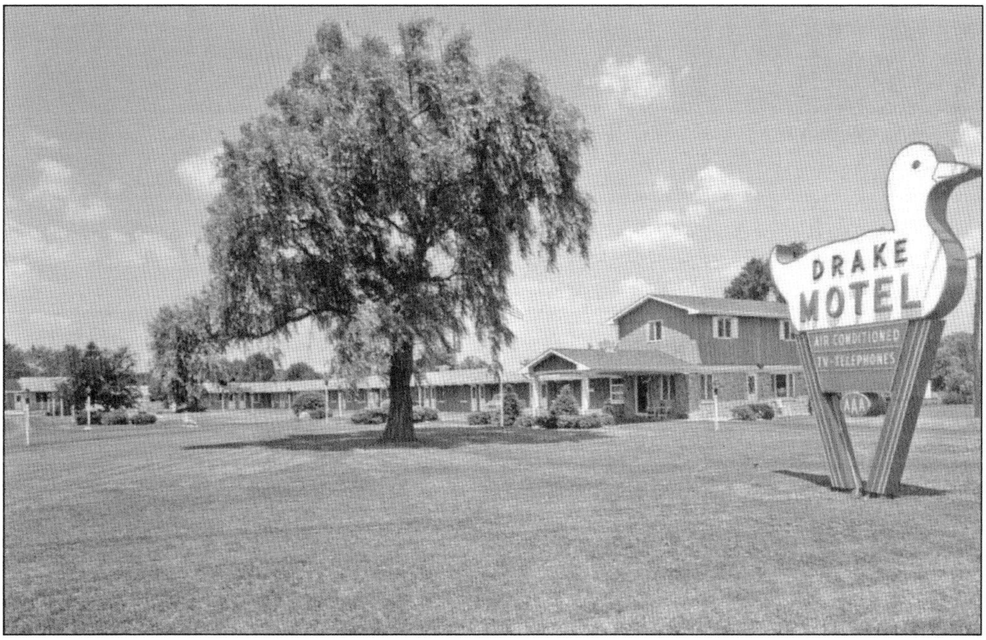

The Drake Motel was located at 60971 US Route 31 on Dixieway South. The motel was built on the northwest corner of the intersection of US 31 and Kern Road. The large Drake sign was lit with neon and advertised the AAA–approved hotel's air conditioning, television, and telephone services. The motel was replaced with a Comfort Inn several years ago, but locals miss the Drake as part of South Bend's southern gateway. (Courtesy Center for History.)

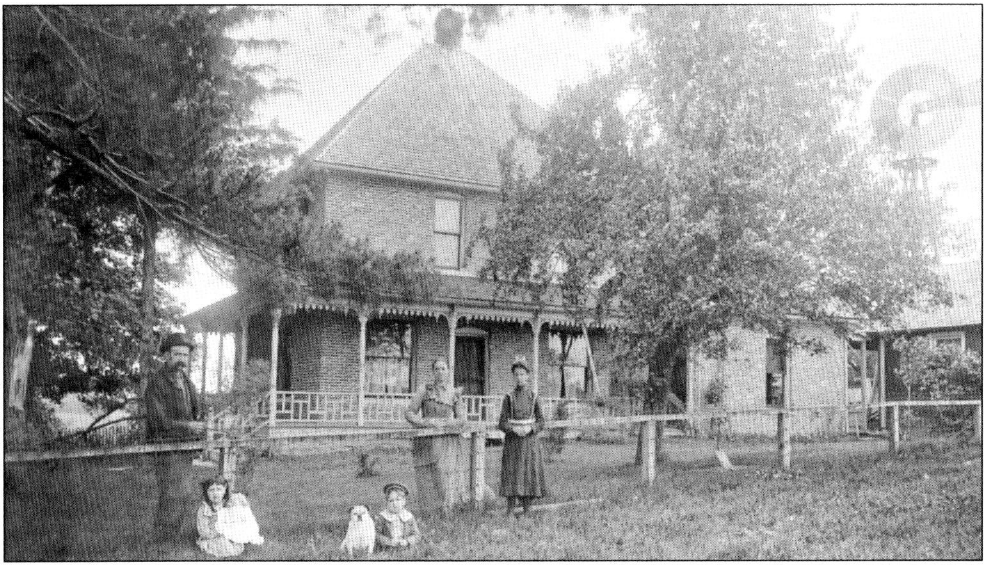

This photograph captures the Phillip Schaffer family farm on US Route 31 in the Gulivoire Park area south of South Bend. The farm is located just south of South Lawn Cemetery and has been in Schaffer family for four generations. The site of the brick farmhouse and large barn was one of several prominent farms on this section of the Dixie Highway. Hogs, dairy herds, sheep, goats, chickens, horses, crops of oats, corn shocks, haystacks, and fields of golden wheat were all common sights. (Courtesy Todd Zeiger.)

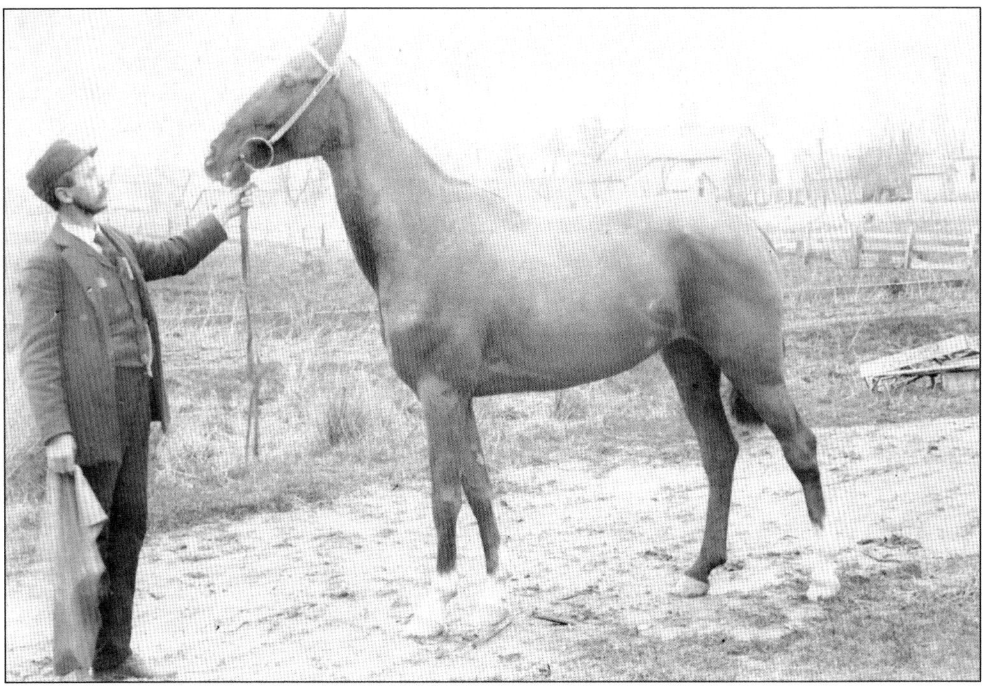

David Sherman was a horse breeder in the Lakeville area and was well known for racing horses up and down the Dixie Highway. In Plymouth, the town council passed an ordinance that prohibited horse racing within the city limits along the old Michigan Road and the Dixie Highway. (Courtesy Jan Shupert-Arick.)

Two

THE DIXIEWAY
TRAVELING THROUGH LAKEVILLE, LA PAZ, AND PLYMOUTH

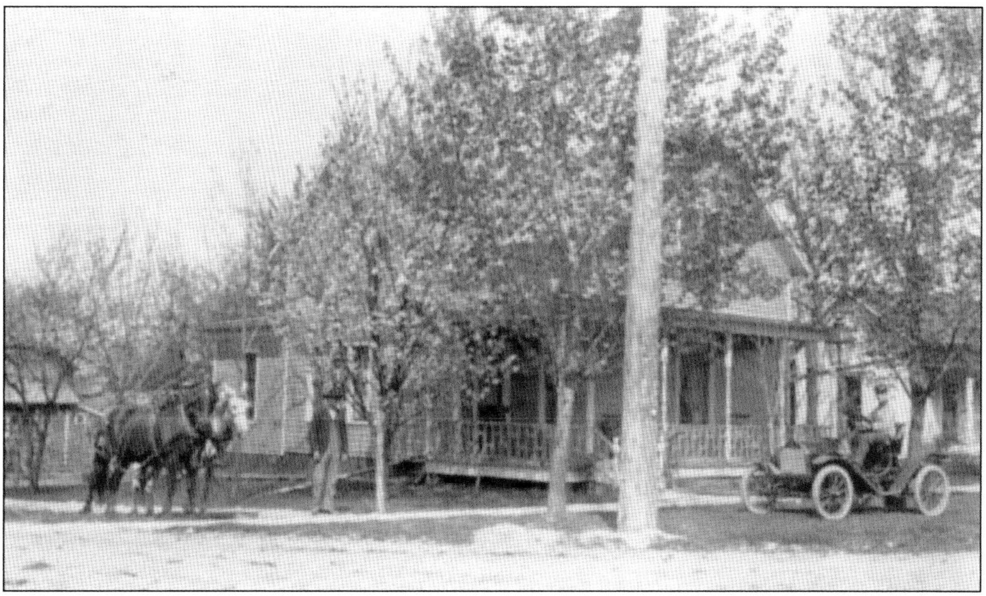

La Paz is a small town in Marshall County's North Township. The town was founded in 1873 and named for La Paz, Bolivia. At the time of its founding, it was served by the Chicago branch of the Baltimore and Ohio Railroad (B&O), now CSX. Following the route of the Michigan Road, the Dixie Highway cut through the heart of the La Paz, which is located just north of US Route 6. (Courtesy Marshall County Historical Museum.)

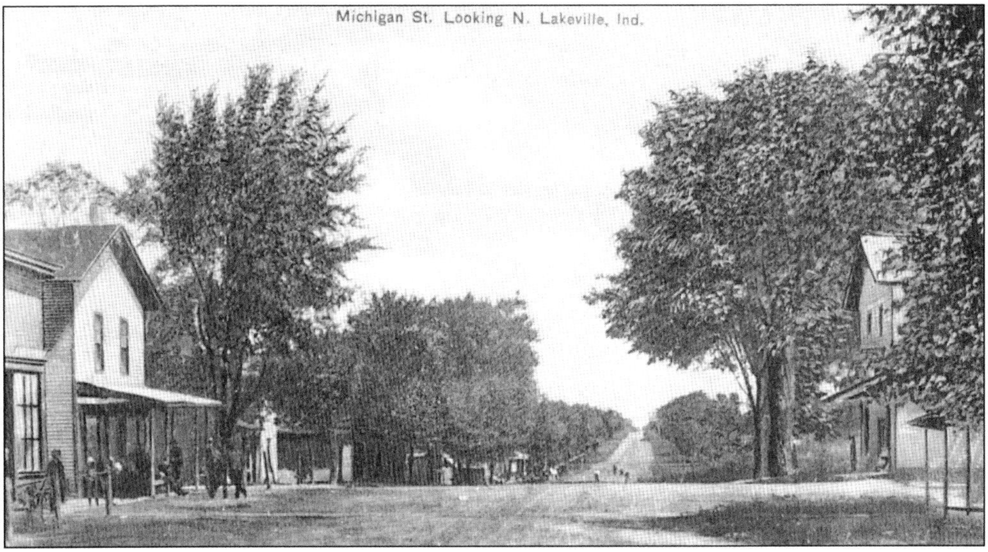

This image shows Michigan Street (originally the Michigan Road through Lakeville). The Vandalia Railroad ran between Logansport and South Bend. The Wabash Railroad ran from Toledo, Ohio, to Chicago. In 1936, a WPA bridge was built over US Route 31 in response to the many accidents that had occurred on the railroad crossing. The bridge was demolished in 2001 after the tracks were abandoned. (Courtesy Russell Rein.)

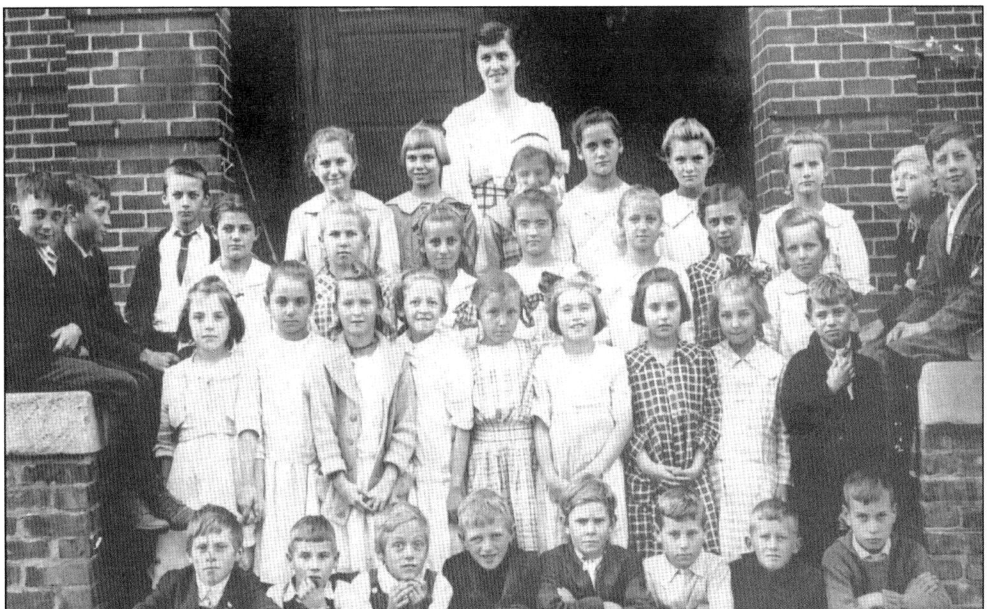

Students and teacher pose for an annual school photograph at Lakeville School in the 1910s. In the 1930s, a new high school was built on the north side of town along the Dixie Highway. In 1989, Robert and Joyce Newton purchased the property. The Newtons, owners of Hoosier Racing Tire (an international racing tire supplier), renovated the complex into a multiuse community center and library. The Newton Center, located at 601 North Michigan Street, is listed in the National Register of Historic Places. An athletic park was added to the north side of the property, providing state-of-the-art sports facilities. (Courtesy Jan Shupert-Arick.)

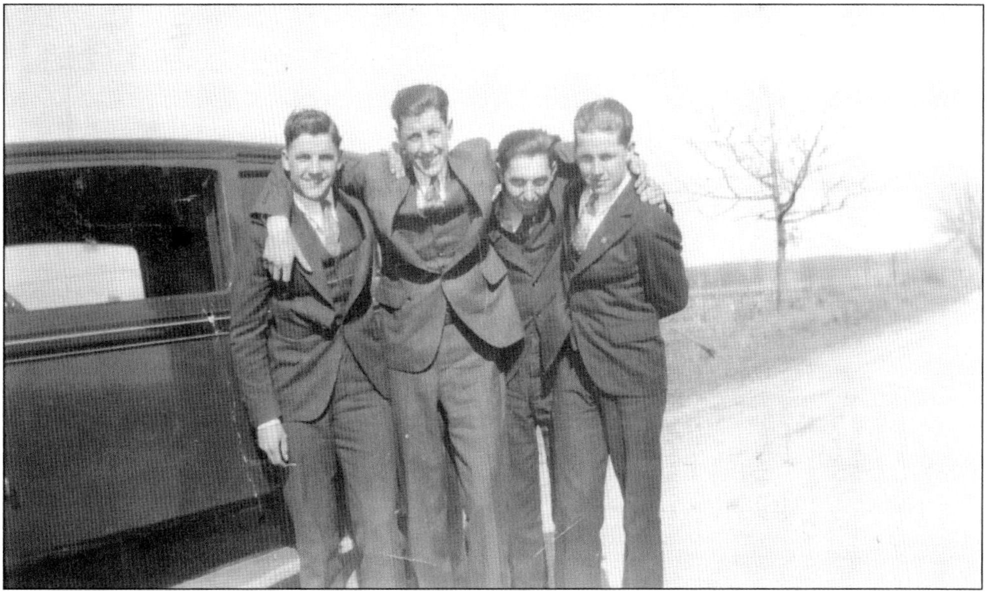

During the Great Depression, many men believed they were not in a position to marry; they remained single until the economy improved. For entertainment, they drove along the Dixie Highway visiting friends, fishing, and exploring roads created by the Good Roads Movement. From left to right, Don and Carl Logan, Alton "Buzz" Wolfe, and Glen D. Shupert pause at the Logan family farm on the Dixie Highway and Road 4 (Pierce Road) to have their photograph taken by a friend with a Brownie camera. (Courtesy Jan Shupert-Arick.)

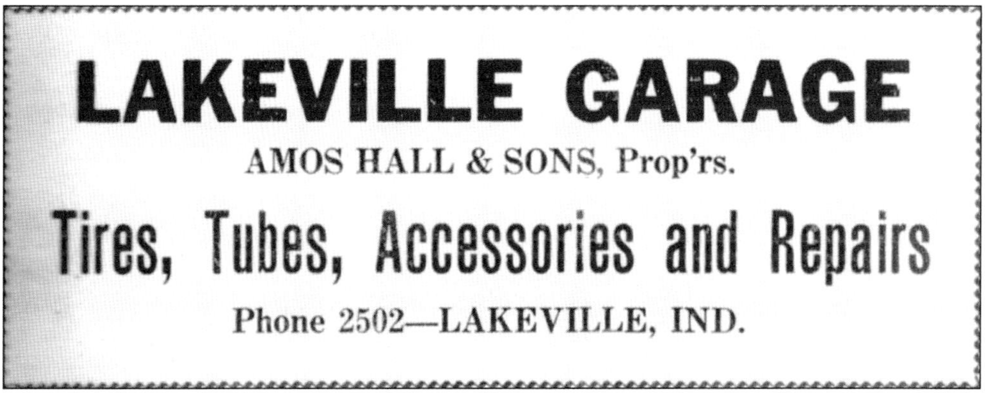

Lakeville provided limited services to travelers between South Bend and Plymouth, but by 1916, O.H. Klopfenstein's Auto Livery was established as a Ford Agency. They sold secondhand Buicks and Fords and offered day and night services. A few miles to the northwest, C.W. Anderson sold automobiles, buggies, harnesses, and sleds. Many years later, the Lakeville Auto Garage was owned and operated by Amos Hall and sons. Garry Hall opened Hall's Twin City south of town on US Route 31 in 1962. (Courtesy Marshall County Historical Museum.)

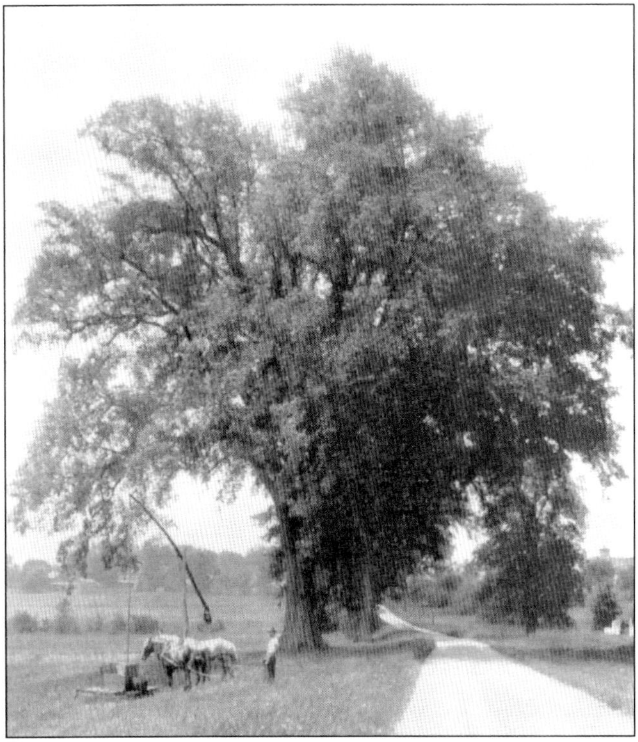

This photograph shows the early Dixie Highway in Marshall County as a long road winding through rural Indiana. A local farmer works with a team of horses in the field at the edge of the road. Good roads, gasoline engines, and the nation's love of personal automobiles that could take them anywhere a decent road led changed the quiet *clip-clop* of rural life. Below, a road construction engineer lifts a wide plank from the old Michigan Road, which had been laid by placing large, flat boards side-by-side to create what became known as a plank road. The planks were unearthed when major road construction to create a four-lane road was under way. (Both, courtesy Marshall County Historical Society.)

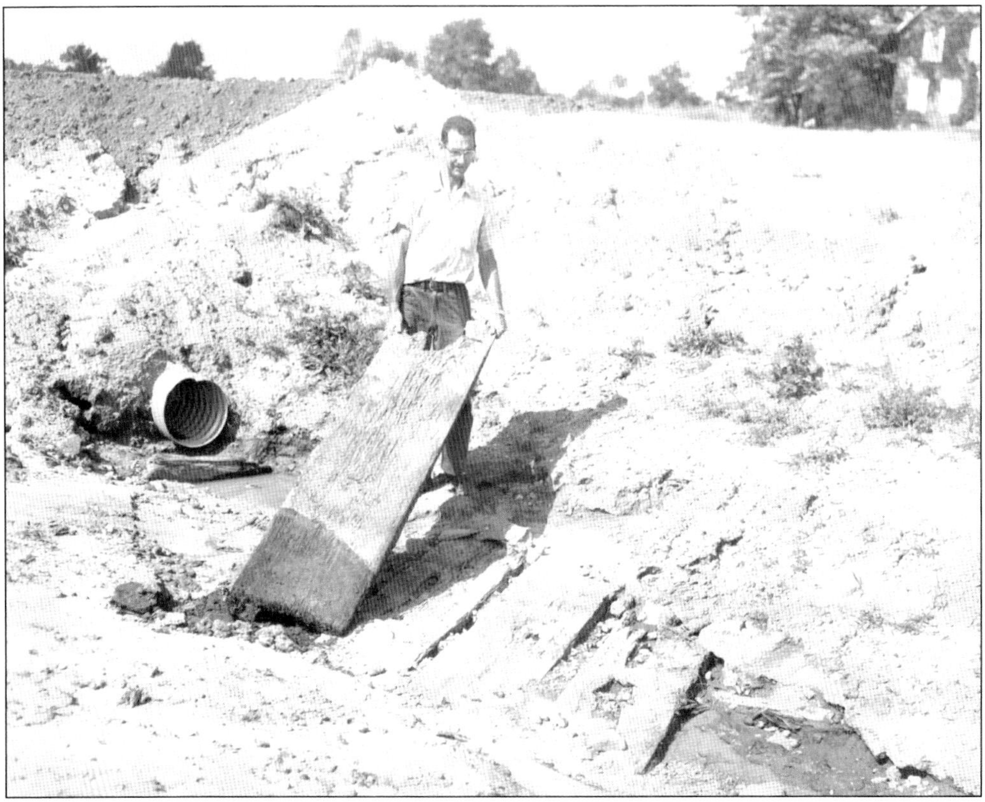

In the 1920s, improvements were made to the US Route 31 corridor through southern St. Joseph and Marshall Counties, including the paving of the highway. In 1947, streets were widened to four lanes, the curve south of town was relocated, and a hill was removed to provide a view of Pleasant Lake. Homes were relocated and demolished to create a path for the highway. The old section of the highway looping south from Lakeville was renamed Quinn Trail. (Courtesy Marshall County Historical Museum.)

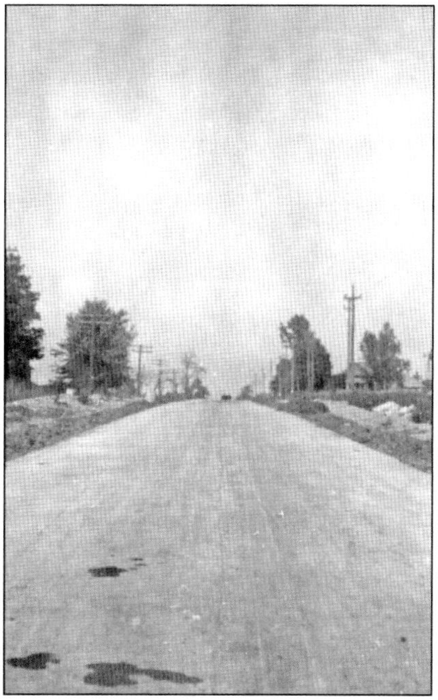

This photograph shows an early open automobile owner heading down the Dixie Highway in Marshall County after a winter snowstorm. Notice the ice on the electric lines and a man walking down the road. Few people owned automobiles before Henry Ford mass-produced the affordable Model T in the early 1920s. (Courtesy Marshall County Historical Museum.)

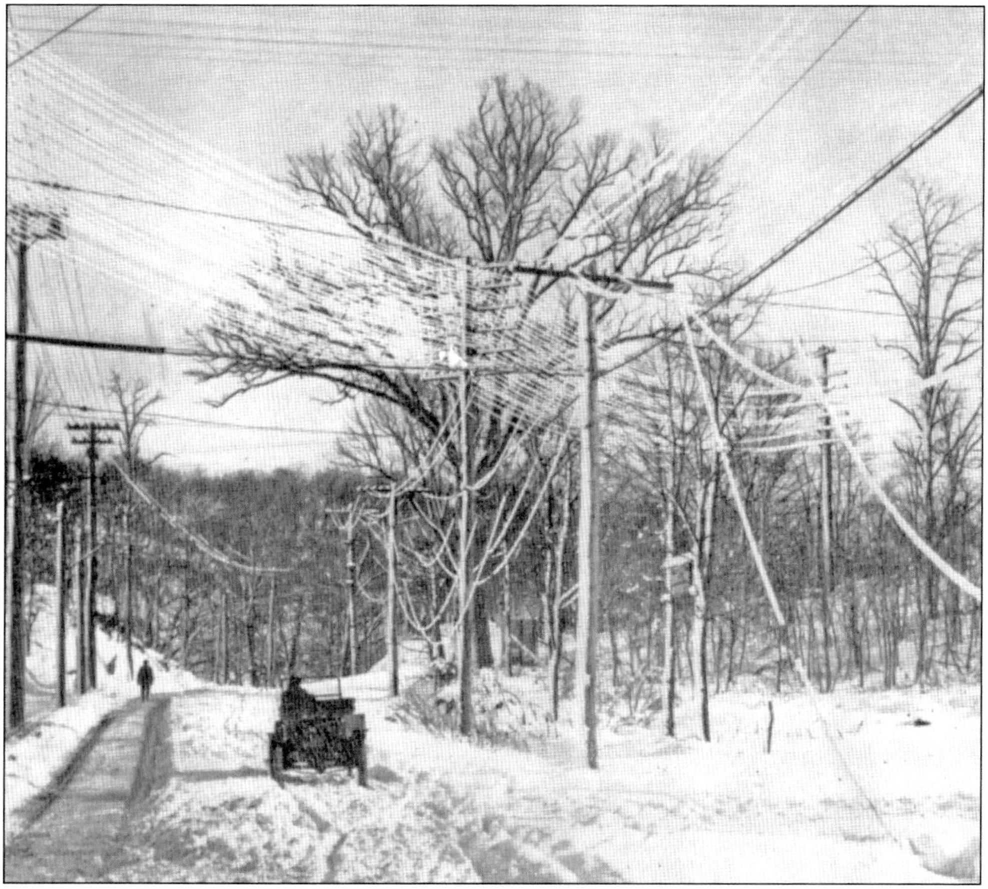

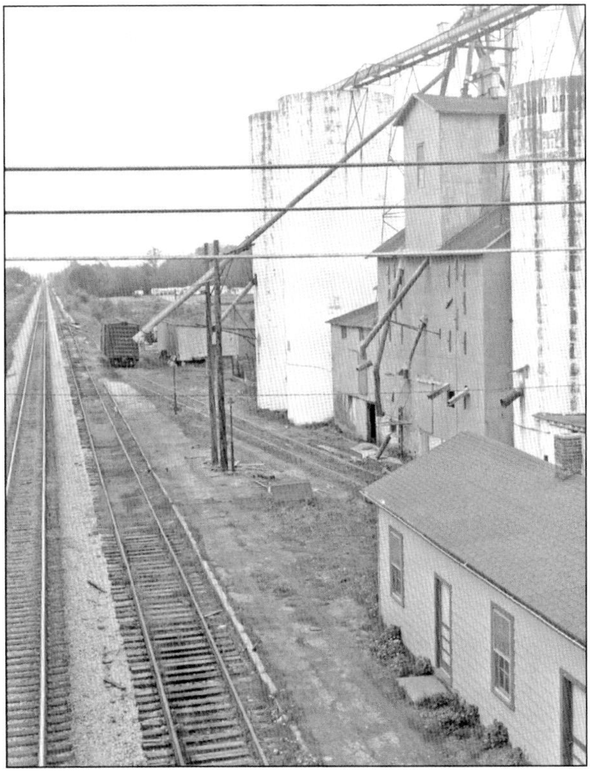

The La Paz grain elevator on the Dixie Highway served a large number of farmers in northern Marshall County. The good road was a benefit to farmers, helping them get their grain to market. At the time of its founding, La Paz was served by the Chicago branch of the B&O Railroad, which is now CSX. (Courtesy Marshall County Historical Museum.)

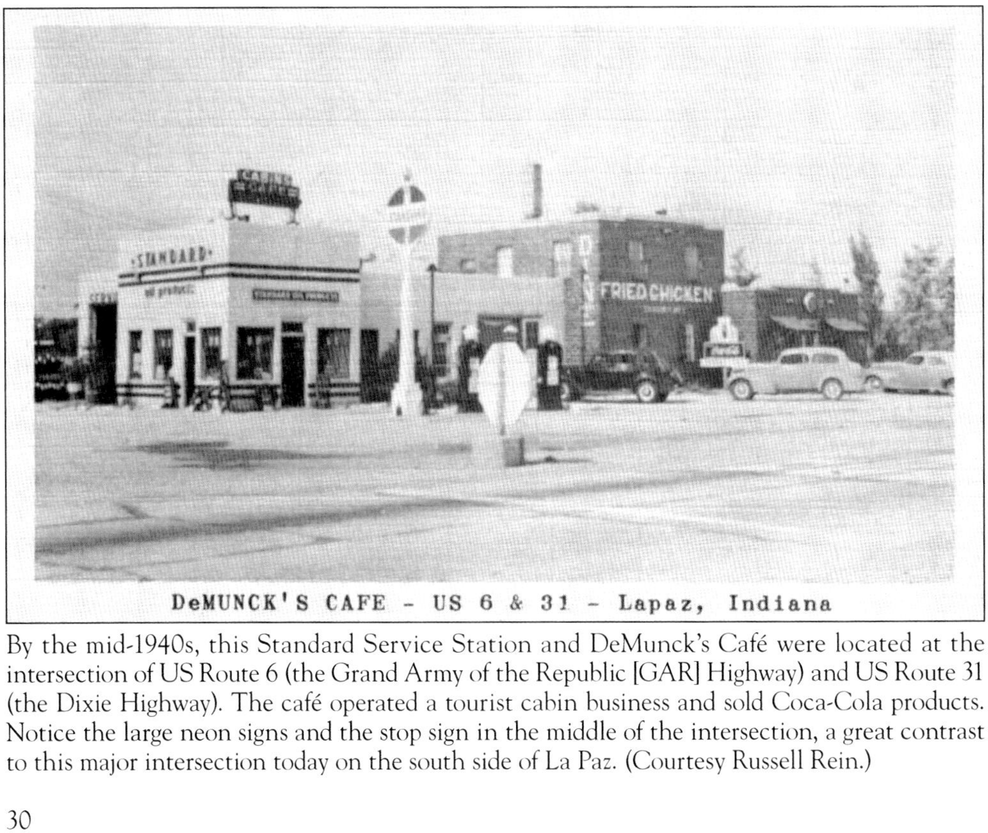

By the mid-1940s, this Standard Service Station and DeMunck's Café were located at the intersection of US Route 6 (the Grand Army of the Republic [GAR] Highway) and US Route 31 (the Dixie Highway). The café operated a tourist cabin business and sold Coca-Cola products. Notice the large neon signs and the stop sign in the middle of the intersection, a great contrast to this major intersection today on the south side of La Paz. (Courtesy Russell Rein.)

The justice of the peace lived in this home near the railroad crossing in La Paz, Indiana. La Paz was founded in 1873 and named for La Paz, Bolivia. The Dixie Highway between South Bend and Plymouth was paved by 1925. The highway crossed a railroad grade at the north edge of town. Travelers crossed numerous other railroad grades in the next five miles to Plymouth. (Courtesy Marshall County Historical Museum.)

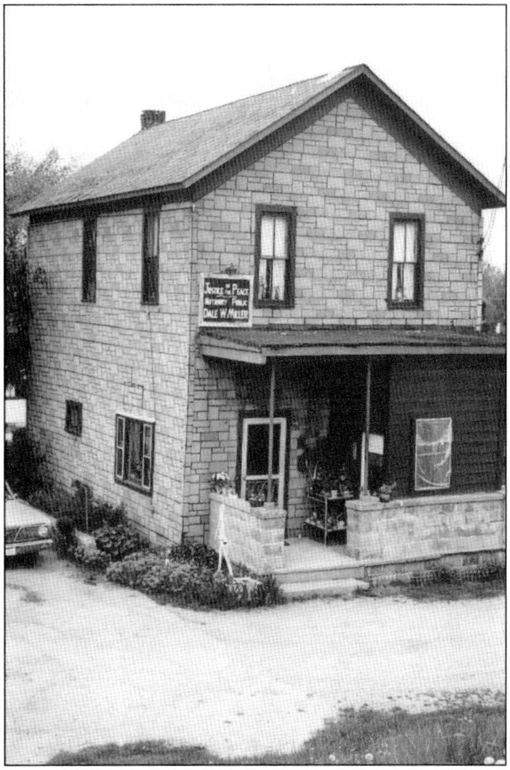

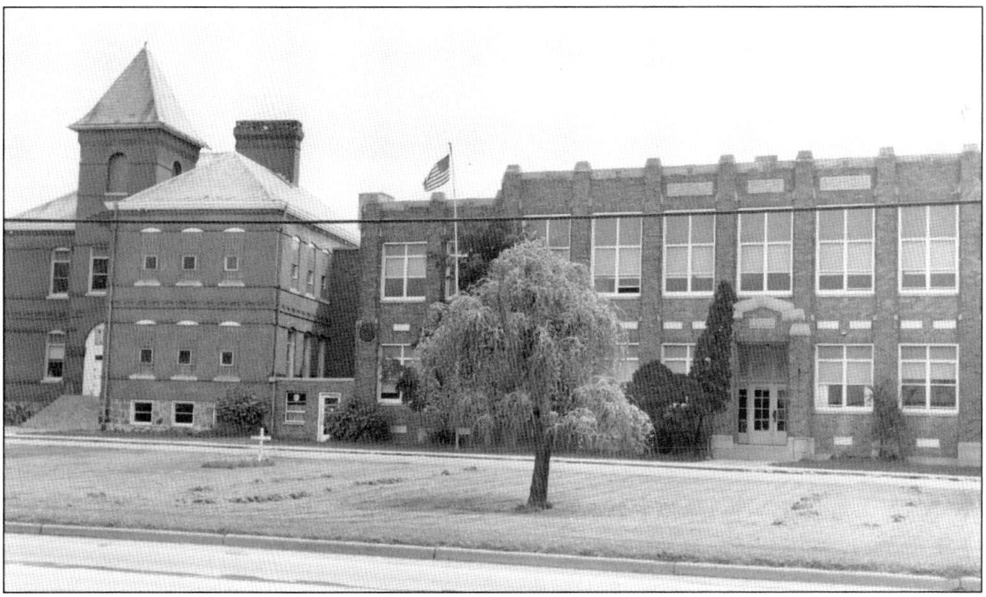

La Paz High School (right) and La Paz Grade School (left) are shown before 1962 when Lakeville and La Paz merged in the Union-North United School Corporation. The district comprises Lakeville in St. Joseph County and North Township, including La Paz in Marshall County. La Ville Elementary School and La Ville Junior-Senior High School are sandwiched approximately 15 miles south of South Bend and 8 miles north of Plymouth on the Dixie Highway. (Courtesy Marshall County Historical Museum.)

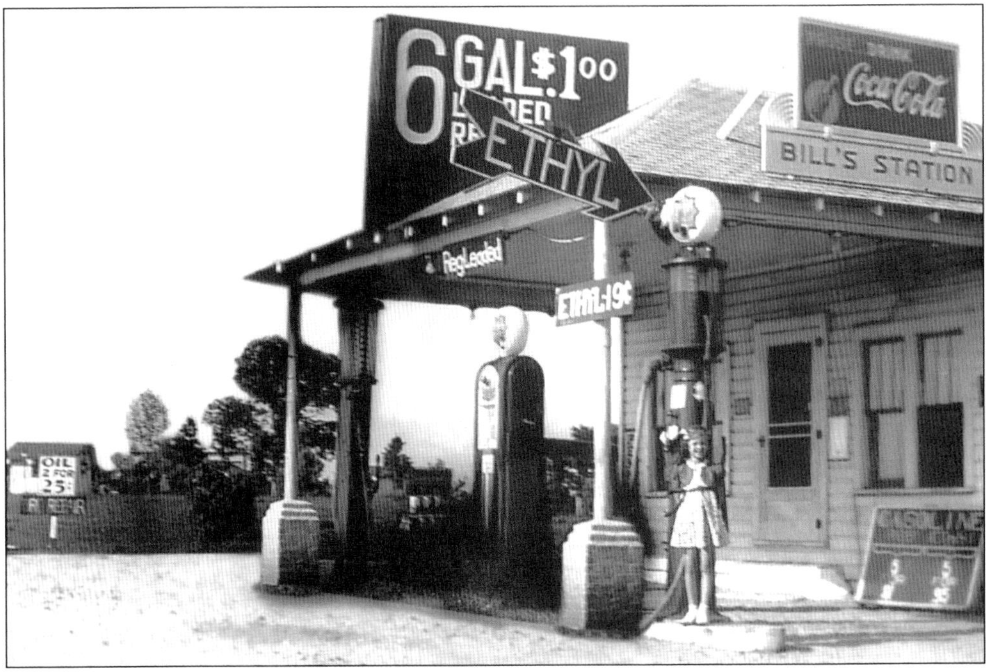

South of La Paz, a young girl poses in front of Bill's Station at the intersection of US Route 6 (the GAR Highway) and US Route 31 (the Dixie Highway). Bill's Station sold Ethyl gasoline at six gallons for $1 and oil at two for 25¢. They also sold Coca-Cola products and root beer and offered cabins for rent. (Courtesy Marshall County Historical Museum.)

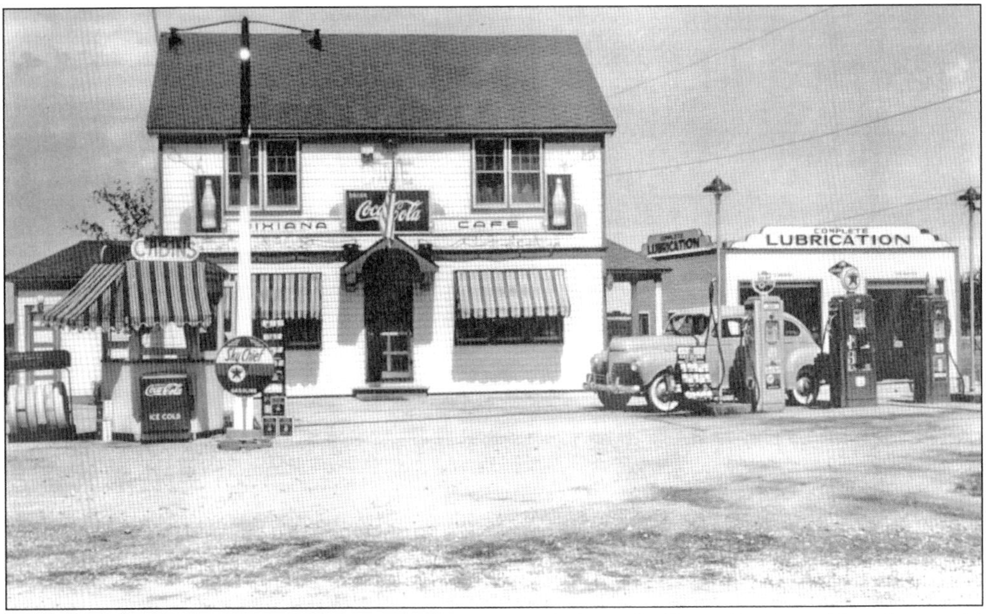

The Dixiana Café and Service Station was a one-stop hub on the Dixie Highway. Travelers could purchase Texaco gasoline, have their automobile lubricated, rent a cabin for the night, or eat in the café. The building is still a residence, but it was moved behind Mac's Market and Grocery at 2083 US Route 31 south of La Paz. This image was taken in the 1930s. (Courtesy Marshall County Historical Museum.)

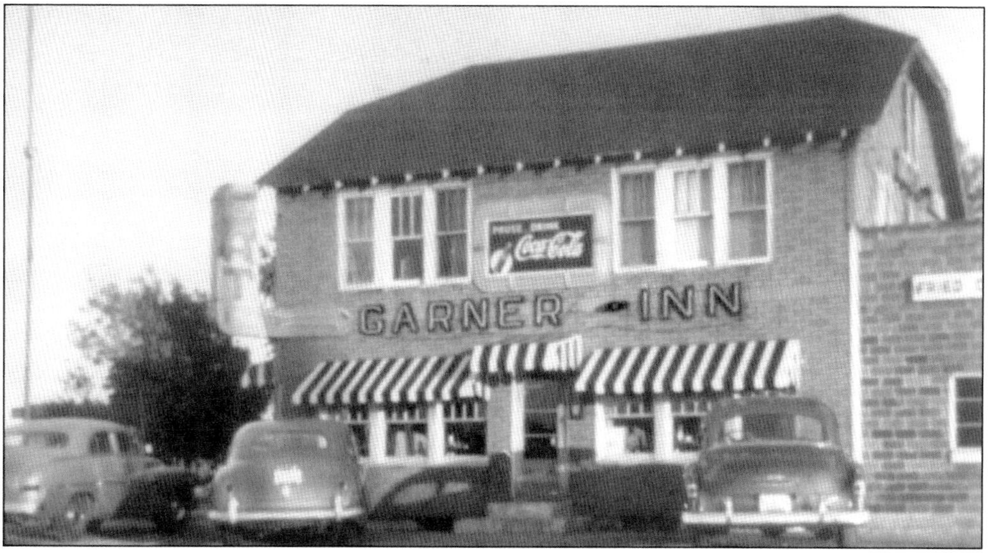

Located south of La Paz, the Maddox family originally operated this inn beginning in the 1920s. In 1950, Jack and Alice Garner traded their farm near Tyner for the Maddox family's inn, at which time it became the Garner Inn. When US Route 31 was widened to four lanes in 1956, the inn was demolished, and the Garners constructed a new truck stop a mile east of Route 31 on US Route 6. Garners Truck Stop was operated by the second-generation owners, Jack Jr. and Cindy Garner, until 1996; the building was razed in 2009. (Courtesy Marshall County Historical Museum.)

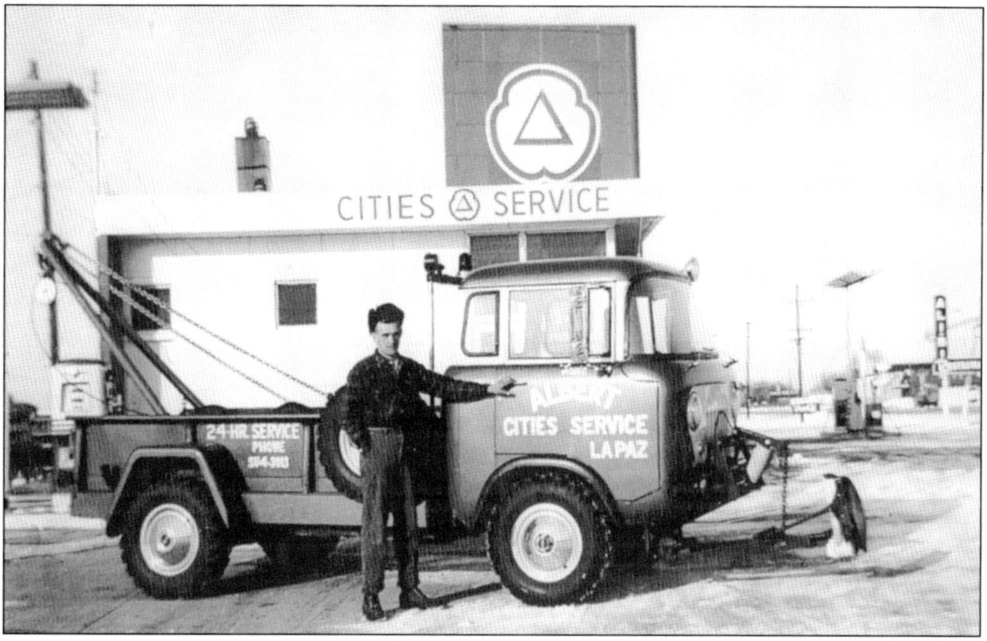

The Cities Service Station was located at the intersection of Route 6 and Route 31 just south of La Paz. The service station sold gasoline and oil and provided a towing service to automobiles and semitrucks traveling through this part of Indiana. The truck traffic was heavy along Route 6 because it was on the route to Chicago. The Alibi Restaurant is in the background. It was located on the northwest corner of the intersection, which had an electric traffic signal by the early 1960s. (Courtesy Marshall County Historical Museum.)

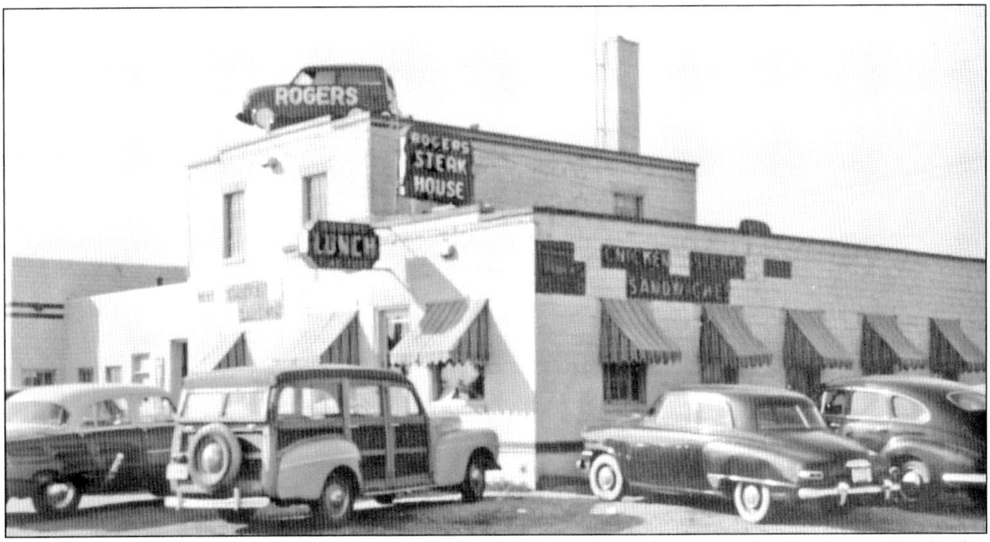

In the 1950s, Roger's Steak House served travelers and locals in the La Paz area. With the introduction of the motor car in the 1920s, the road that became US Route 6, then called the Toledo-Chicago Pike or State Road 17, became a popular east-west route to and from Chicago. It intersected with the Dixie Highway on the south edge of La Paz. (Courtesy Russell Rein.)

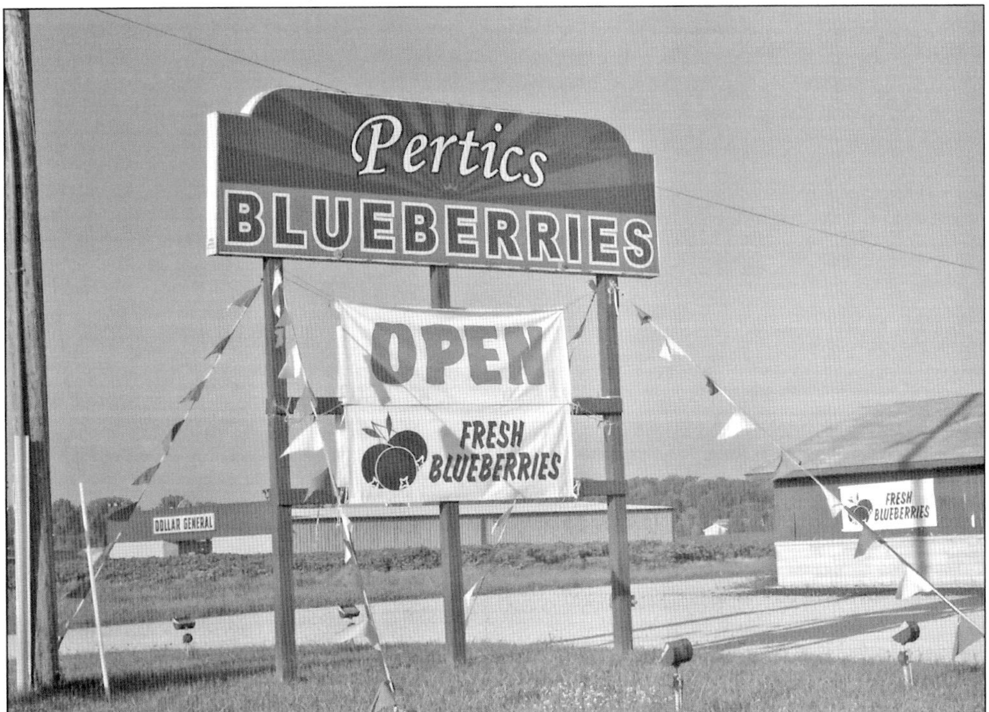

Pertics Blueberries is located at 618 South Michigan Street in La Paz. Pertics is one of a number of fruit farms in the area, which is well known for its orchards and roadside produce stands. Pertics welcomes customers to pick their own berries, but also offers picked berries for sale along the road—although during berry season, their sign often reads, "Sold Out." (Courtesy Jan Shupert-Arick.)

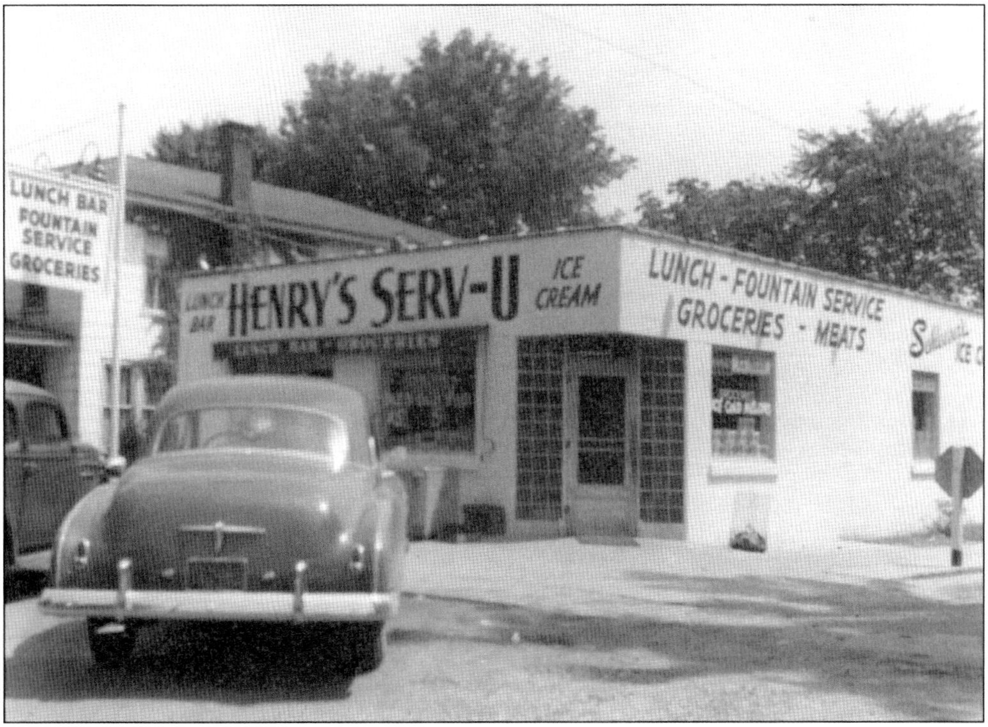

Located at 1535 North Michigan Street, Henry's Serv-U carried groceries and had a full-line meat counter and a soda fountain that offered a variety of ice cream selections. The Open Window was a simple, block-style building owned by the Merton Snider family in 1949. The establishment sold the ever-popular root beer and popcorn, and it was the first place in Plymouth to offer frozen custard and pizza. Notice the walk-up window with an awning. Later, the business changed names and became the Snyder Drive-In. Locals remember hanging out here as teenagers. (Both, courtesy Marshall County Historical Museum.)

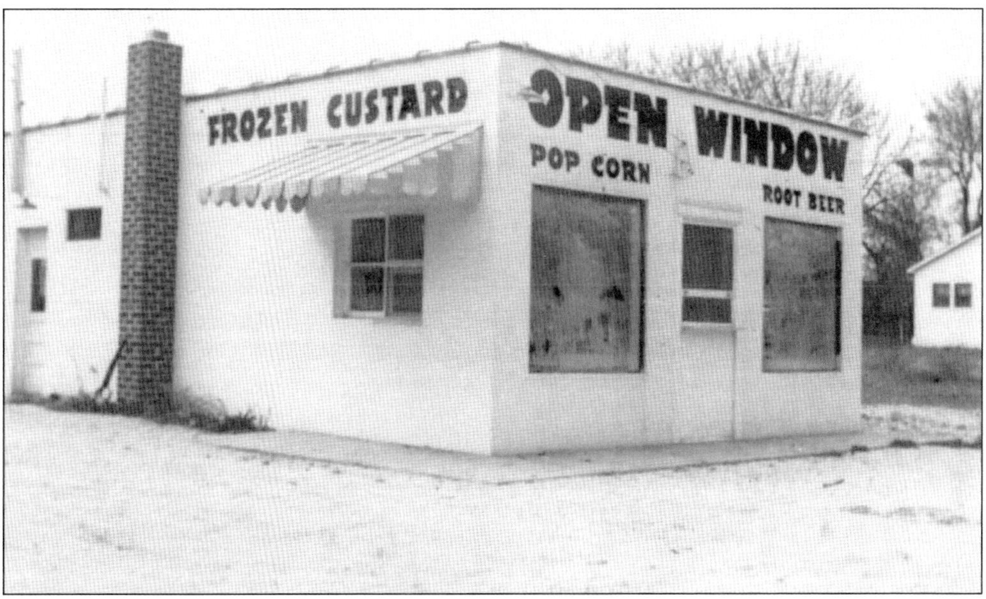

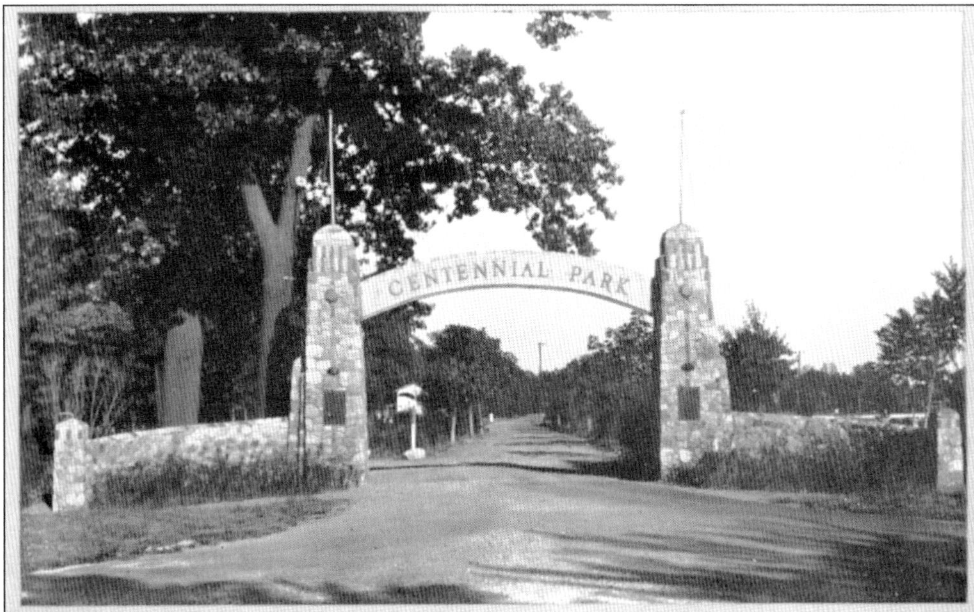

ENTRANCE CENTENNIAL PARK, PLYMOUTH, INDIANA G-563

Located at 1616 North Michigan Street in Plymouth, Indiana, Centennial Park has served as a centerpiece for Marshall County since it was established in 1916. In the early 20th century, the area was used as a county fairground. In the 1930s, the Works Progress Administration (WPA) built a fieldstone clubhouse that is still in use today. In 1973, fifty-seven acres across the Yellow River were added to the park; the two sections were joined with a covered bridge built over the river. Plymouth holds three annual festivals in the park; the largest is the Blueberry Festival held each Labor Day weekend. Attended by over 500,000 people each year, the festival is second in size only to the Indianapolis 500 for any Indiana weekend event. Today, Centennial Park contains a wide variety of active recreational facilities, including lighted baseball and softball fields; lighted basketball and tennis courts; facilities for shuffleboard, horseshoes, and swimming; playgrounds; a skateboard area; and passive recreational facilities, such as picnic areas, shelters, nature trails, and fishing. (Above, courtesy Russell Rein; below, courtesy Marshall County Historical Museum.)

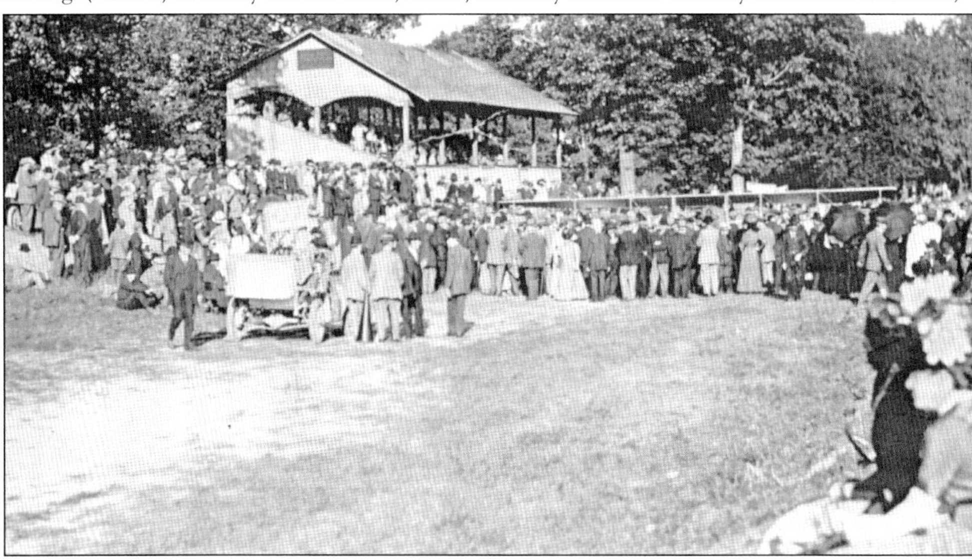

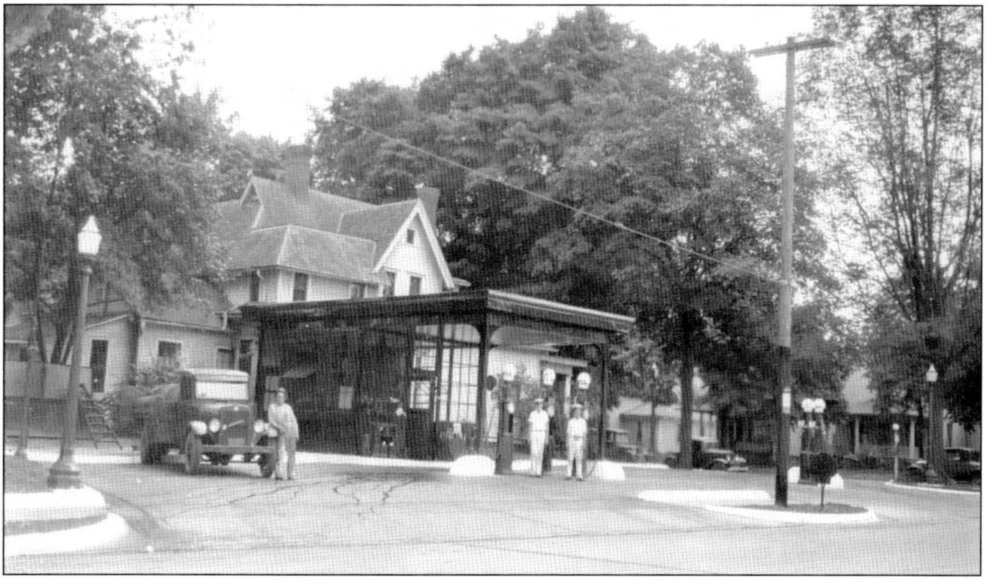

This photograph from the 1930s shows the Shell Service Station at the intersection of the Dixie and Lincoln Highways in Plymouth just after the Lincoln Highway route across Indiana was shortened. Plymouth became the crossing point for the Lincoln and Dixie Highways in the state. The original Lincoln Highway route of 1913 from Fort Wayne to South Bend, La Porte, and Valparaiso was rerouted. In 1926, the road became US Route 30, meandering to Columbia City, Warsaw, Plymouth, and finally Valparaiso. (Courtesy Marshall County Historical Museum.)

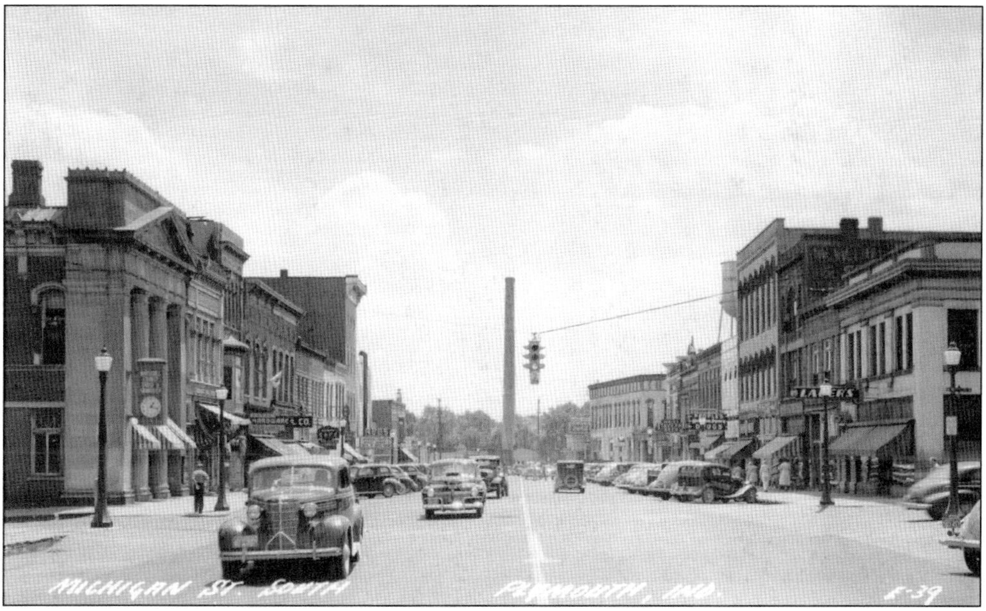

Often called the crossroads of America, Plymouth was incorporated on April 25, 1873, in Marshall County. The city serves as the county seat. The courthouse is located on Jefferson Street, one block west of the Dixie Highway. The Lincoln Highway, the Dixie Highway, the GAR Highway (US Route 6), and the Yellowstone Trail all run through Marshall County. Marshall County was formed in 1836 in an area occupied by the Potawatomie Nation. (Courtesy Marshall County Historical Museum.)

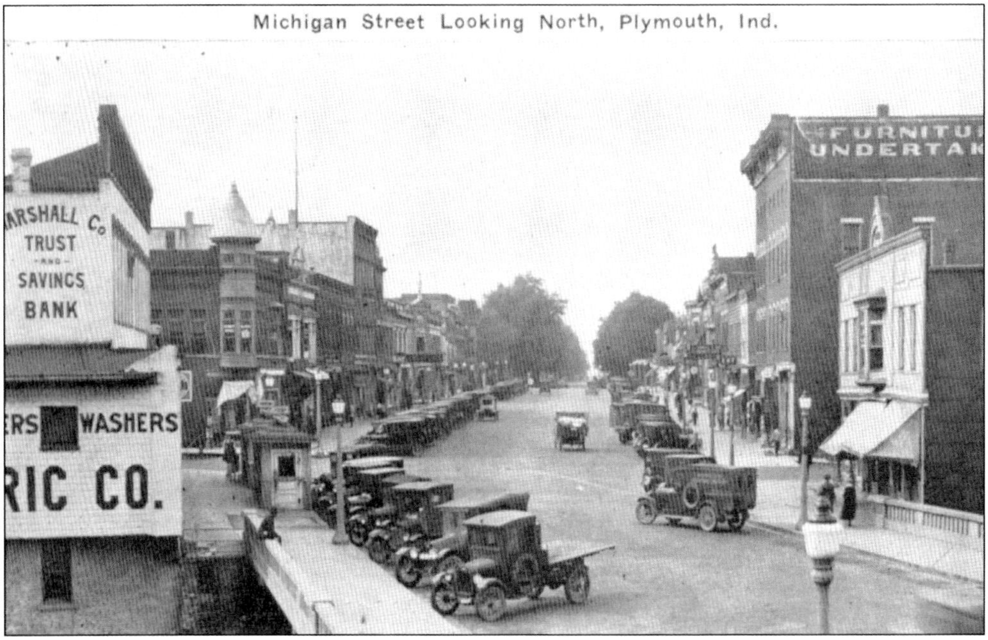

These photographs show Plymouth's South Michigan Street Bridge in two evolutions. The modern concrete span took the place of the ornate through-truss bridge over the Yellow River, a tributary of the Kankakee River. The old iron bridge could not safely accommodate heavier vehicles and increased traffic, which required greater bridge capacity. Built in the 19th century, the old bridge included separate side walkways for pedestrians going to and from the immediate downtown shopping district. The modern bridge utilized the space for a wider span that provided space for angled parking. (Both, courtesy Marshall County Historical Museum.)

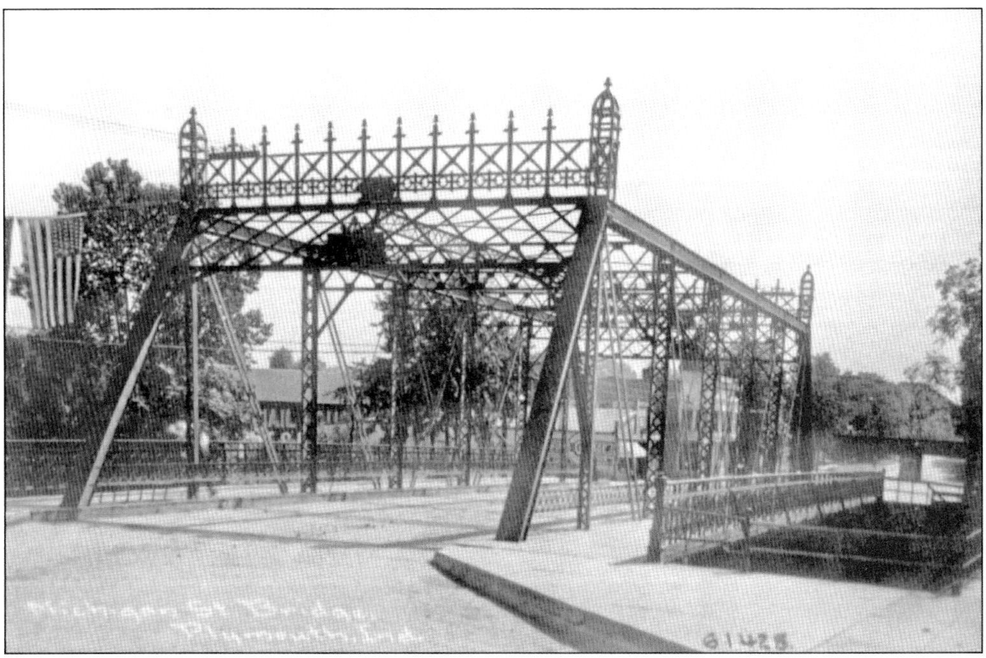

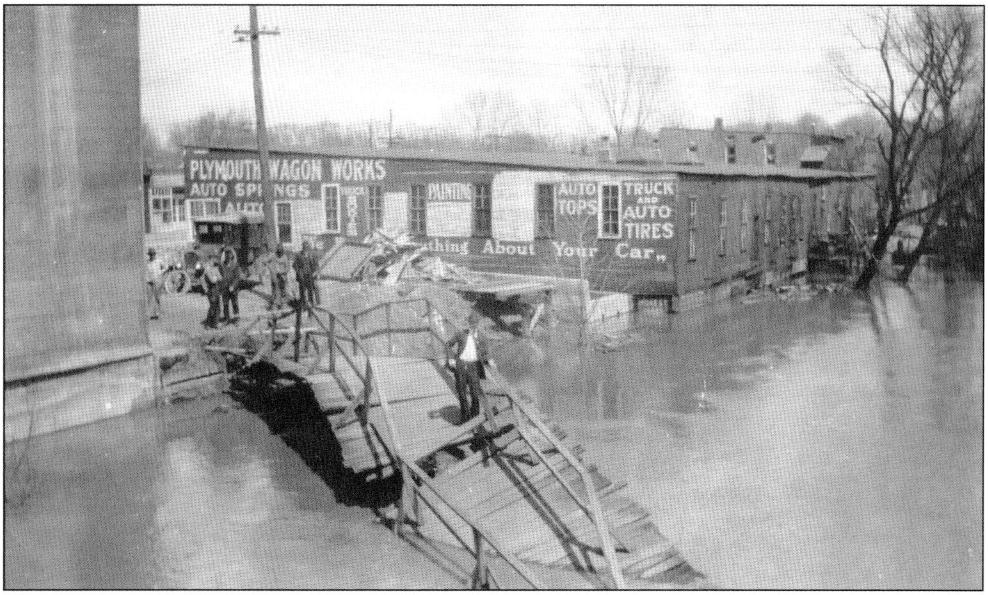

This photograph was taken of the Plymouth Wagon Works at Yellow River upon the collapse of the wooden pedestrian bridge. The Yellow River appears to be in a flood stage. The wagon works sold automobile springs, automobile tops, and truck and automobile tires. Notice the truck with wooden wheels next to the building. (Courtesy Marshall County Historical Museum.)

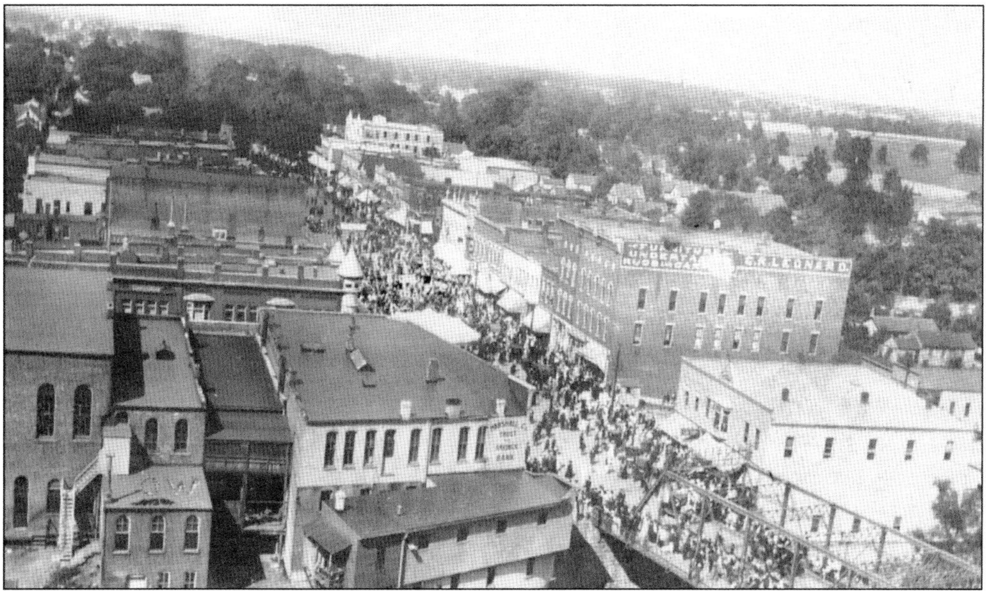

This aerial view of downtown Plymouth includes the iron through-truss bridge on South Michigan Street. The photograph appears to have been taken from the South Michigan Street viaduct, built in 1874 on the south end of downtown. Many of the buildings have been restored as a historic district. The first Montgomery Ward store in the nation was located on the east side of Michigan Street and is now the home of the *Plymouth Pilot*, the local newspaper. (Courtesy Marshall County Historical Museum.)

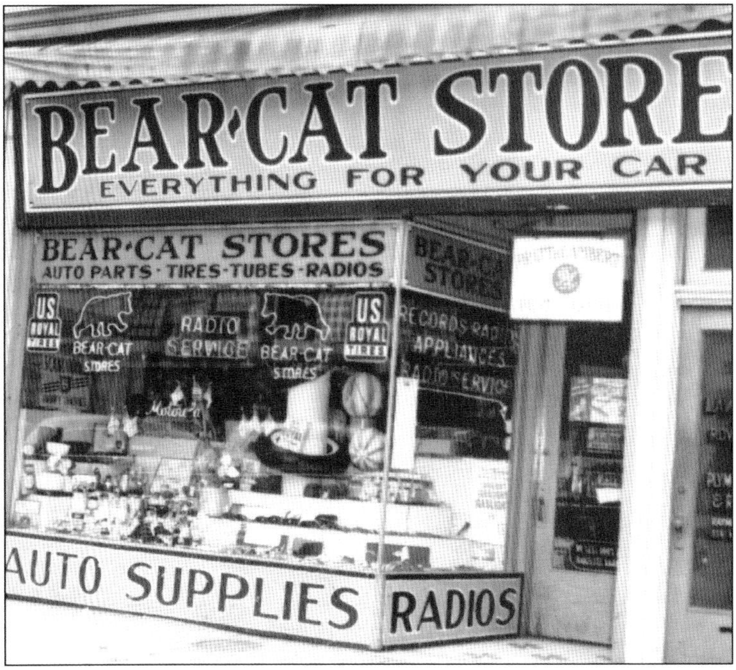

Located on Michigan Street in downtown Plymouth, the Bearcat Store had everything for the car owner. They also sold and serviced radios, sold vinyl records, US Royal tires, tubes, and appliances. (Courtesy Marshall County Historical Museum.)

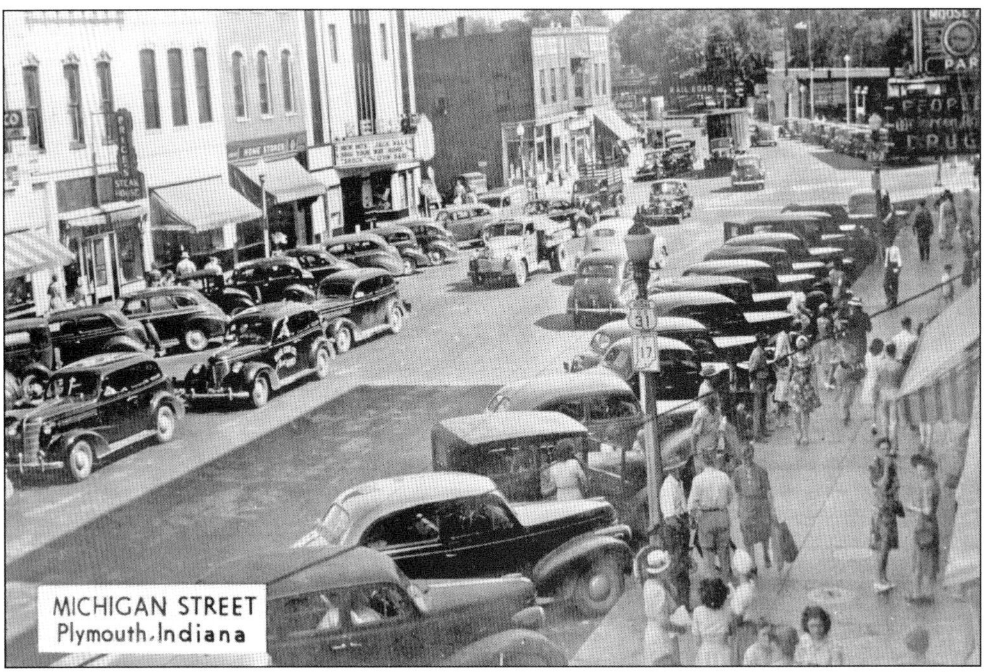

This photograph from the 1940s shows downtown Plymouth on a typical weekday. Included are the theater, streetlights, and street signs that mark US Route 31 and State Road 17. (Courtesy Marshall County Historical Museum.)

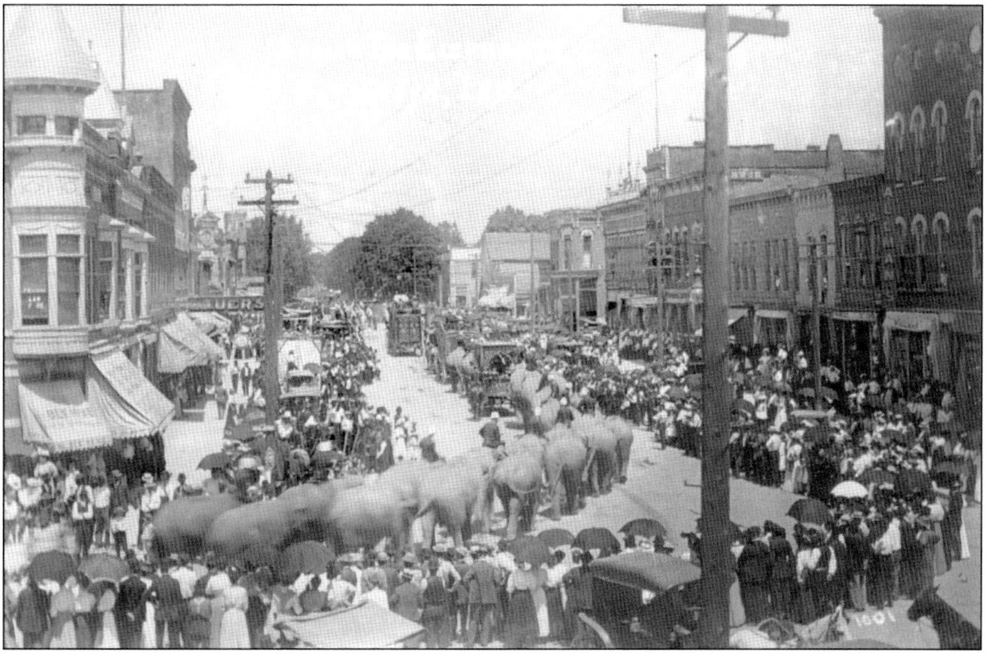

Hoosier communities welcomed small circuses through the fist half of the 20th century. To promote the arrival of the circus and draw locals to the performances, the elephants were paraded down main streets in the mornings or afternoons as the big top was setting up. The parade also included lions in their special wagons, the strange-sounding calliope, fancy horses and riders, and the clowns showed off their talents. Taken around 1915 on Michigan Street in Plymouth, this real-photo postcard reads, "Seeing the Elephants!" (Courtesy Marshall County Historical Museum.)

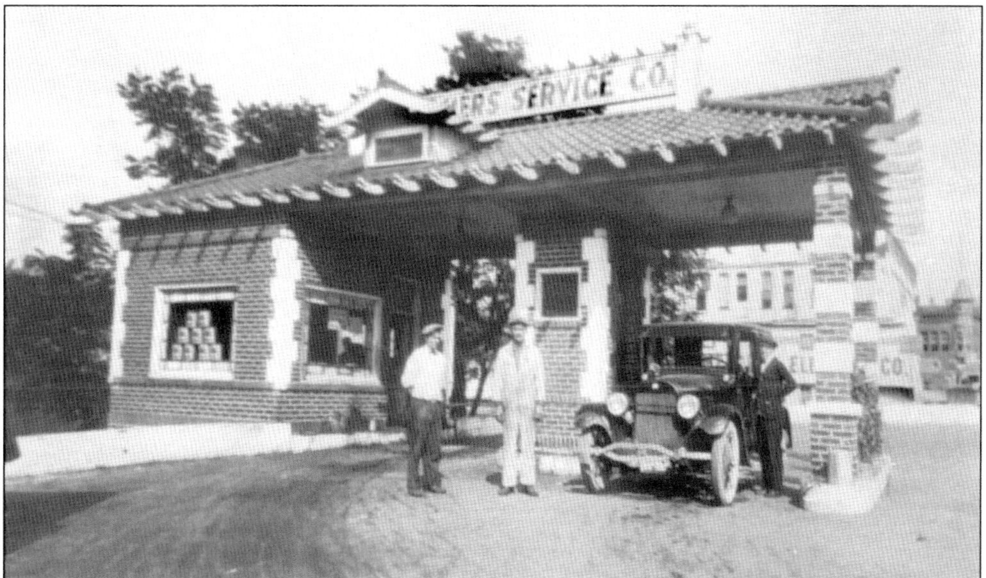

According to local newspaper advertisements published in 1908, the Consumers Service Company on South Michigan Street in Plymouth sold petroleum products that provided "the energy your car needed to get the job done with less carbon and more miles." Managed by Walter Inks, the business boasted prompt service. (Courtesy Marshall County Historical Museum.)

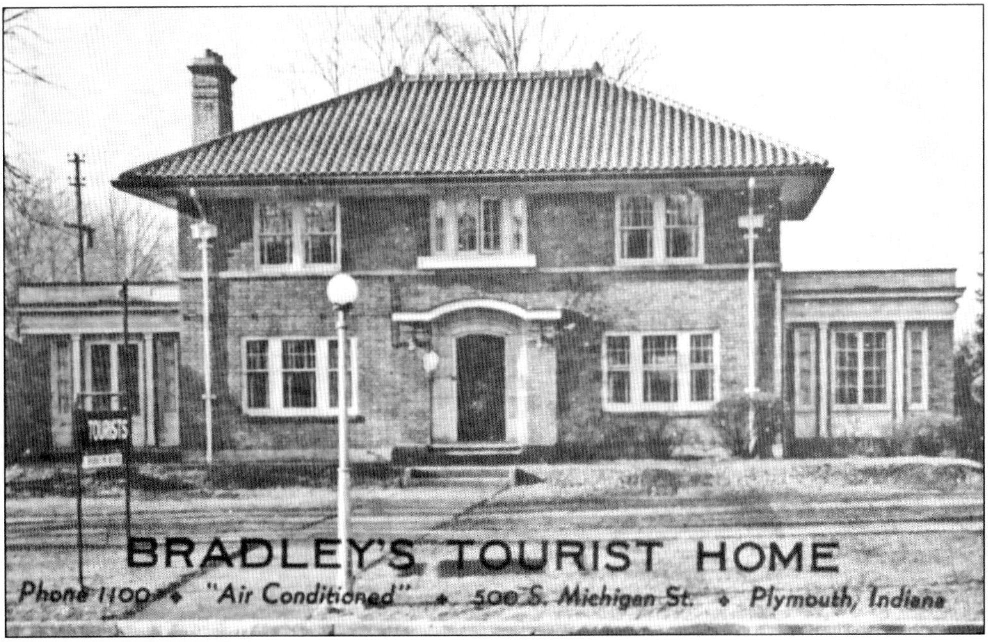

Many historic homes are located along South Michigan Street in Plymouth. The two-story brick home at 500 South Michigan was built in the Prairie style, with solariums on the north and south ends, a red-tile roof, wide overhangs, and a large central front entry. In the 1940s, a sign in the yard welcomed travelers, and postcards promoted the home as "air conditioned." Today, this home is a private residence. (Courtesy Russell Rein.)

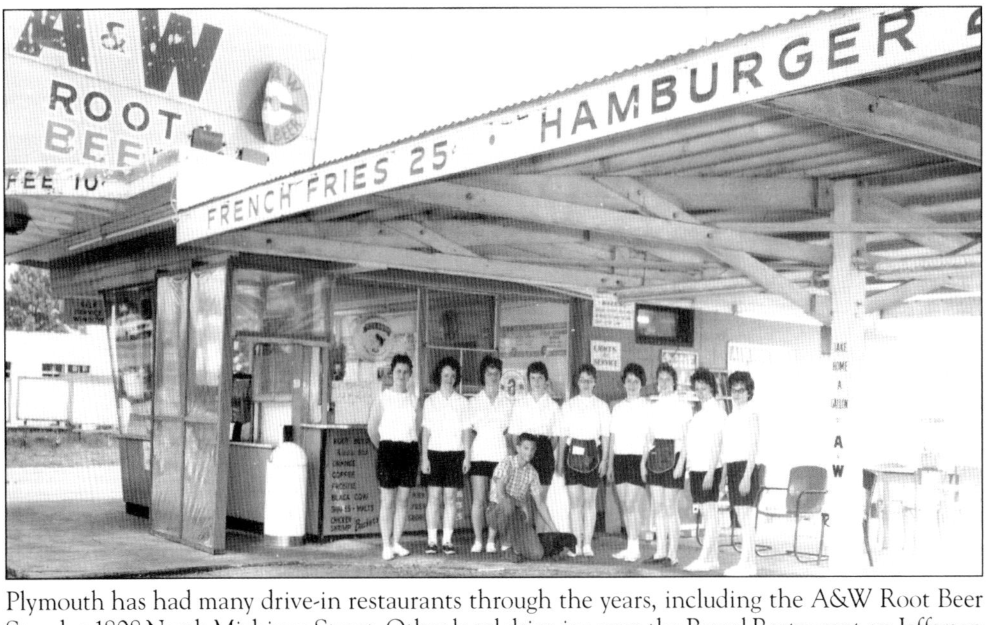

Plymouth has had many drive-in restaurants through the years, including the A&W Root Beer Stand at 1808 North Michigan Street. Other local drive-ins were the Barrel Restaurant on Jefferson Street (on the 1928 route of the Lincoln Highway) and the Big Mug, a popular gathering place on US Route 30 West in the 1950s. (Courtesy Marshall County Historical Museum.)

This aerial image shows the modern US 31/US 30 cloverleaf east of the old Dixie Highway on the north side of Plymouth. (Courtesy Marshall County Historical Museum.)

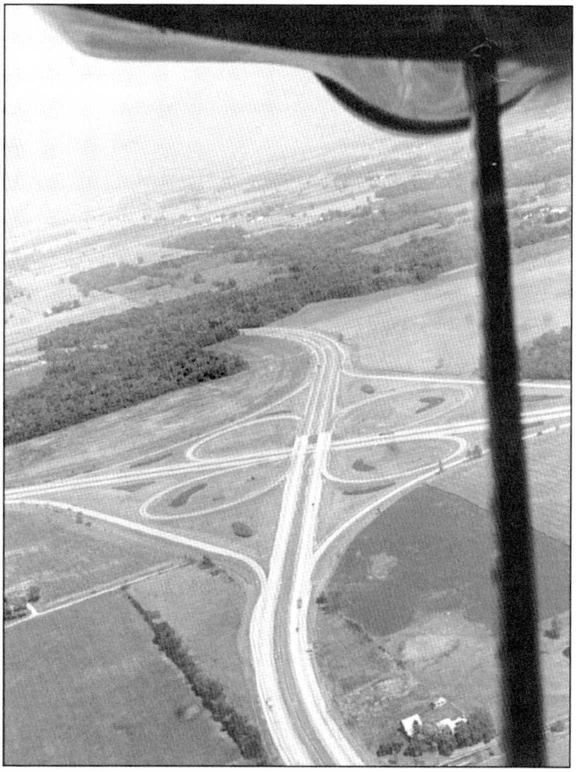

Standing in front of the Marshall County Historical Museum and Crossroads Center, Linda Rippy, the museum director, and Kurt Garner, a local preservationist and architect, pose to have their photograph taken at the opening of the Crossroads Center. The museum serves as the official archive for the Indiana Lincoln Highway Association. (Courtesy Marshall County Historical Museum.)

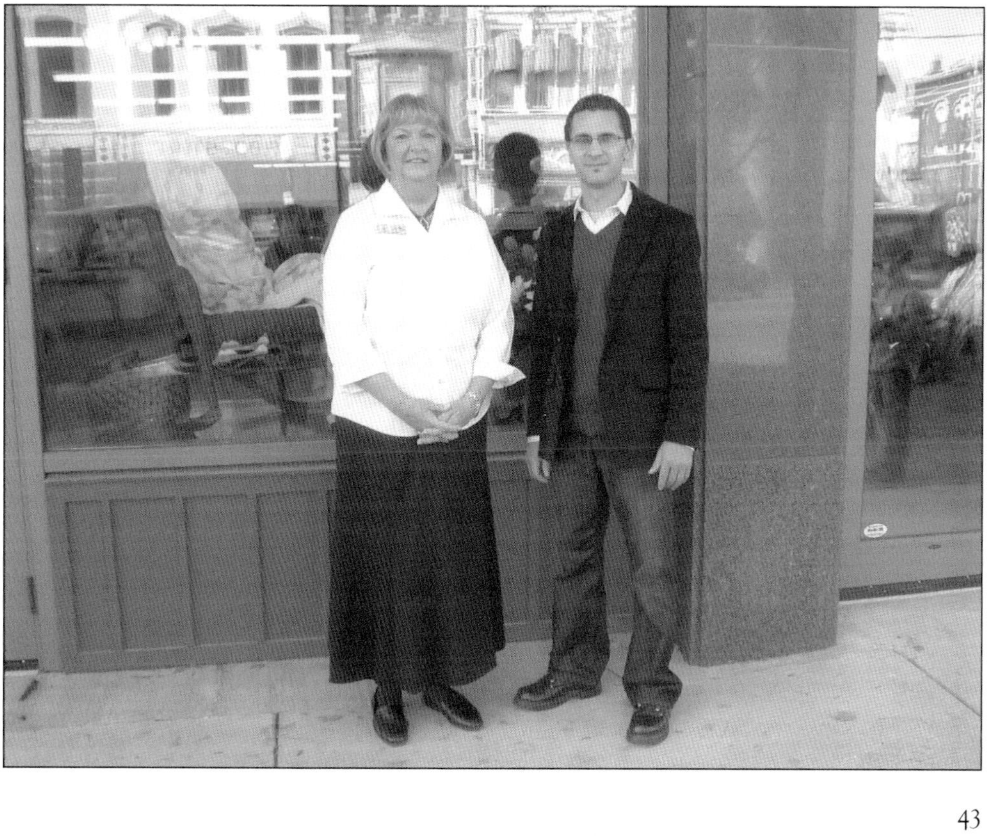

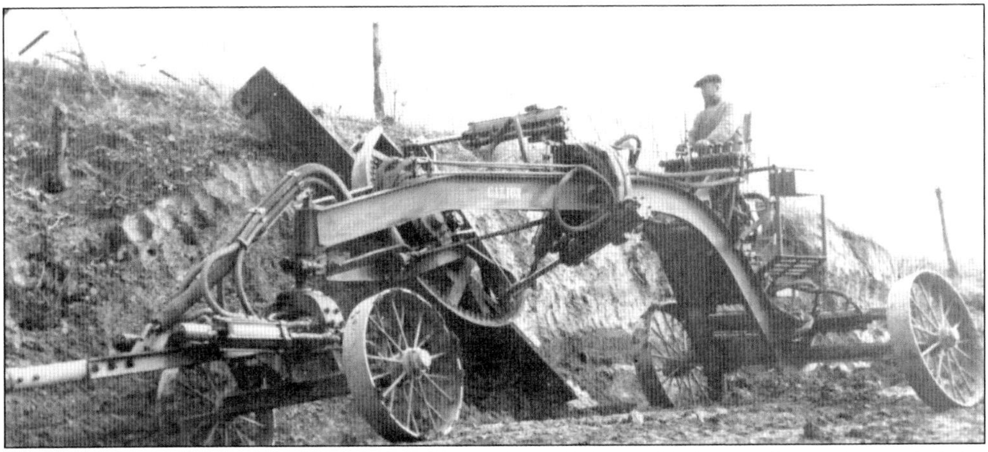

A Galion Iron Works pull-type grader works on the early Dixie Highway. The grader leveled the ground in preparation for road construction. The operator scrapes the road side to widen the highway, making it safer. Realizing the potential of the machine early, Galion was one of the first grader manufacturers to market a motorized grader. The first self-propelled grader was made by Russell Grader Company in 1919. (Courtesy Marshall County Historical Museum.)

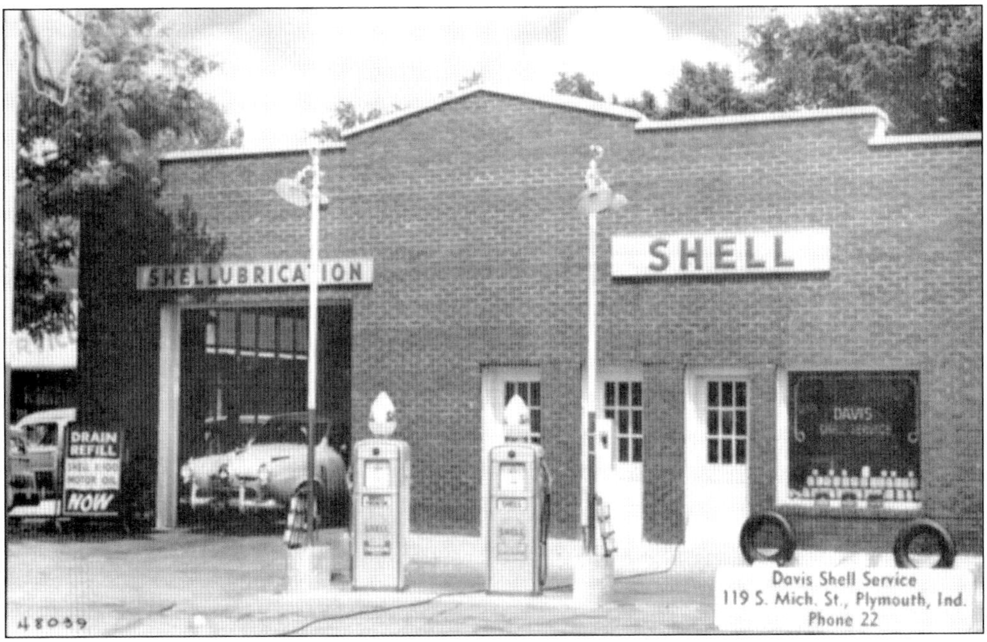

Located at 119 South Michigan Street in Plymouth, the Davis Shell Station was a one-bay garage with a single island with two glass-globe-topped gas pumps. A South Bend–manufactured, bullet-nose Studebaker was being serviced in the bay. (Courtesy Russell Rein.)

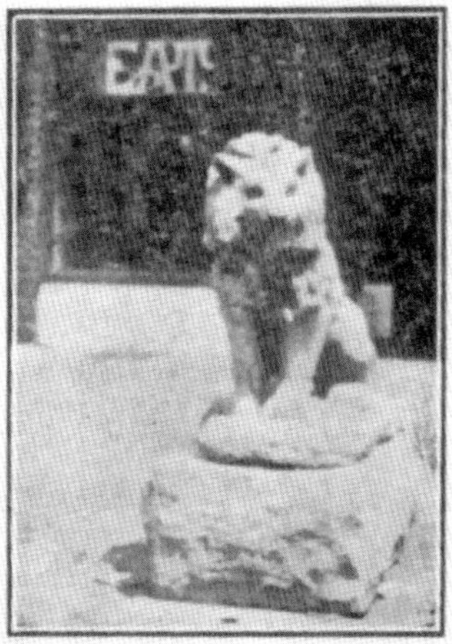

THE LION CAFE

E. H. RINGGENBERG

100Ate North Michigan St.

PLYMOUTH, IND.

(OVER)

The Lion Café handed out small promotional cards with a poem that promoted the town of Plymouth in the early 20th century. This Lion Café was located at 100 North Michigan Street. (Courtesy Russell Rein.)

Plymouth On The Map

They may talk about the sunny south
Also the growing west,
But this old town of Plymouth can
Give cards to all the rest.

Old Frisco has its golden gate,
Niagara has it's falls
New York it's population, Newport
it's fancy balls,
But for all around enjoyment and
living at your best,
This old town of Plymouth can
Give cards to all the rest.

I've seen Chicago's packing plants
And things of which we here,
Like Boston's school of learning and
Milwaukee's famous beer,
But I'm back again in Plymouth and
I will never leave it more.
Till I get a one-way ticket to that
far famed Golden Shore.

And perhaps when I'm a singing
before that throne of grace,
Or frizzen like a doughnut in that
other unnamed place,
I'll hunt up a railroad station and
hand it to them flat,
I want to go right back again to
Plymouth on the Map.

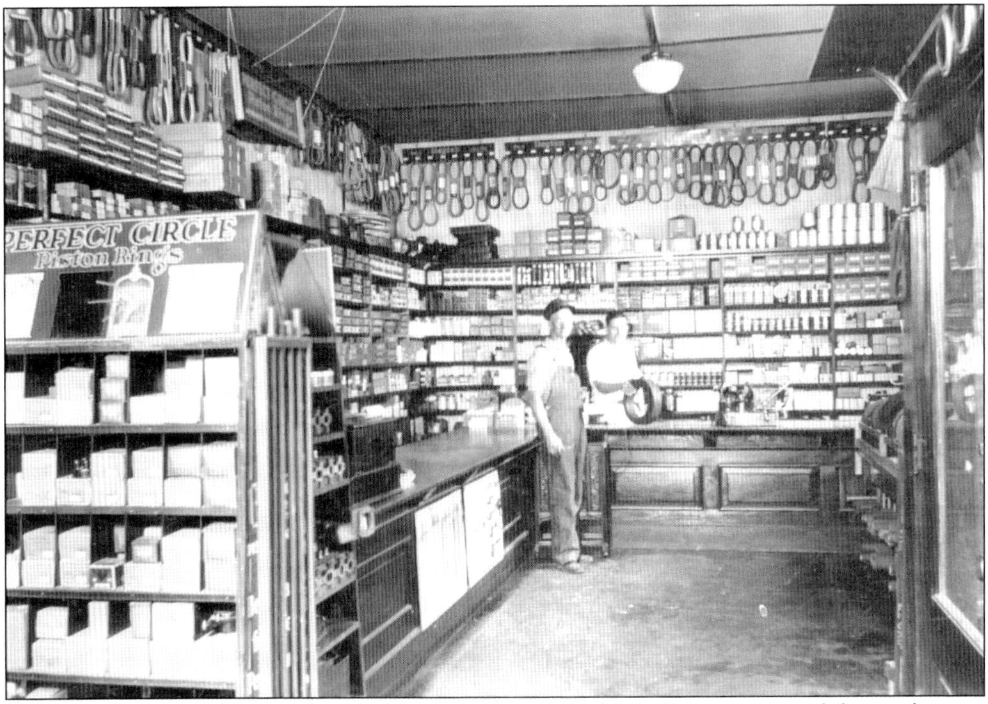

Taken in downtown Plymouth, this image shows a typical, small-town automobile supply store with all the necessary spare parts a person would need to service or repair an early automobile on hand. The Perfect Circle, a New Castle, Indiana, company, produced piston rings for customers who were serious about maintaining their automobile engines. (Courtesy Marshall County Historical Museum.)

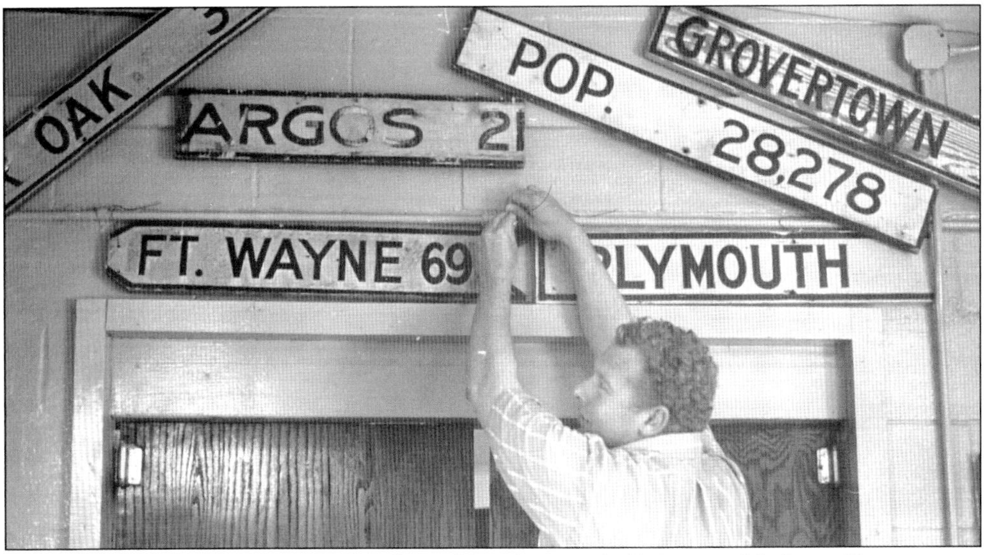

This image shows the road signs collected by the Marshall County Highway Department. As new signs were placed along the road, the old signs from towns in the region were taken down and attached to the wall in the maintenance shop. They must have appreciated the changing road numbers, names, population counts and signage styles. (Courtesy Marshall County Historical Museum.)

Three

Pass with Care

Traveling from Argos to Rochester and on to Logansport

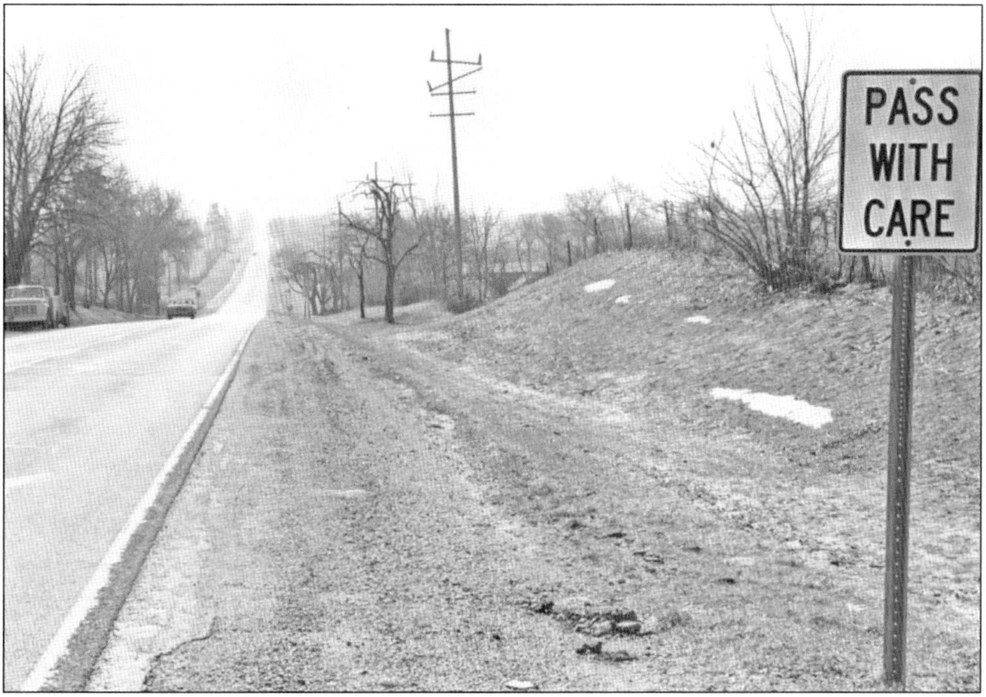

This photograph was taken in the early 1960s on Route 31 in the Argos, Indiana, area. The road had been improved by that time. Its wide berms, white and yellow lines, road signs, and modern pavement made traveling less dangerous. The four-lane Route 31 would bypass Argos by the early 1970s. Local residents said it was hard to sleep at night once the highway was rerouted because the night was so quiet without the truck traffic. In the earlier days, the Dixie Highway ran through this area on US Route 31 to Rochester, where it picked up State Road 25 to Logansport. (Courtesy Marshall County Historical Museum.)

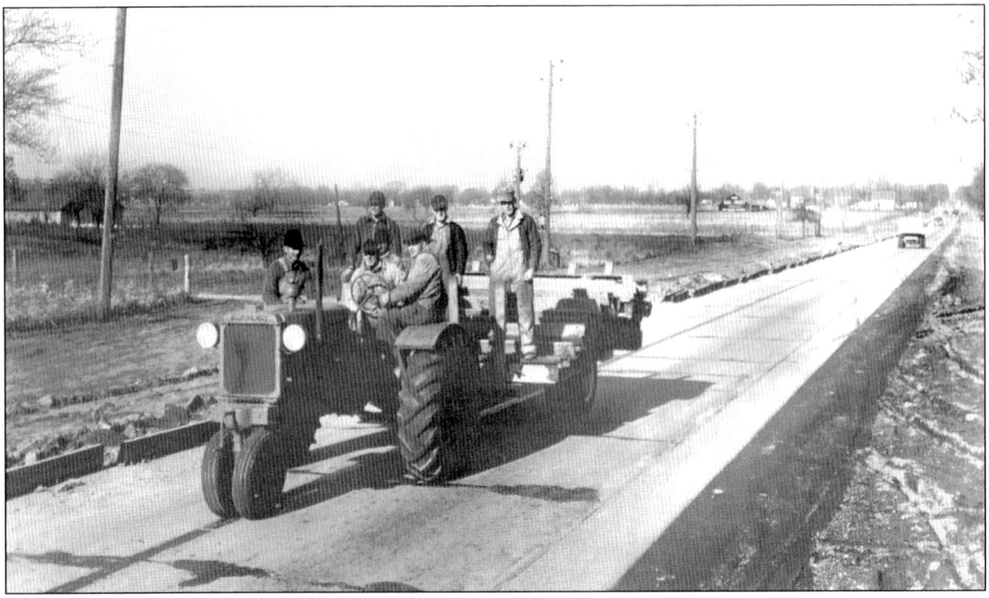

A road construction crew is shown on the Dixie Highway with a tractor and wagon. This crew was working on the road just south of Argos. Paving the Dixie made the highway easier to maintain than in the days when it was graveled and, later, tarred. (Courtesy Marshall County Historical Museum.)

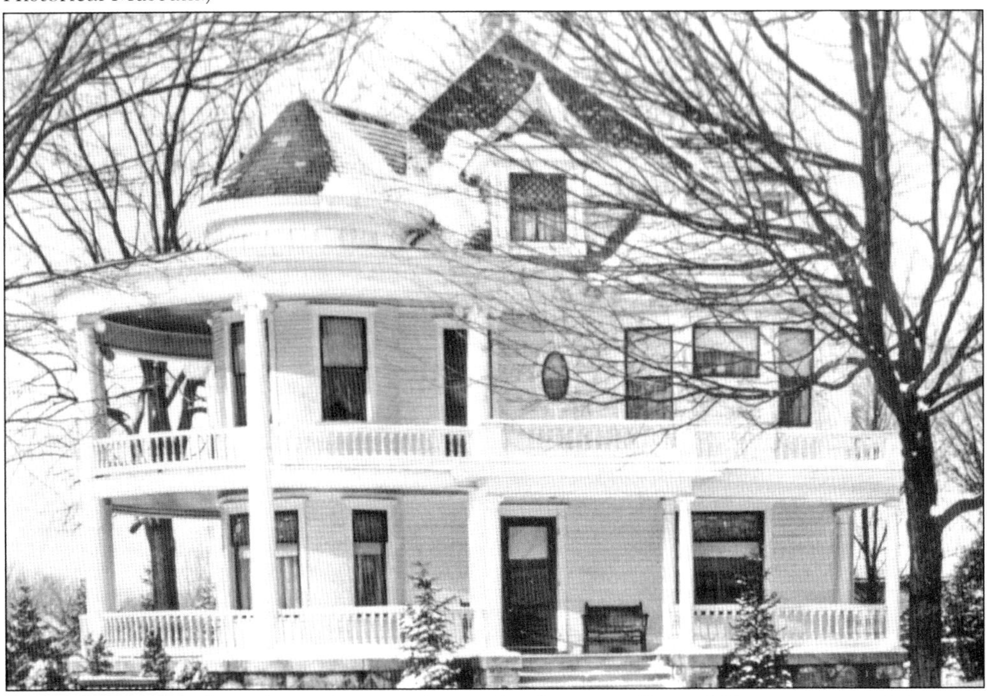

Located at 110 North Michigan Street in Argos, the Grossman Funeral Home was one of the most beautiful homes in the area. The funeral home has been in business for over a century and is now called the Earl Grossman Funeral Home. Previously, it was listed as the O.L. Grossman Furniture and Undertaking business. The business sold rugs, carpets, linoleums, sewing machines, picture frames, refrigerators, pianos, and talking machines. (Courtesy Marshall County Historical Museum.)

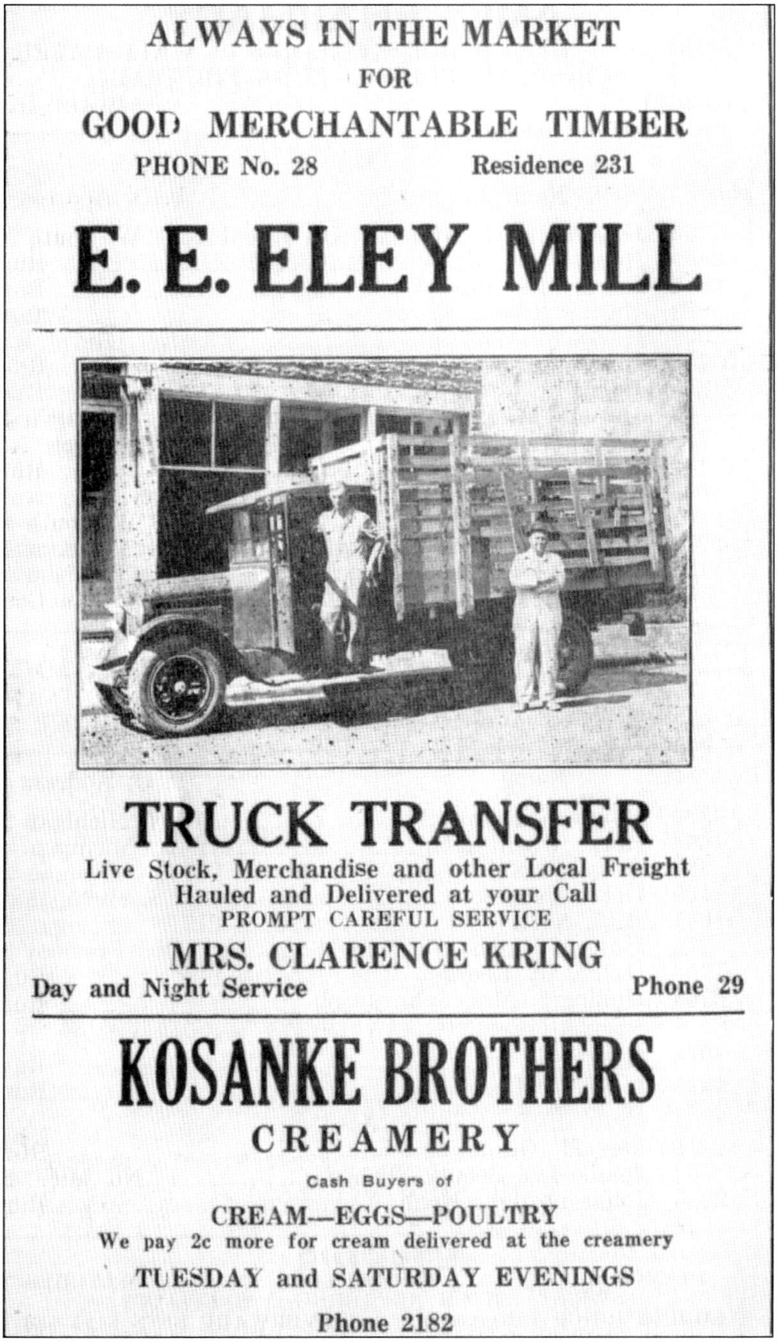

In the 1920s, local businesses promoted their products and services in the Argos newspaper. Beneath the advertisement for the E.E. Eley Mill is an advertisement for Mrs. Clarence Kring's truck transfer company. The advertisement shows the company's early flatbed truck. At the bottom is an advertisement for the Kosanke Brothers Creamery. The area around Argos had an abundance of hardwood lumber to be milled, rich farmland, and dairy farms. Good roads helped Indiana farmers get their goods to market, which meant higher profits. (Courtesy Marshall County Historical Museum.)

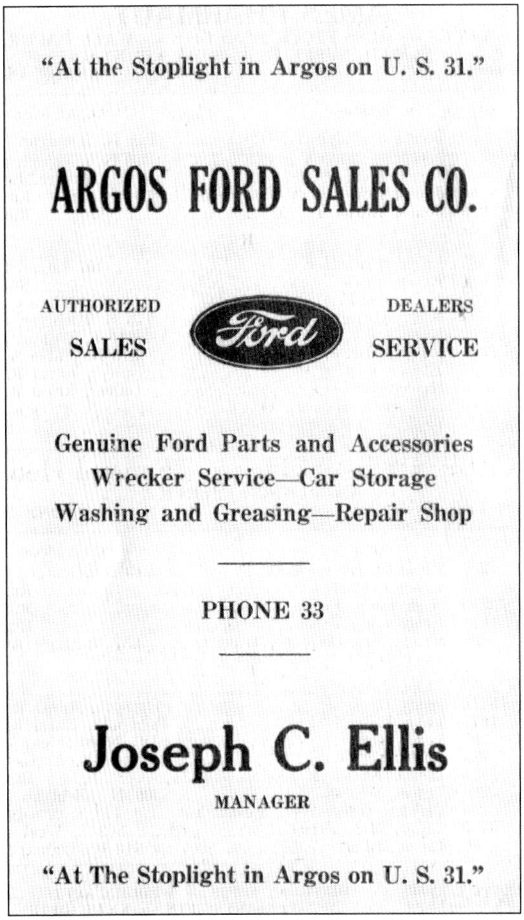

This advertisement is for the Argos Ford Sales Company that was located at the only stoplight in downtown Argos. Route 31 (the Dixie Highway) and State Road 10 intersected at this point. This advertisement appeared in the Argos newspaper in the 1950s. Note the short telephone numbers; all calls were routed through a central operator. (Courtesy Marshall County Historical Museum.)

Operated by Mr. and Mrs. Ardith P. Davis, the Allen Hill Motel was built in the 1950s north of Argos on the Dixie Highway. The Dixie was a main thoroughfare until a new four-lane highway that rerouted truck traffic away from the town was completed. (Courtesy Russell Rein.)

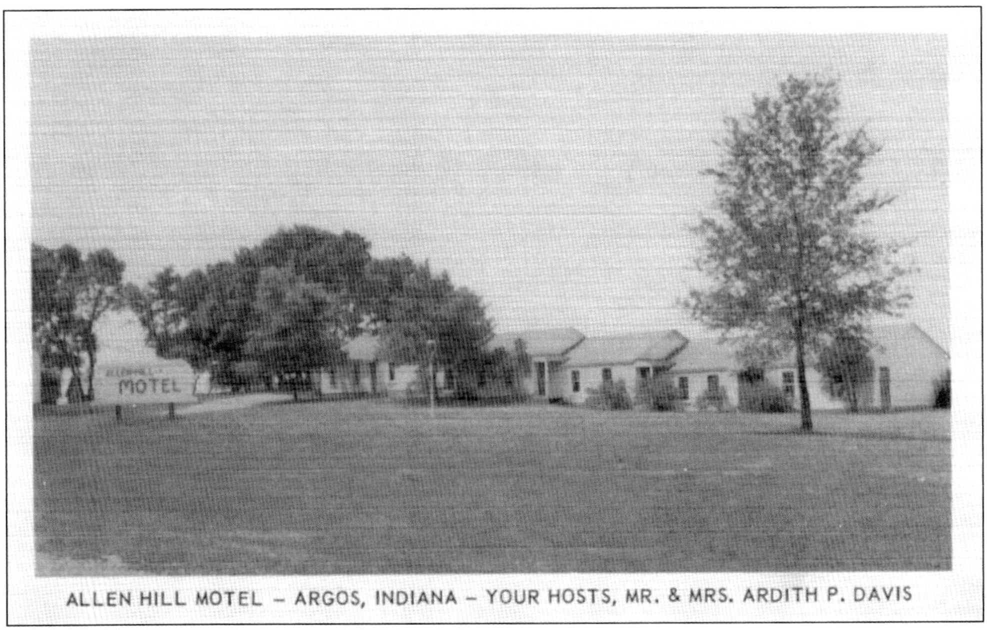

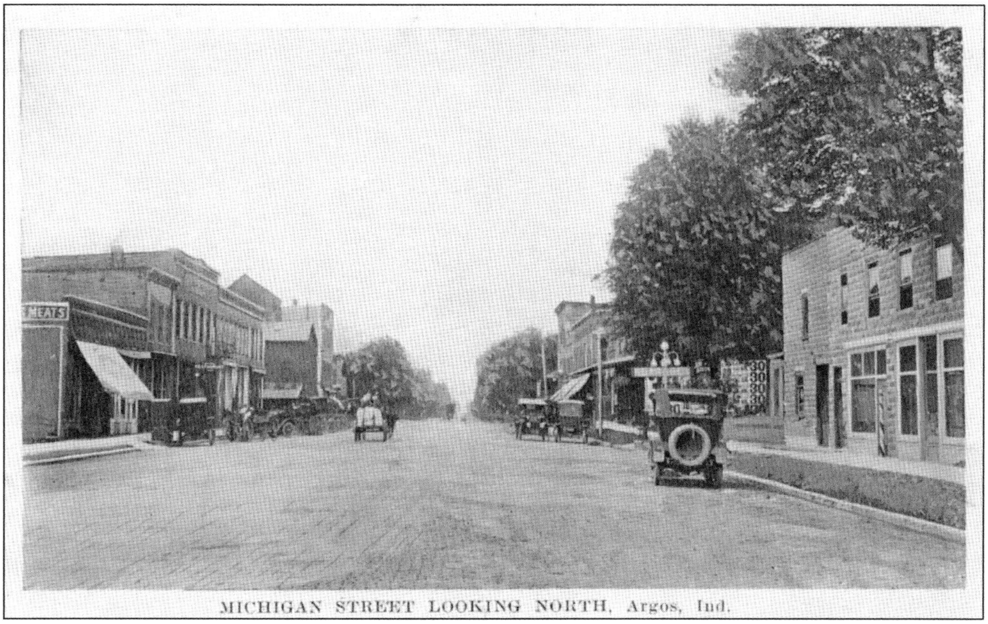

This postcard image captures a glimpse of downtown Argos in the 1910s. The streets are lined with brick pavers and curbing. Small businesses included an auto garage with a gas pump and electric lighting to guide travelers, a barbershop, a grocery, and a small restaurant. The time period between 1910 and 1920 was a major transition between the horse and buggy and the new gasoline-powered automobiles. (Courtesy Russell Rein.)

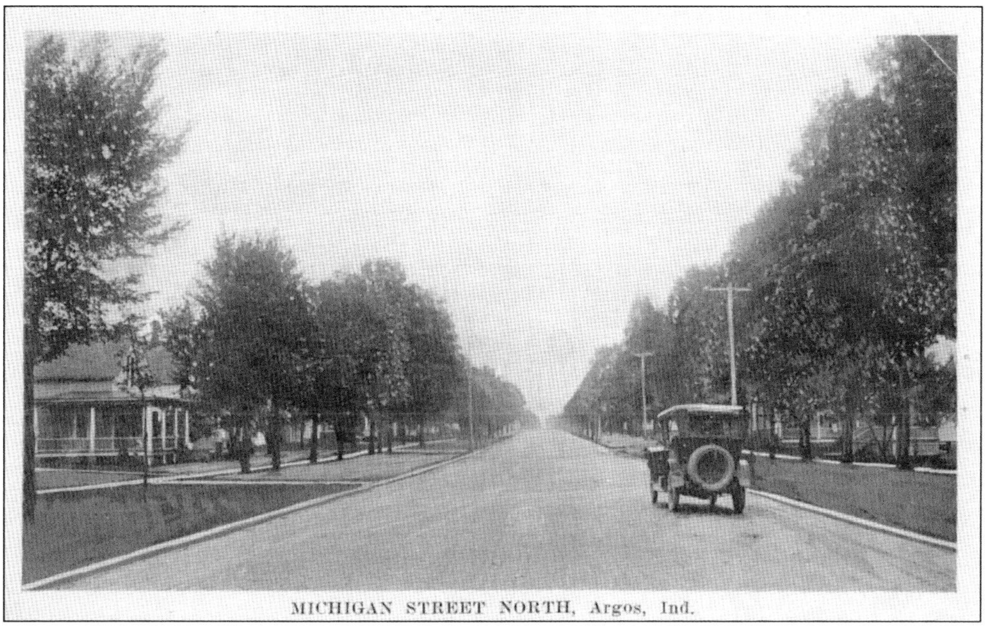

By 1920, traveling through Argos on the Dixie Highway (formerly the Michigan Road) was a pleasant experience. Tree-lined streets with pavers and curbing provided a smooth ride. Notice the concrete sidewalks and beautiful homes along this historic section of the town. (Courtesy Russell Rein.)

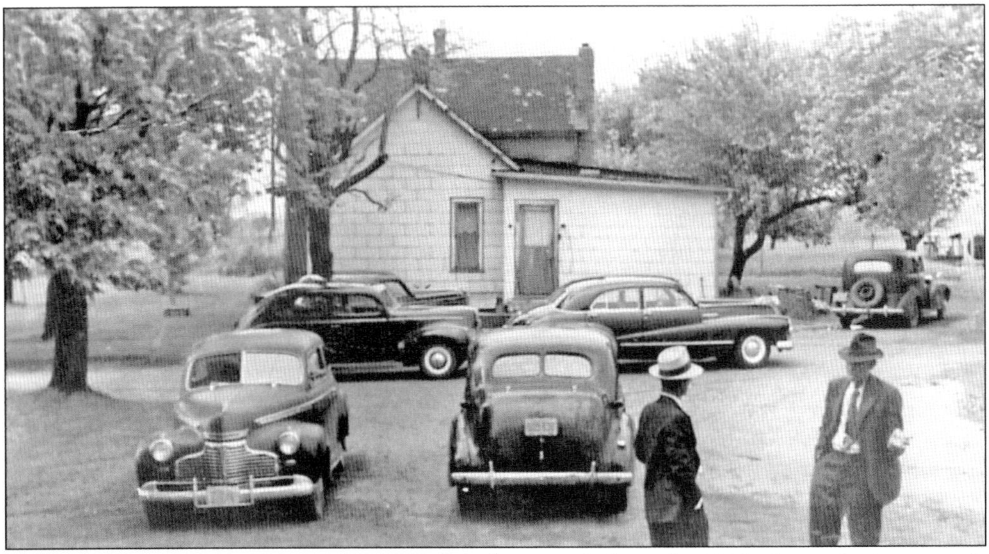

Taken during a holiday family gathering, this photograph from the 1940s shows the Longstreth farm, a typical family farm on the Dixie Highway south of Argos. Catering to the Dixie Highway traffic, the Longstreths sold homegrown vegetables, watermelons, and pumpkins at a roadside stand on their property. (Courtesy La Donna Weber.)

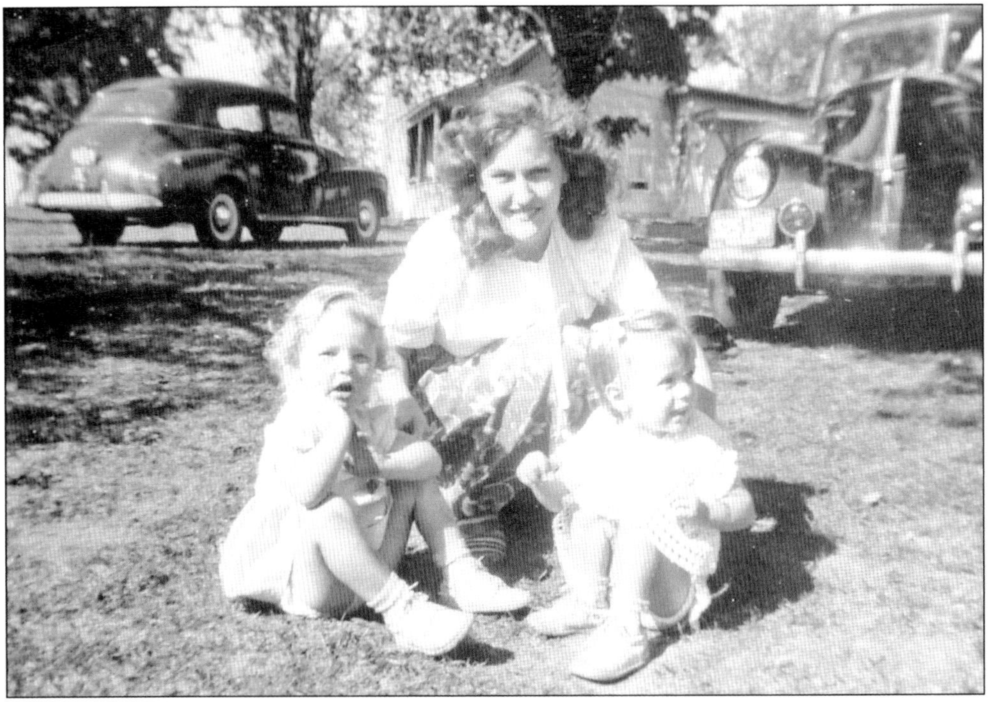

Martha Grossman Longstreth and daughters Karen and Barbara pose at the Longstreth farm south of Argos on the Dixie Highway. The farm included a corn crib, a chicken house, a tool shed, and a German-style bank barn that advertised Mail Pouch tobacco and, later, Kreamo Bread. The highway advertisements were painted on the south side of the barn and served as highway billboards. The family was paid a small fee for allowing the advertiser to paint their barn. (Courtesy La Donna Weber.)

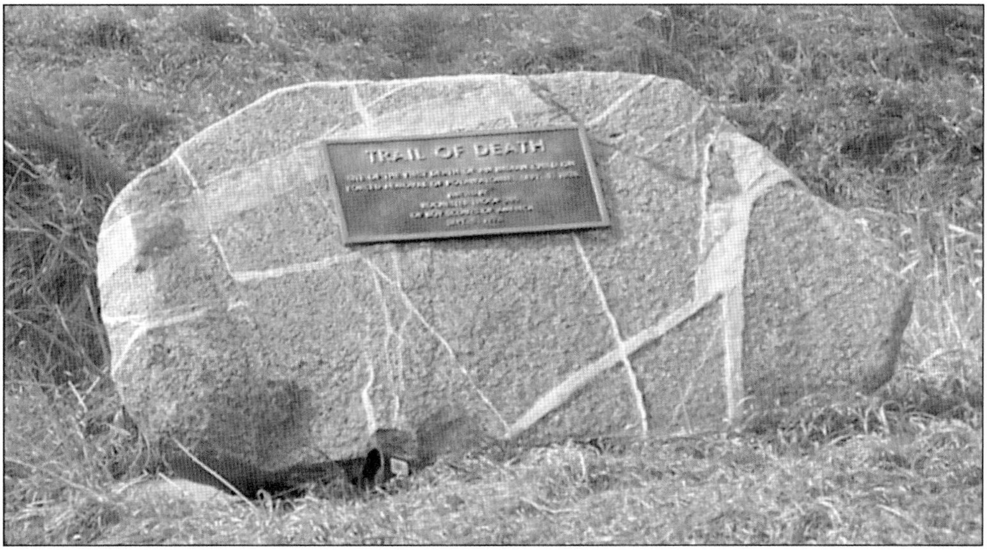

In the fall of 1838, the Potawatomi were forcibly moved from north-central Indiana to eastern Kansas. It was a year of terrible drought, and water was scarce. What water they found was stagnant and caused a fever believed to be typhoid. Of the 859 Potawatomi who started, 41 died along the way and were buried in unmarked graves. The start of the Potawatomi Trail of Death is marked by the Chief Menominee statue south of Plymouth. The Trail of Death marker in this photograph was placed on a stone at the Tippecanoe River at the site of the old iron bridge over the river north of Rochester. This spot marks the gathering place where Potawatomi people met before their departure from Indiana. A concrete span has replaced the metal through-truss bridge. (Both, courtesy Jan Shupert-Arick.)

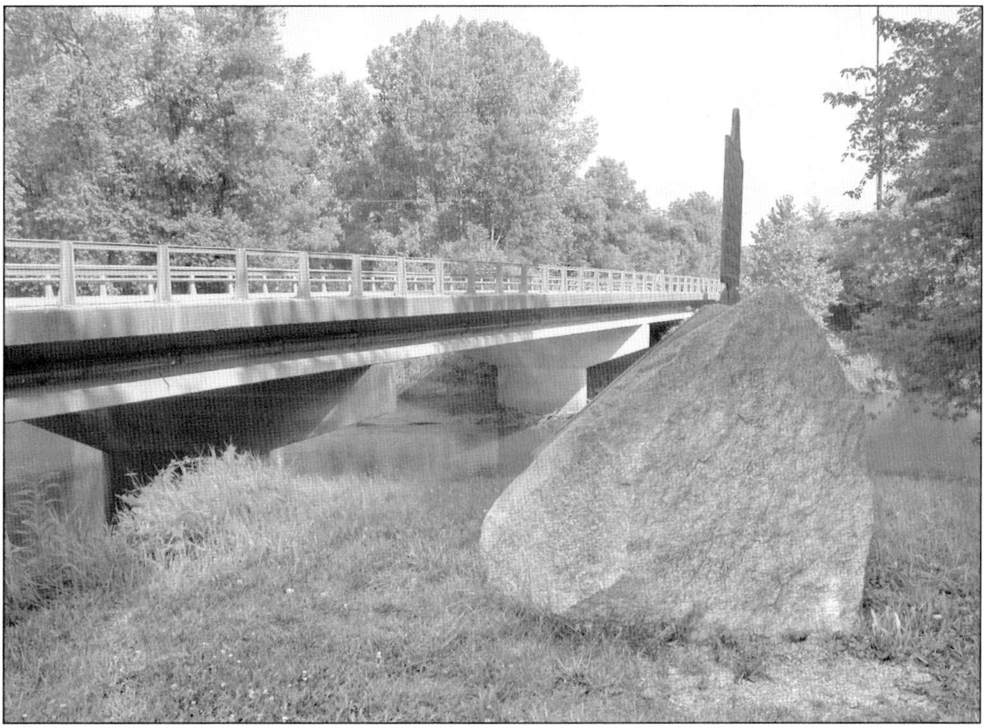

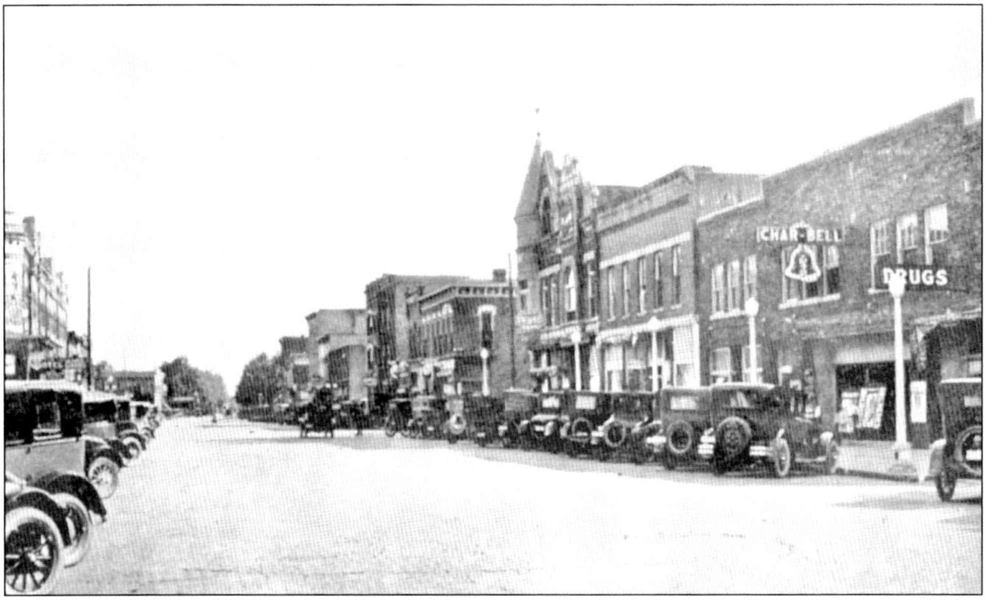

Looking north from the center of town, this 1920s image of downtown Rochester shows the Char-Bell restaurant and the drugstore on Michigan Street. The main street was surfaced in brick pavers. Automobiles line the street as a horse and wagon pass. The first automobile arrived in Rochester in 1901 with a minstrel show. The automobile had a steam horn that sparked the public's curiosity enough to attend the evening shows. (Courtesy Russell Rein.)

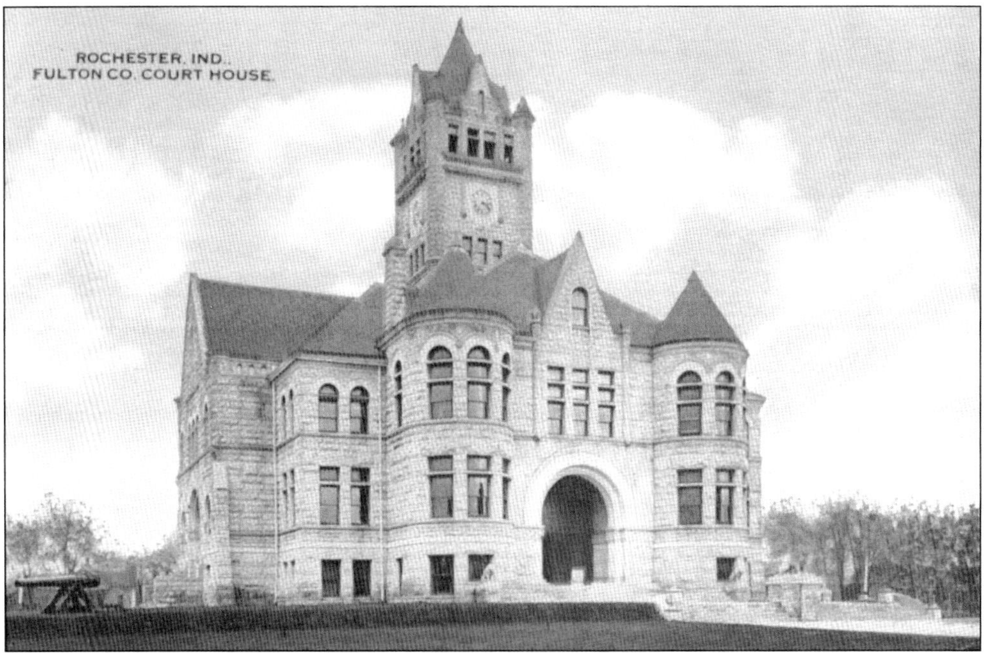

Built in 1896, the Fulton County Courthouse was designed in the Richardsonian Romanesque style of architecture, which featured round-headed Romanesque Revival arches, a large recessed entrance, and cylindrical towers. The exterior is limestone from Bedford, Indiana. The 10 guardian lions were carved by a German stonecutter who brought his 10-year-old son as his interpreter when he came from Europe to work on the courthouse. (Courtesy Russell Rein.)

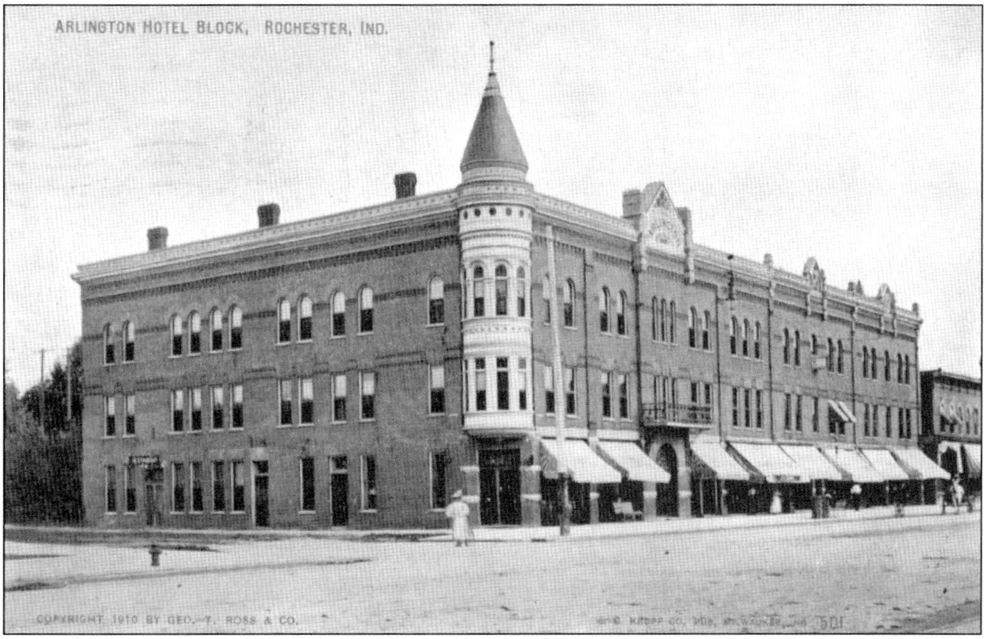

This early image from 1910 shows the Arlington Hotel block in downtown Rochester. The hotel operated from 1890 to 1962. In 1975, a fire destroyed the entire building. (Courtesy Russell Rein.)

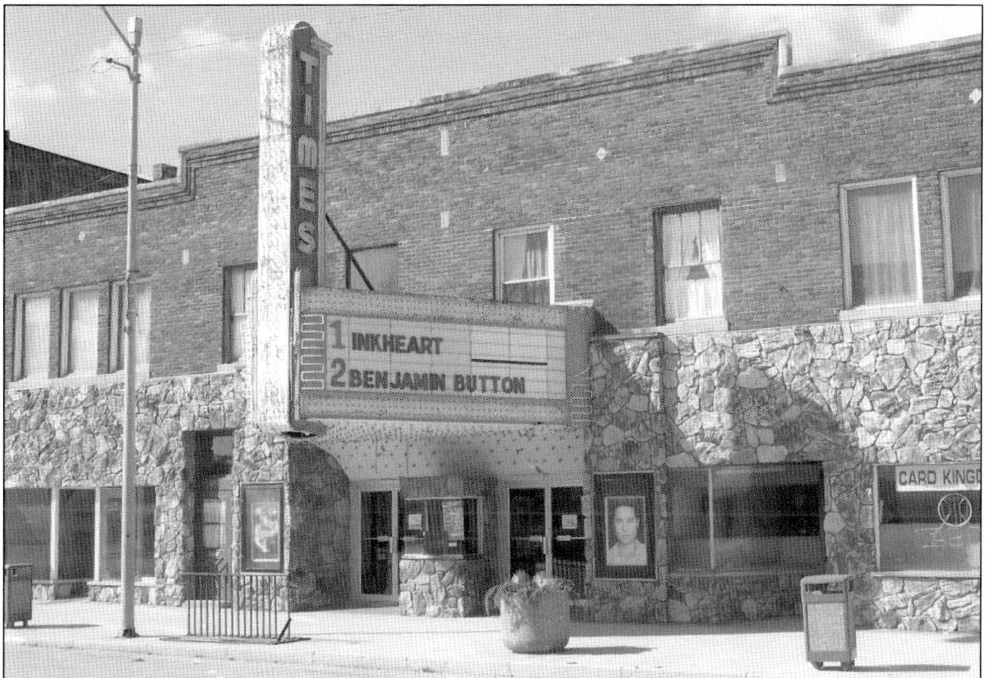

In 1924, the Char-Bell opened on Main Street in Rochester. The 780-seat theater was constructed in a building that formerly housed an automobile dealer. Under new ownership, the Char-Bell was renamed the Times Theatre in 1942. In 1979, the Times was twinned. In 1985, a fire caused damage, however, the theater was repaired. Note the updated marquee with running neon lights. Movie posters lure moviegoers to purchase tickets at the old-fashioned ticket booth. (Courtesy Russell Rein.)

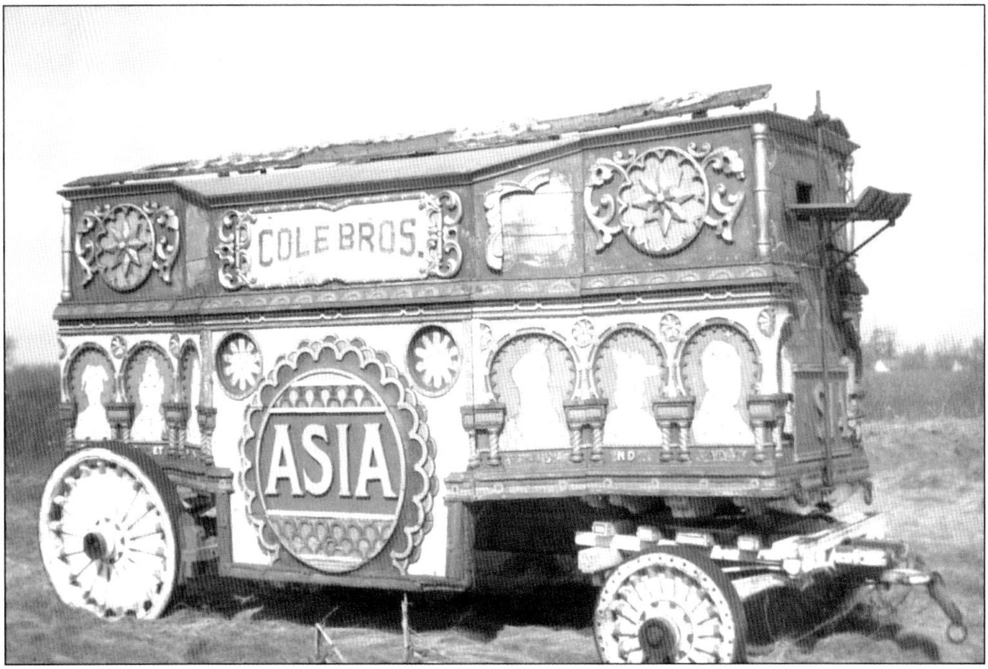

This photograph captures the artistic detail of a Cole Brothers circus wagon. Rochester was the original home of the circus named after W.W. "Chilly Billy" Cole in 1906. Cole was the first man to make over a million dollars in the circus business. The Rochester and Peru communities were the winter homes of Indiana's nationally famous circuses. (Courtesy Russell Rein.)

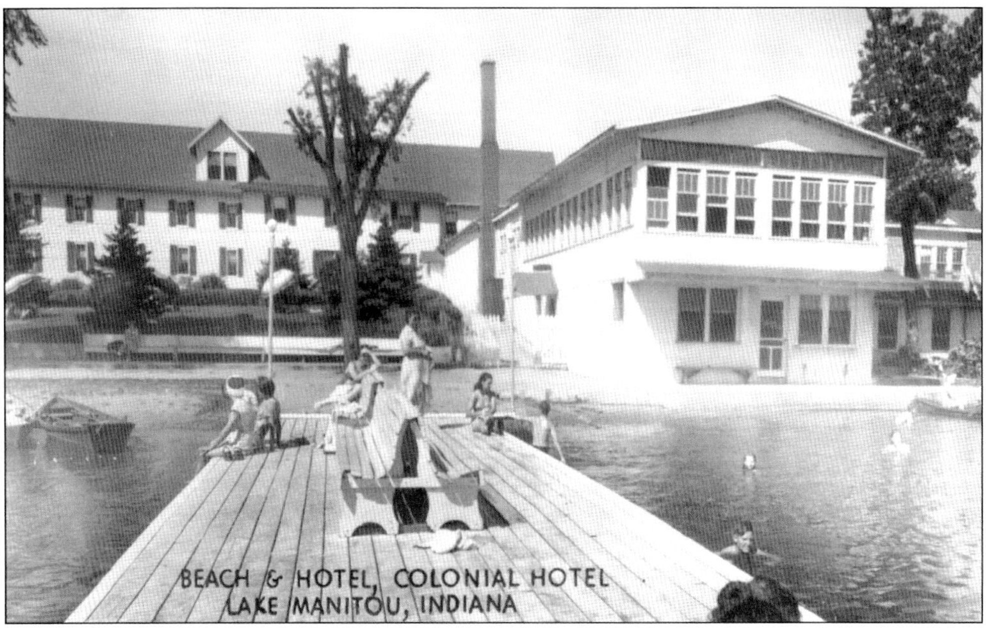

This beach and the Colonial Hotel at Lake Manitou were a tourist destination just east of the Dixie Highway near Rochester. Today, the Colonial Hotel contains condominiums, but in its heyday in 1915, this hotel had become a very popular dance resort. (Courtesy Russell Rein.)

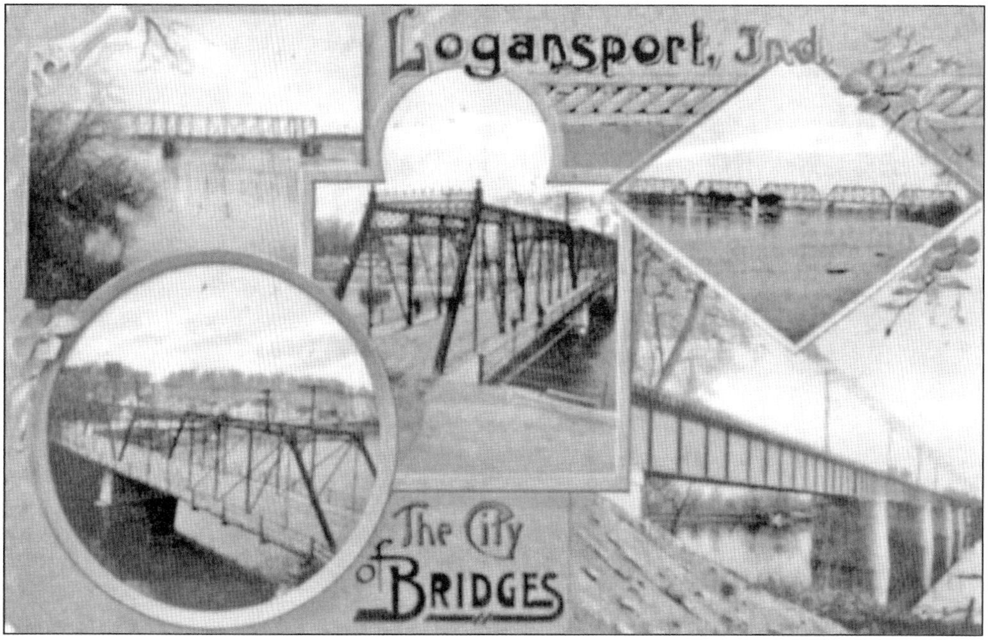

Logansport was known as the city of bridges. Above shows five bridges in and around the city of Logansport. Below is the Third Street Iron Bridge that carried the Dixie Highway. The road was originally crossed by wooden bridges and, later, an iron through-truss span. Fort Wayne and Wabash Valley Traction Company had a track across the east side of the iron truss bridge for a period until its abandonment. Later, a concrete arch bridge was here. Called by the locals the Lost Bridge over Wabash River, it was on Third Street on the north side of Biddle Island. (Both, courtesy Russell Rein.)

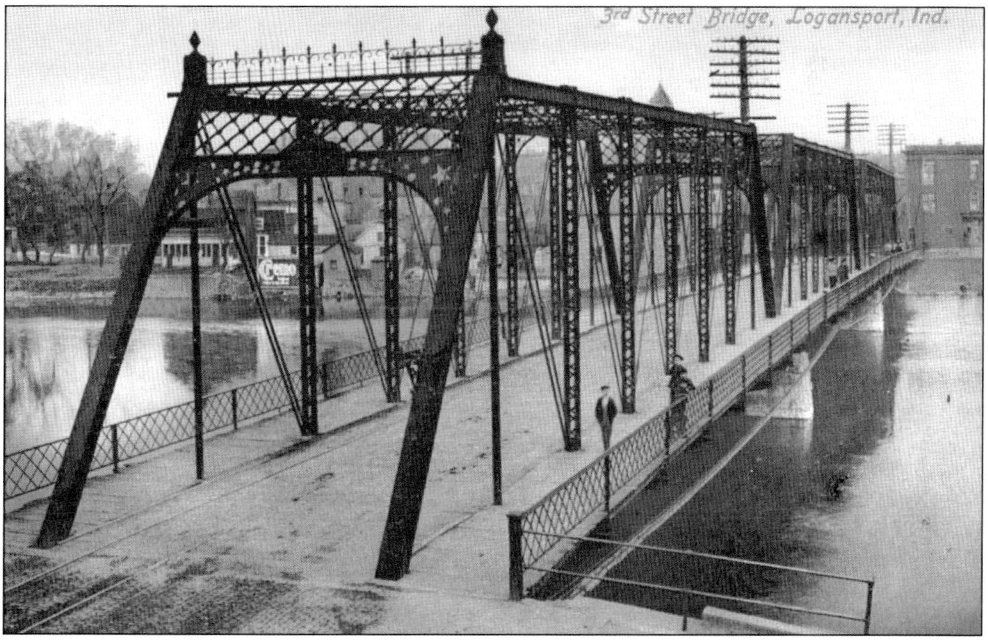

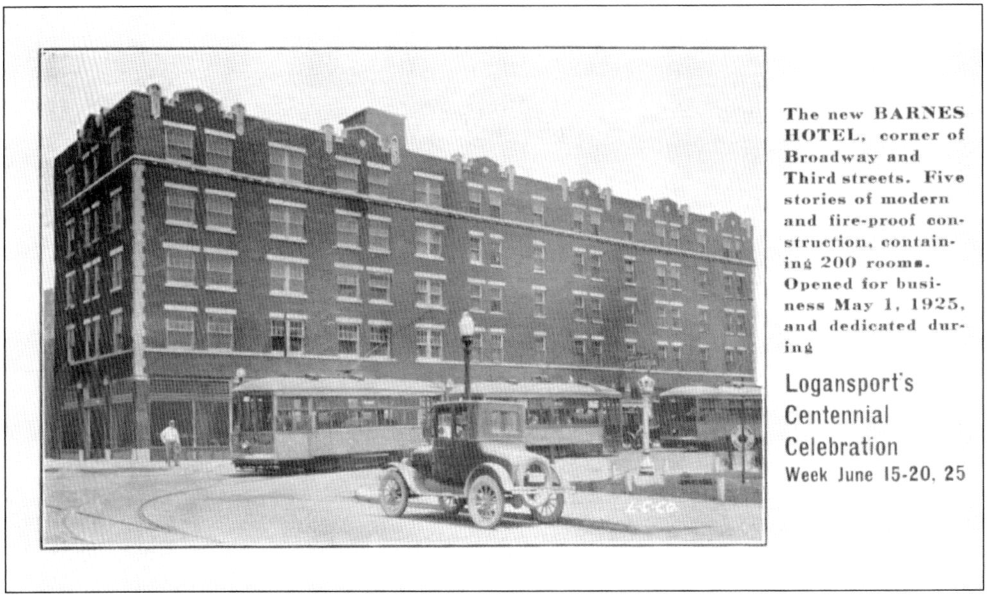

This early image is of the Barnes Hotel, located in downtown Logansport at 300 East Broadway Street. In the photograph are an early train and car, the Barnes Hotel, the Logan Theater, Rite-Way Shoe Shop, and a taxi stand. The Barnes Hotel was later renamed the Captain Logan Hotel. The building is now used as an office building known as Logan Square. (Courtesy Russell Rein.)

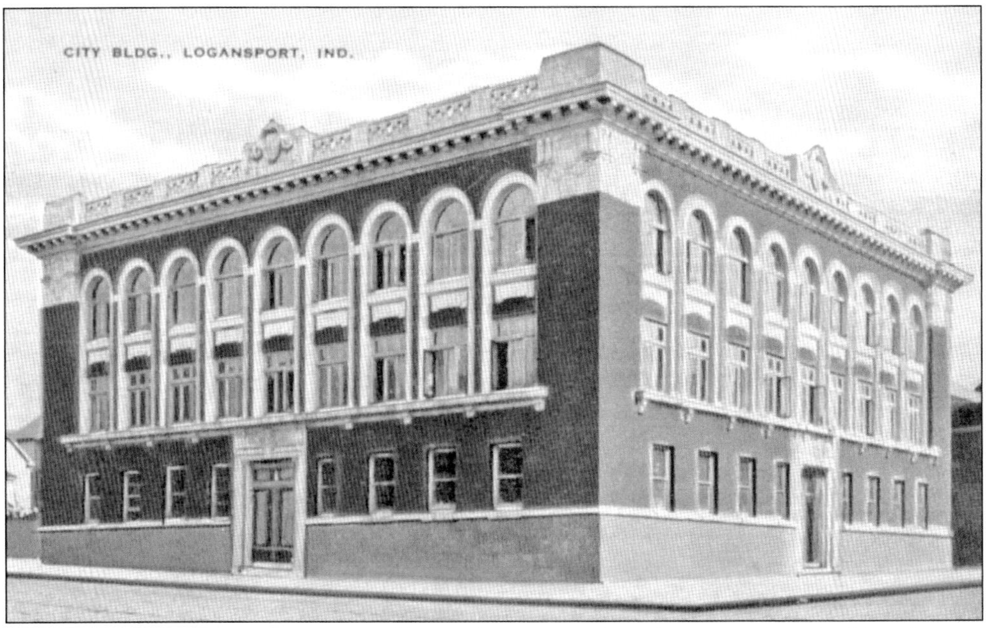

This image captures the unique city building in Logansport. The three-story brick building features an elaborate interior, a central staircase, and a stained-glass skylight. The building continues to serve the community and has been fully restored. The building is listed in the National Register of Historic Places. (Courtesy Russell Rein.)

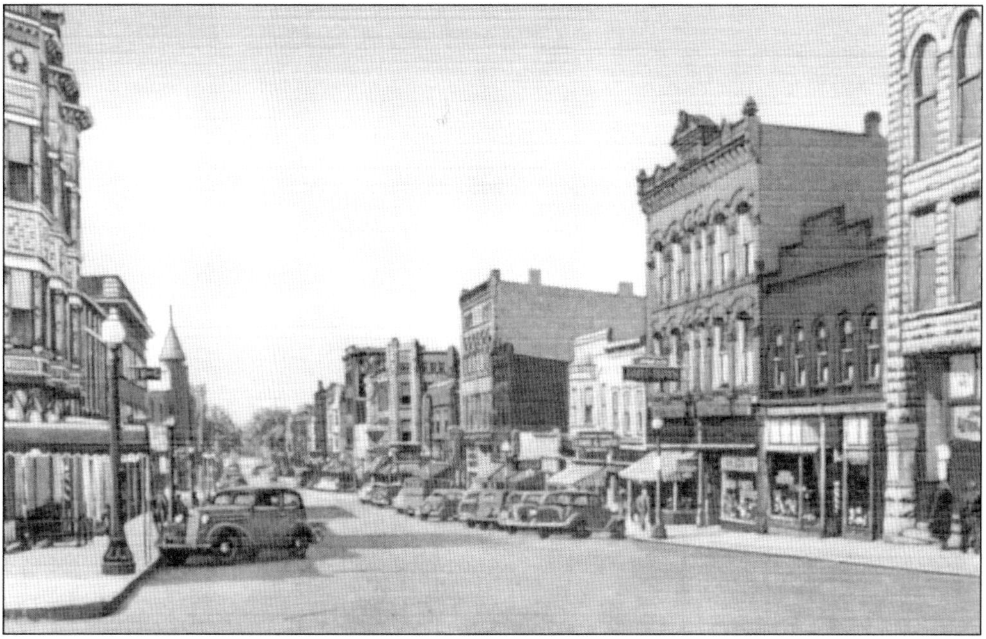

Pictured in the 1940s, this section of East Broadway Street looking west in Logansport is the Dixie Highway before it turns left onto Third Street to continue south. In Logansport, travelers cross two Wabash River bridges because part of the city is actually built on Biddle's Island. The land was purchased from Gen. John Tipton by Judge Horace Biddle. Biddle permitted a Miami chief named No'Kamena to be buried on the island. (Courtesy Russell Rein.)

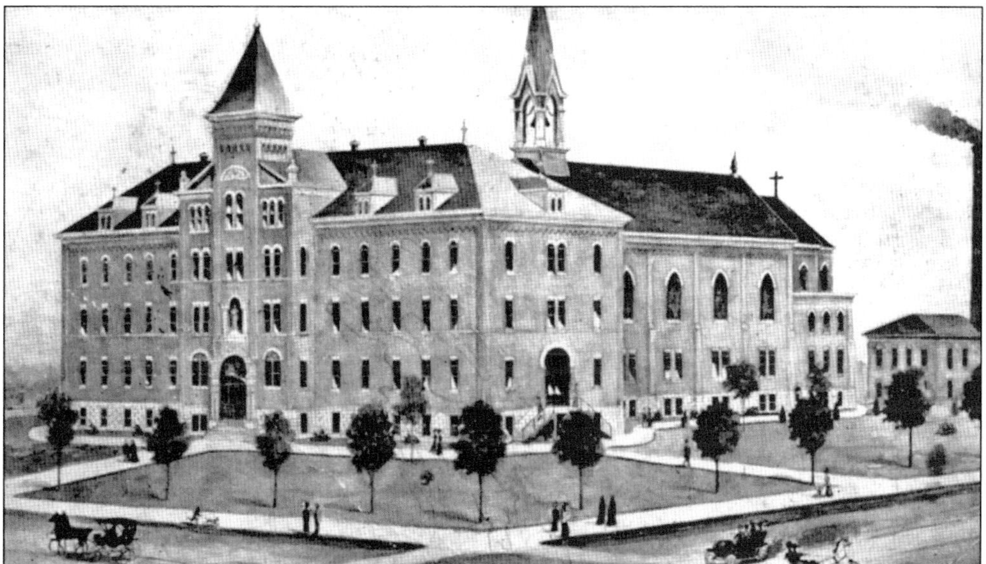

An early image of the Logansport Hospital captures the change in transportation that was taking place in the early 20th century. Notice the horse-drawn vehicle and the early automobile. (Courtesy Jan Shupert-Arick.)

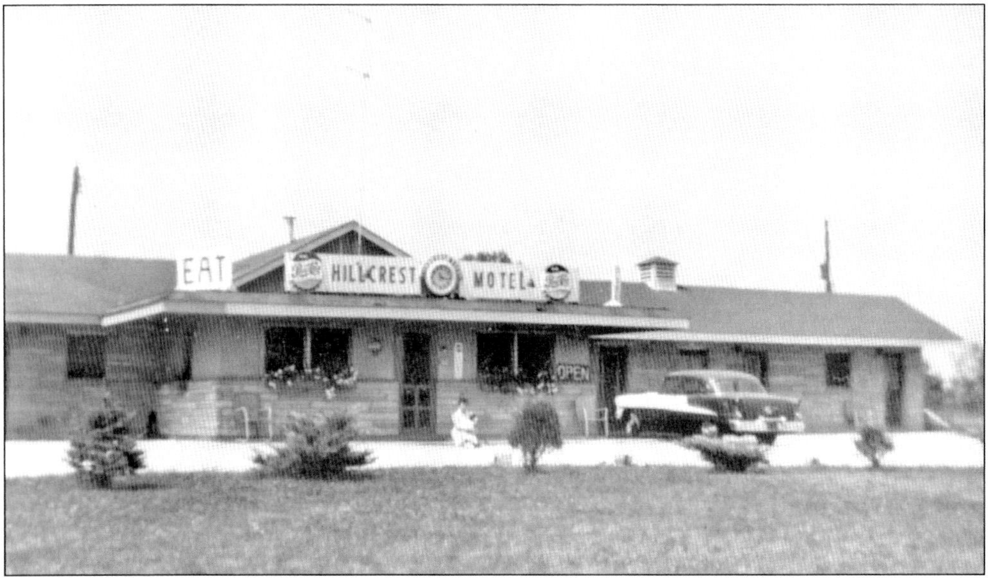

This postcard shows the Hillcrest Motel and Restaurant, located in Logansport. It was a ranch-style structure with a partial limestone facade. The motel sign included a neon-lit clock and advertised Pepsi-Cola products. Notice the 1950s-style lawn chairs and the 1956 Chevy in front of the motel. (Courtesy Russell Rein.)

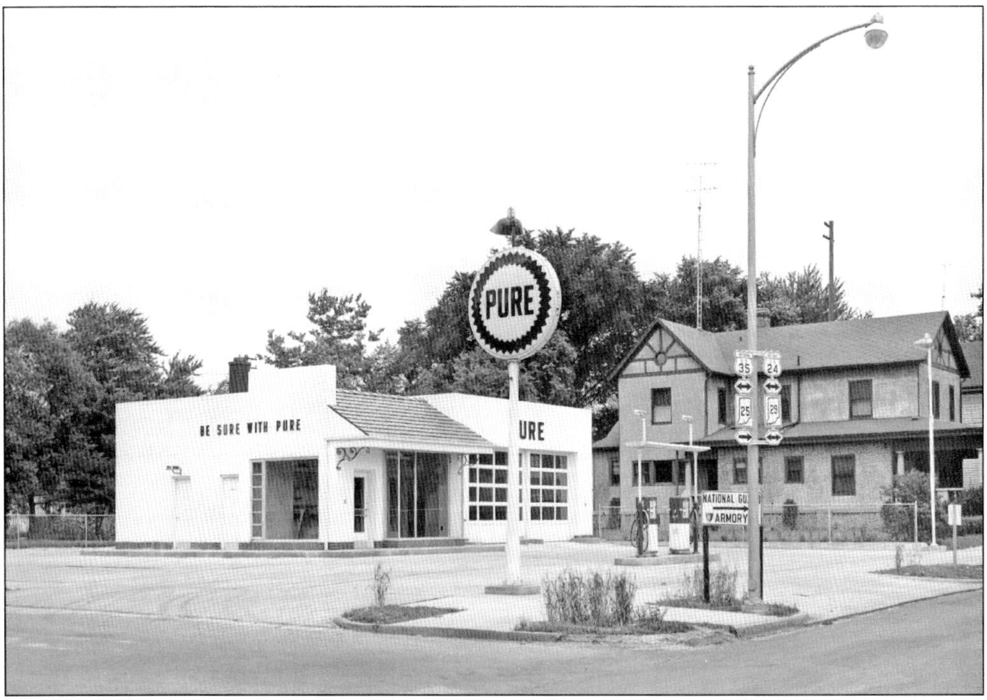

In Logansport, this Pure Oil double-bay service station was built at the corner of US Highways 35 and 24 and State Road 25 (the Dixie Highway). A single island provided Ethyl and regular gasoline. Both gasoline types contained lead, but the Ethyl brand was a higher octane for larger engines. This image was purchased from the file collection of the Pure Oil Corporation, and it appears to have been taken in the 1960s. (Courtesy Russell Rein.)

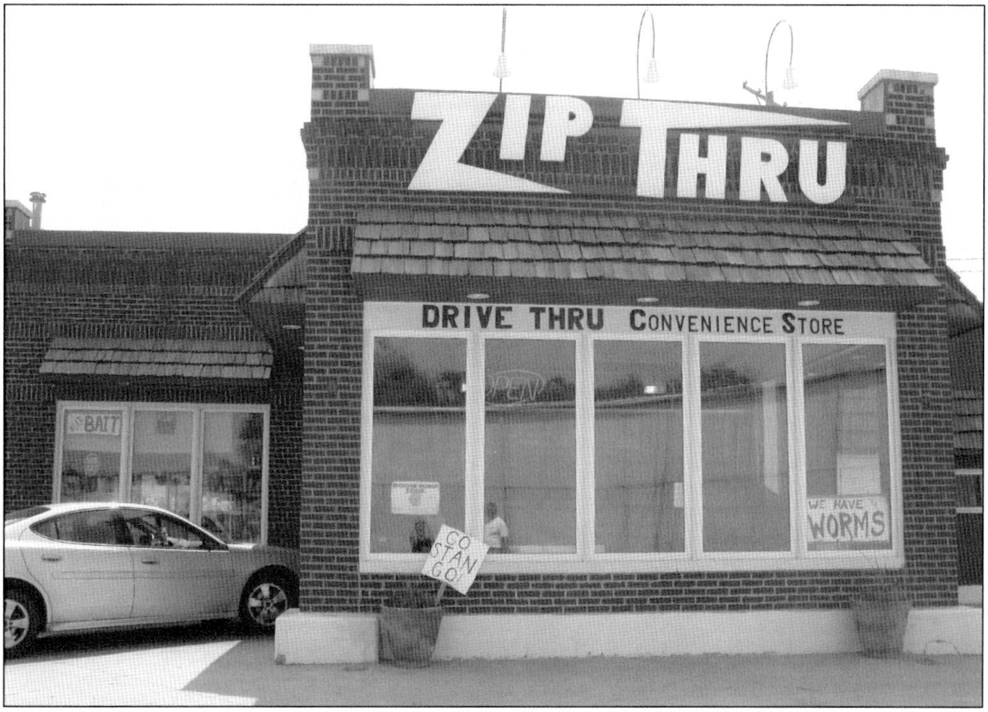

An unusual business in Logansport, the Zip Thru, is an old gas station converted to a grocery store. This is the ultimate in convenience stores; with its drive-thru ordering and pickup, customers can shop without leaving their cars. (Courtesy Jan Shupert-Arick.)

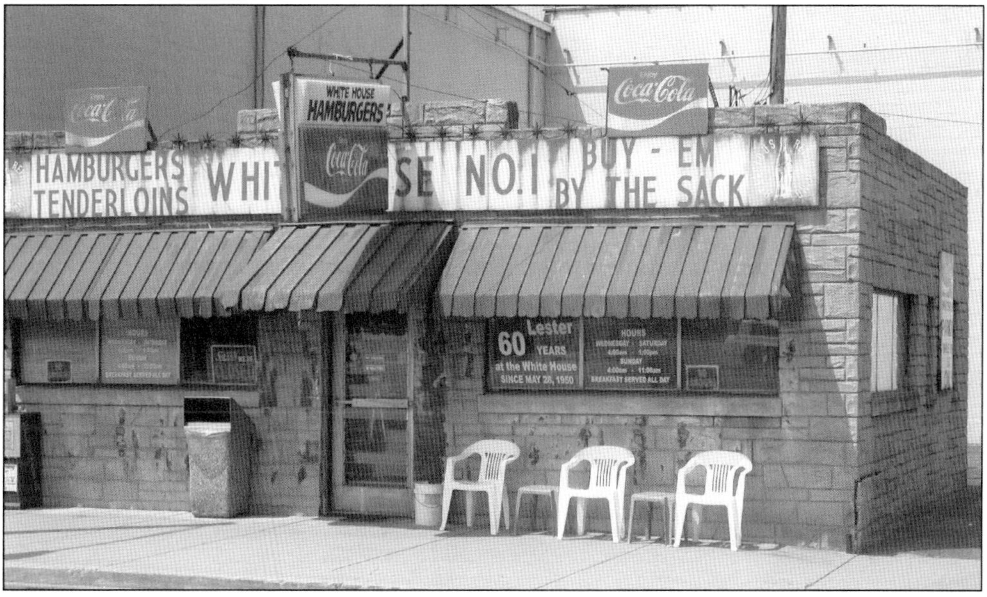

The White House No. 1 Restaurant windows advertise 60 years in business and is an icon in Logansport. Proprietor Lester Hettinger opened this place in 1950 and has been flipping burgers ever since. The White House is set up like a diner with a few booths and ringside seats at the counter that overlook the grill. Hanging on pegs along the back wall are coffee cups of all logos, brought in by regulars to use on their visits. They also serve tenderloins. (Courtesy Jim Grey.)

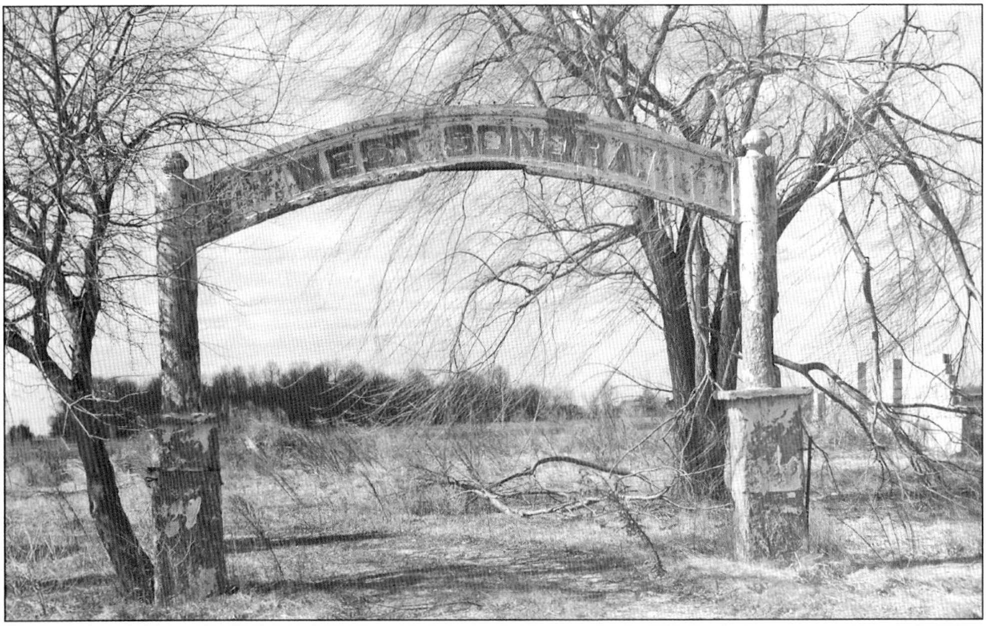

Carroll County was formed in 1828 and named for Charles Carroll, the last surviving signer of the Declaration of Independence, who died in 1832. The county seat is Delphi. Approximately nine miles south of Logansport a careful observer can spot an old arch marking the small community once known as West Sonora and renamed Deer Creek. The West Sonora name can still be seen on the arch. (Courtesy Russell Rein.)

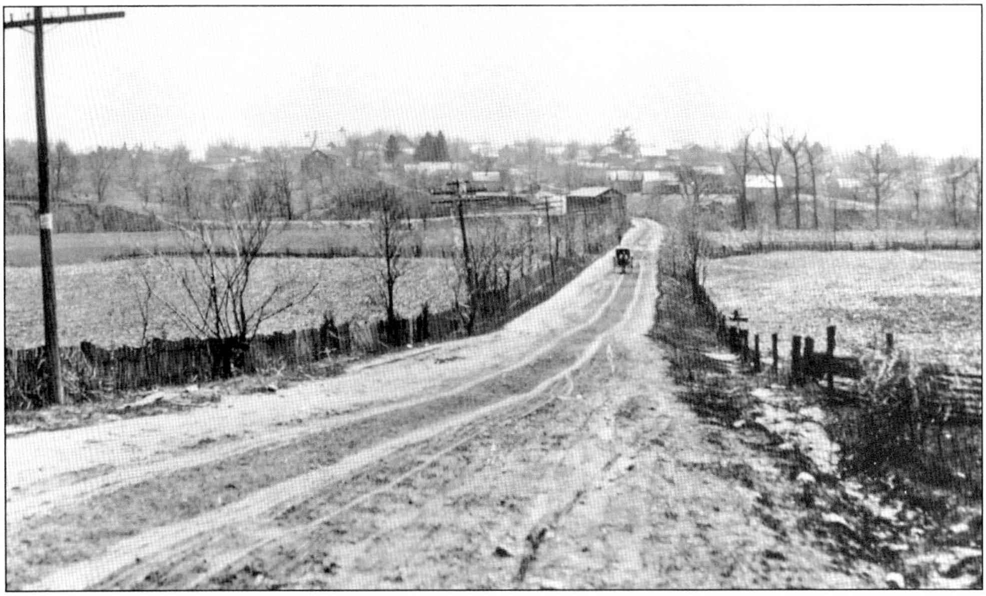

This section of road was located between Logansport and Indianapolis on this stretch of the Dixie Highway. A covered bridge over Wildcat Creek headed south to Burlington. Burlington was founded in 1832 and named for Chief Burlington of the Wyandotte Indian tribe. Burlington was a stagecoach and tavern stop on the Michigan Road. A tollgate at the south edge of the village charged vehicles 10¢ to pass. A Ford Auto Garage opened for business there in the 1920s. (Courtesy Carroll County Historical Society.)

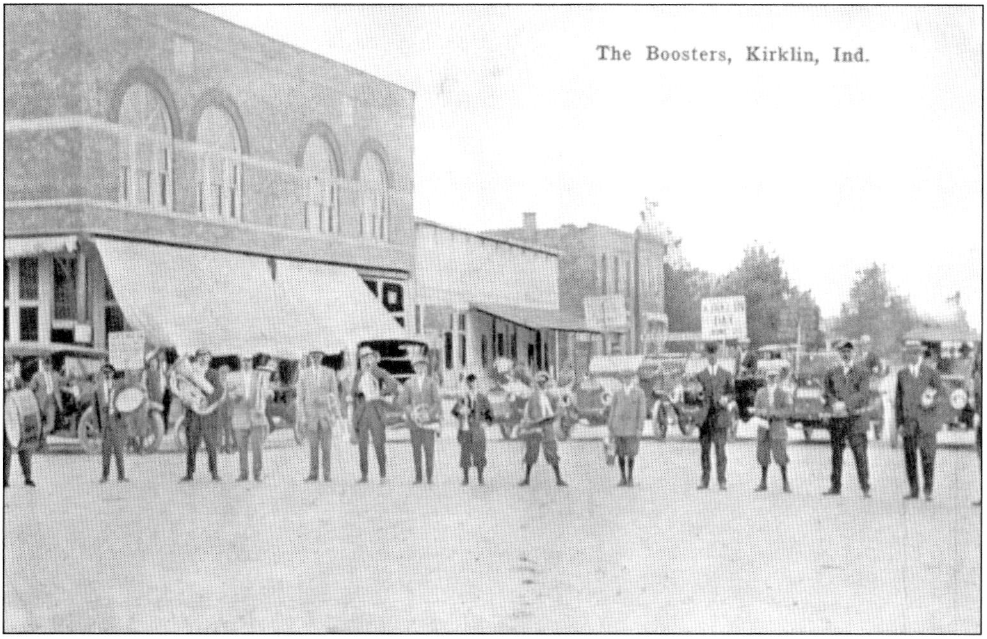

Kirklin, Indiana, is located in Clinton County. Nathan Kirklin laid out the town in the early 1830s and operated a tavern on the Michigan Road. Edward Miller established the first general store in a log building, and William Wynkoop built the first hotel. Kirklin hosted horse shows and street fairs along its modern, paved Main Street. In this photograph from the 1920s, the local band boosters played in a parade in Kirklin. A number of antique shops now occupy much of Kirklin's downtown. (Courtesy Russell Rein.)

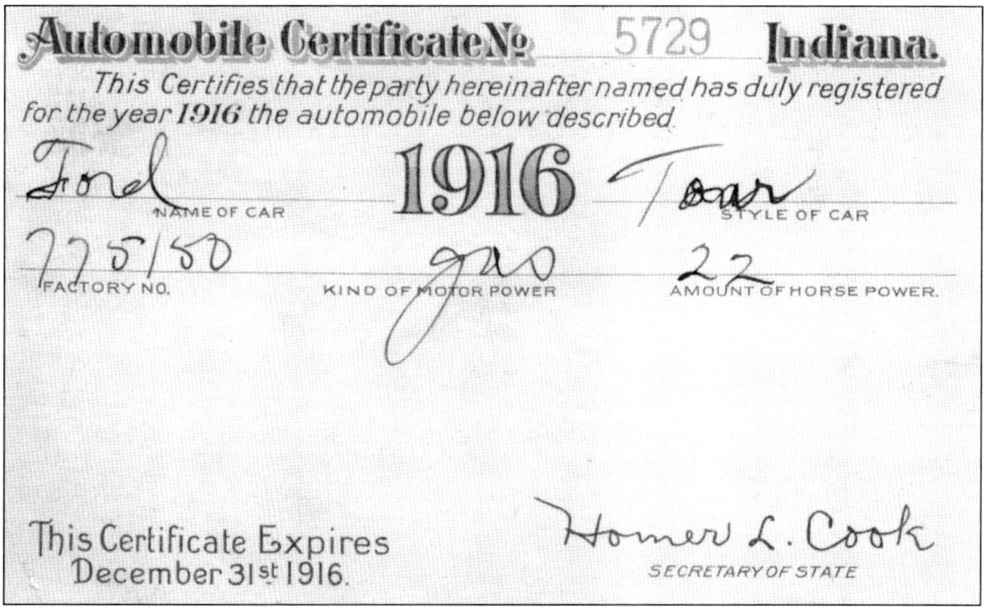
Automobile Certificate No 5729 Indiana.

This Certifies that the party hereinafter named has duly registered for the year **1916** *the automobile below described.*

Ford — NAME OF CAR — 1916 — Tour — STYLE OF CAR

775180 — FACTORY NO. — gas — KIND OF MOTOR POWER — 22 — AMOUNT OF HORSE POWER.

This Certificate Expires December 31st 1916.

Homer L. Cook
SECRETARY OF STATE

As automobiles became more common, state laws required annual registration of each vehicle. Pictured is an authentic registration certificate issued by Indiana in 1916. The state was celebrating its centennial, and automobiles and good roads were on the rise in 1916. (Courtesy Jan Shupert-Arick.)

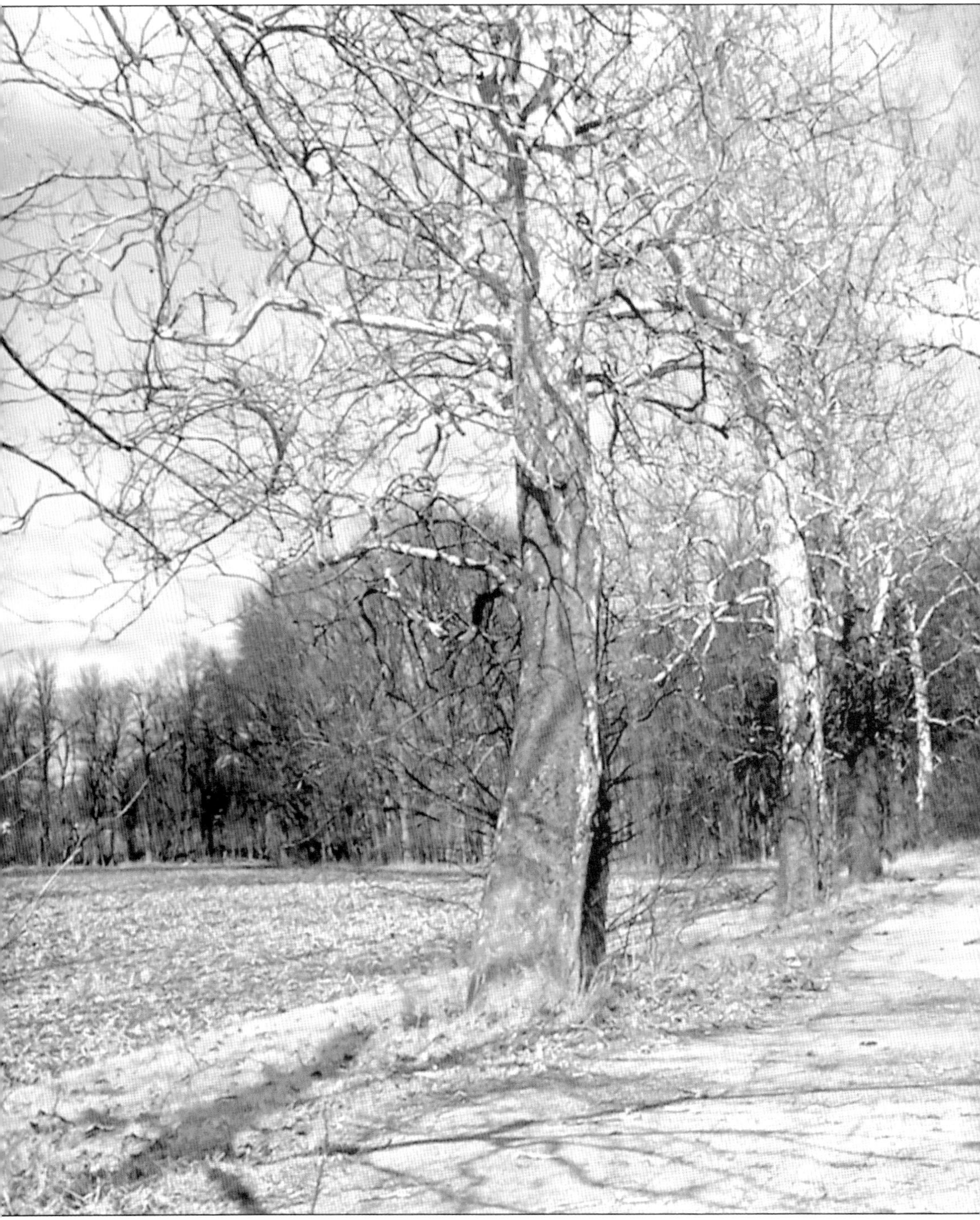

Sycamore Row was a plank road on the old Michigan Road (Dixie Highway) between Logansport and Indianapolis. Sycamore Row was formed when trees that were felled in this wetland area were used to build a corduroy road to fix the Michigan Road's muddy condition. The green sycamore logs sprouted on each side of the road and grew to be mature trees. The 1941 *WPA Guide to Indiana* describes this area as "a tunnel of foliage formed by a 400-foot row of tall sycamore trees

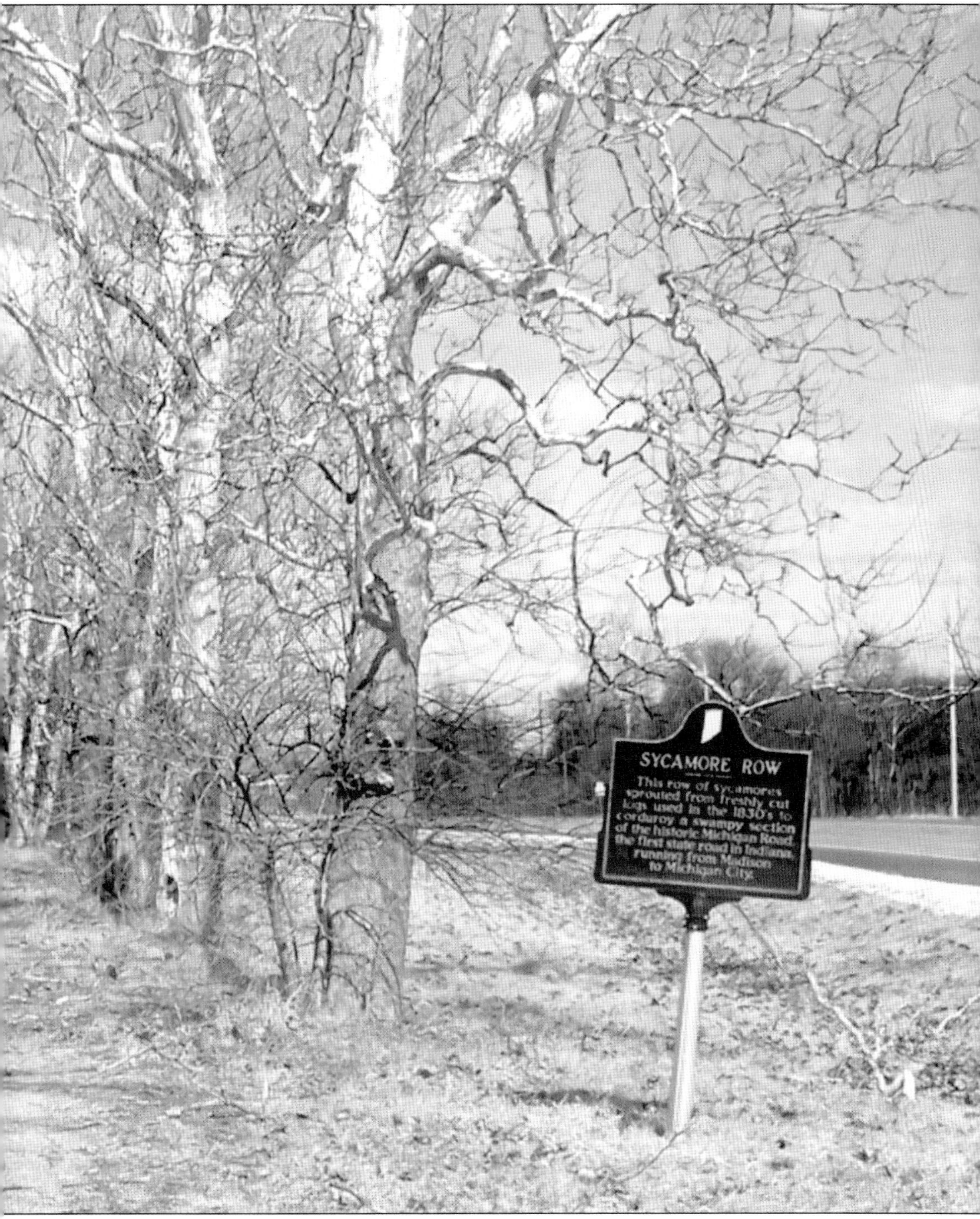

on each side of the roadway, which narrows here to 20 feet." Up until 1987, there was a narrow bottleneck because of an old steel truss bridge over Deer Creek and the Sycamore Row. The old iron truss bridge was demolished, and a new bridge was built to the east to allow widening of State Road 29. Historic-minded Carroll County residents convinced state officials to preserve Sycamore Row as a historic site with a marker. (Courtesy Russell Rein.)

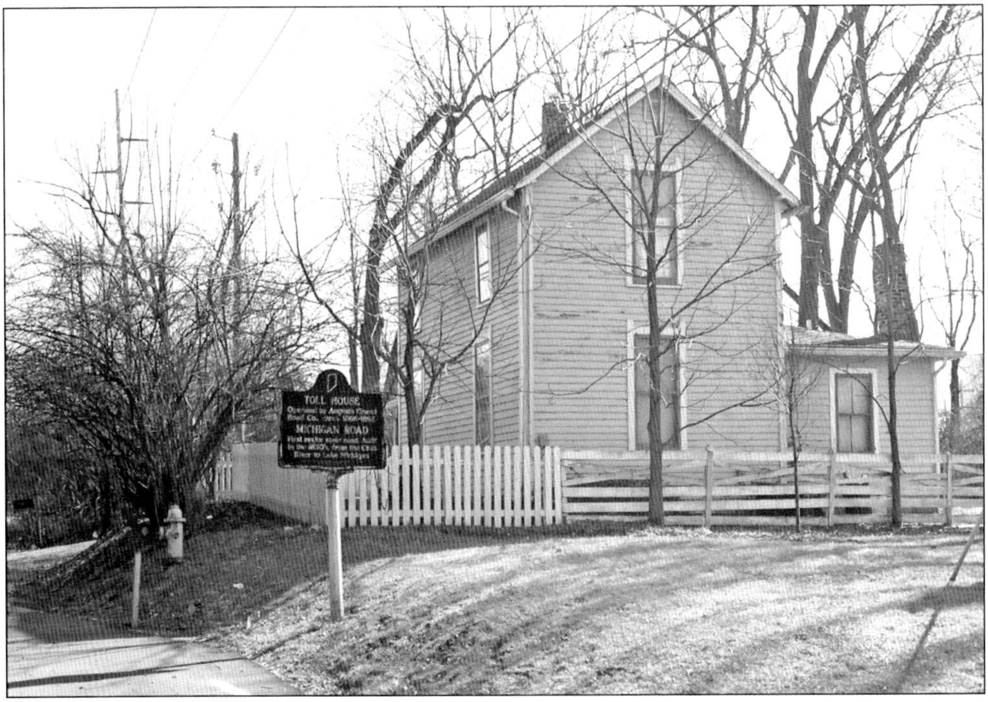

The Toll House and its historical marker are located at 4702 North Michigan Road in Indianapolis. The Toll House was established on the Michigan Road (built in the 1830s and the first major state road) to control traffic to Indianapolis. Allowing private companies to collect tolls on roads they had improved was a common practice in Indiana. The New Augusta Gravel Company had put gravel on parts of the Michigan Road north of Indianapolis and collected the tolls. Samuel Howard was the toll keeper here for 25 years in the late 19th century. Living with his wife, Howard served as toll collector, storekeeper, postmaster, and notary public for travelers and nearby farmers. (Both, courtesy Russell Rein.)

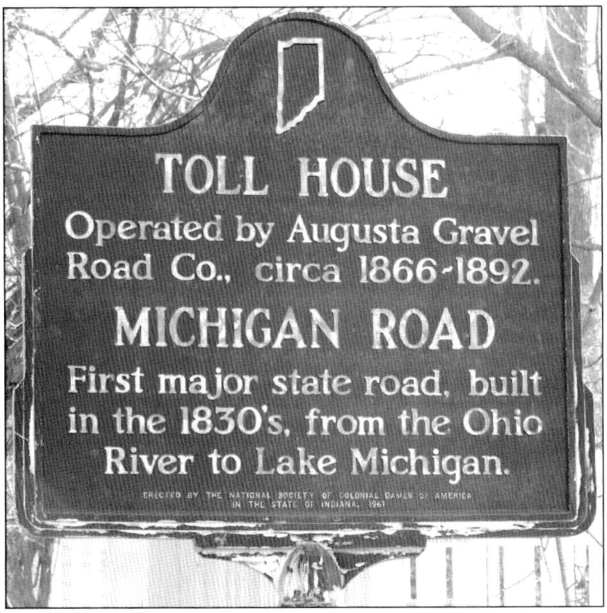

Four

Indianapolis
City of Style, Speed, and the Spectacular

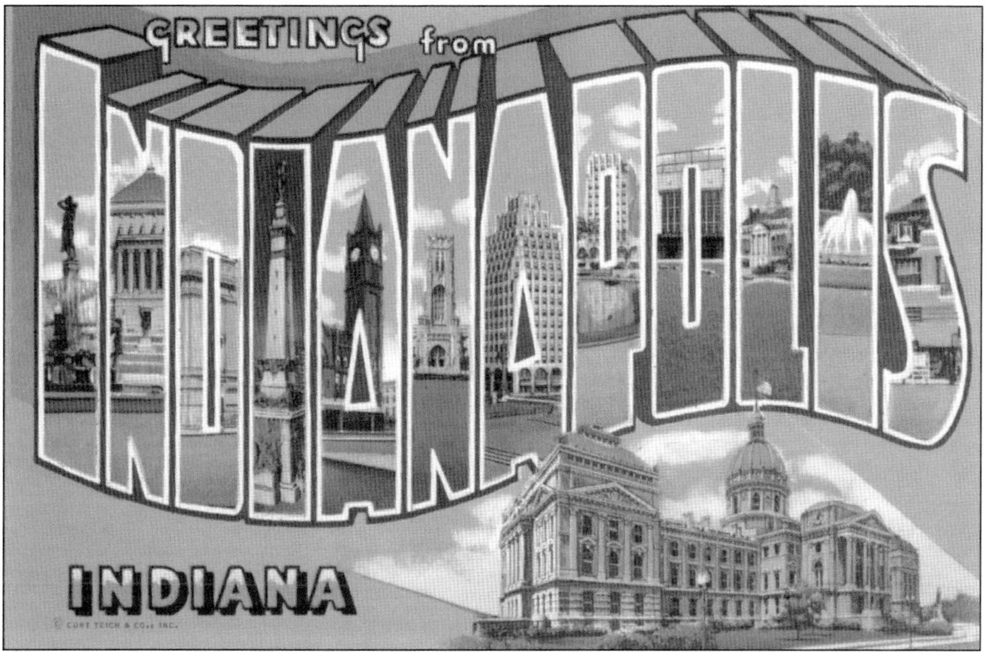

Indianapolis was carefully planned as the state capital. In 1820, the legislature in Vincennes selected 10 commissioners to choose a site for the state capital. Fall Creek, located at the center of the state, was chosen. Alexander Ralston laid out the streets of Indianapolis to radiate from a central circle, like the spokes of a wheel. Today, Monument Circle features the Soldiers' and Sailors' Monument. In 1881, Indianapolis was one of the first American cities to have paved streets and electric streetlights throughout. At the end of the 19th century, the automobile was developed by companies in and around Indianapolis, and the first automobile race was held at the Indianapolis Motor Speedway in 1911. By 1920, Indianapolis became an important industrial city with a population of 300,000. (Courtesy Russell Rein.)

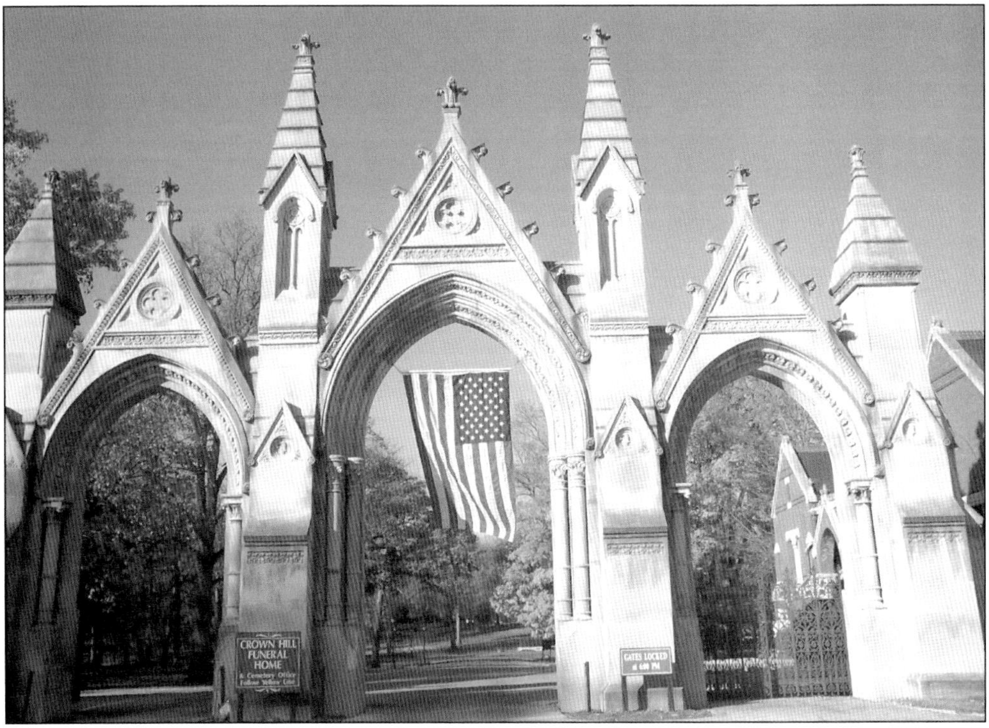

Crown Hill Cemetery is the fourth largest cemetery in the country, comprising 550 acres. Located on the north side of Indianapolis at the intersection of the Dixie Highway (Martin Luther King, Jr. Drive) and Thirty-eighth Street, the cemetery is filled with famous people, including the leaders who built the city and state. The magnificent Gothic-style entrance pictured was built in 1885 at 3400 Boulevard Place. Carl G. Fisher's family mausoleum can be found on the east side of Strawberry Hill (also the final resting place of James Whitcomb Riley, Indiana's poet laureate). Built in the Art Deco style, the mausoleum features copper work and carved limestone columns with Egyptian motifs. Fisher's ashes were brought here following his death in Miami on July 5, 1939, at the age of 65. Fisher is remembered for his marketing genius, his leadership in forming the nation's transcontinental roads, and for building the Indianapolis Motor Speedway, the town of Speedway, and the Indianapolis 500. He was also the operator of the first automobile dealership in the nation. (Both, courtesy Jan Shupert-Arick.)

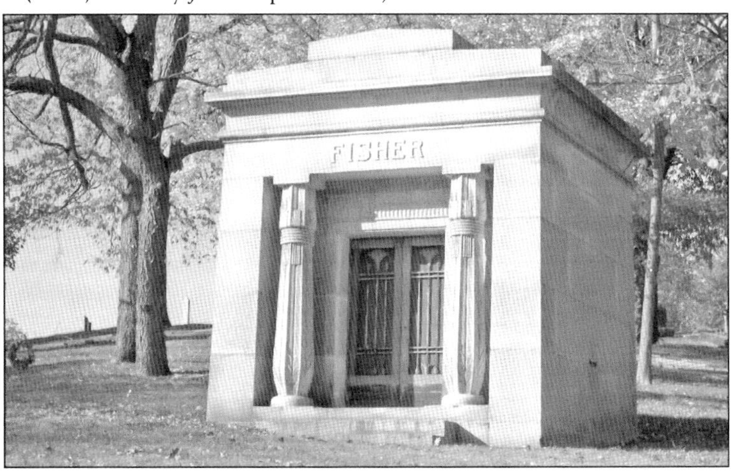

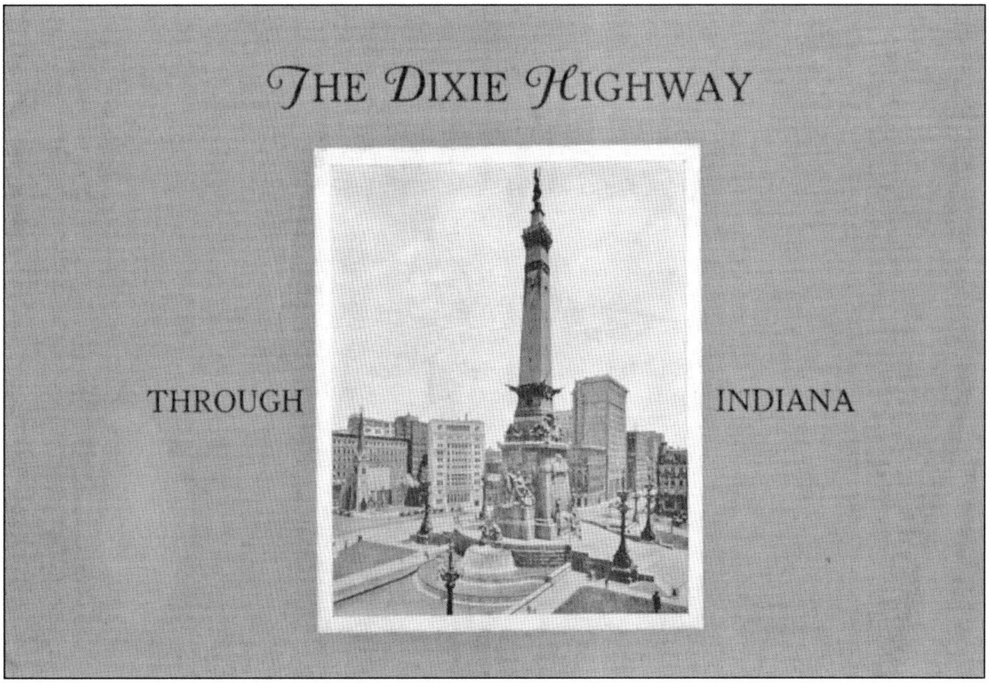

The budding automobile industry created a political advocacy group backed by Carl G. Fisher. The group was known as the Flat Tire Club. The club evolved into the Hoosier Motor Club and established its office on Monument Circle in the center of Indianapolis. The extraordinary Soldiers' and Sailors' Monument stood proud over the circle, which has become a world-renowned site. This image is the cover of an Indiana Dixie Highway promotional booklet published in 1925. (Courtesy Russell Rein.)

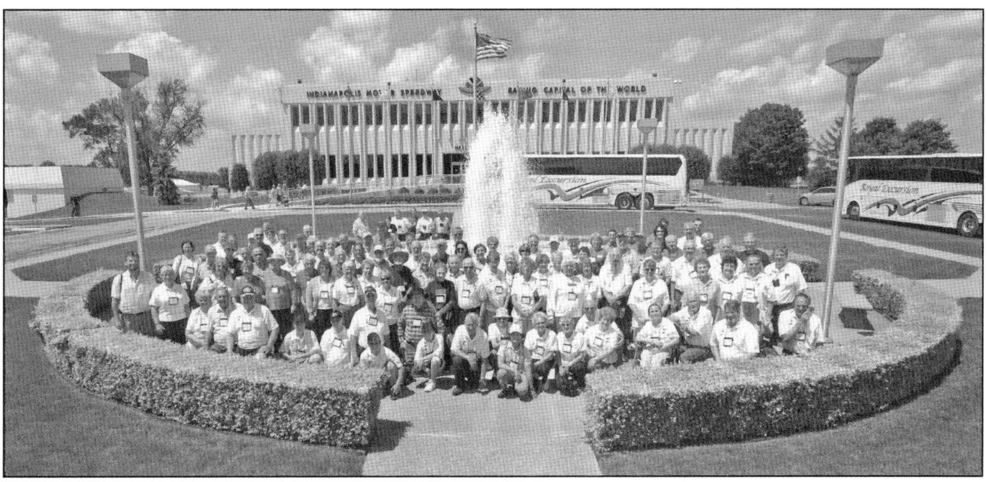

The 2009 Lincoln Highway Association's annual conference was held in South Bend. The conference bus trip to Indianapolis automotive sites included a visit to Carl G. Fisher's Indianapolis Motor Speedway. The group poses here for the official conference photograph. (Courtesy Mike Kelly.)

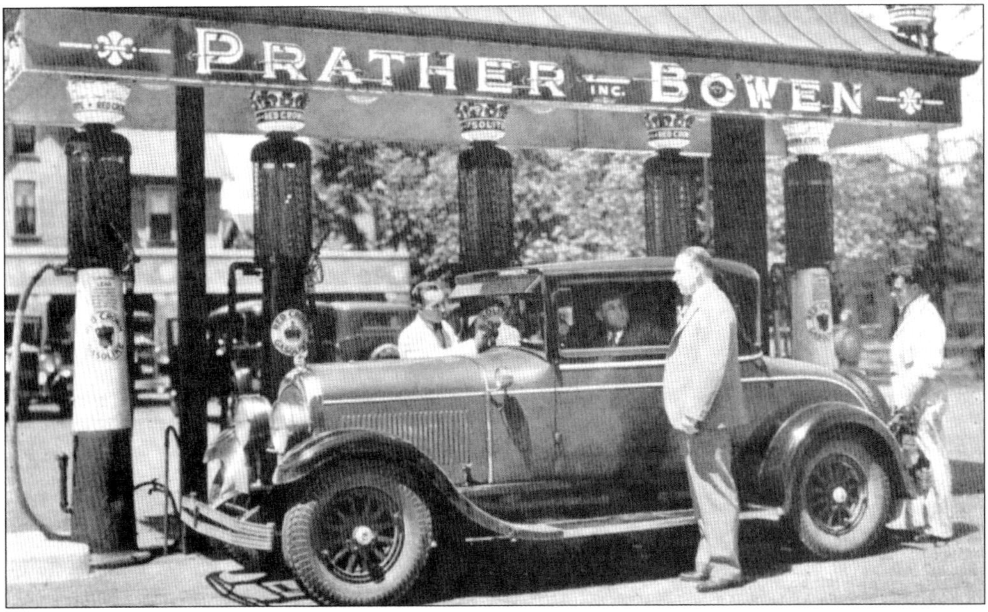

This historic photograph captures the Prather Bowen gas station at Twenty-fourth and Meridan Streets in Indianapolis in the 1930s. A long covered gas pump island includes five Red Crown gas pumps with ornate glass tops and a neon sign. The raised tin roof adds to the character of the station. An automobile repair building with numerous bays sits behind the island. (Courtesy Russell Rein.)

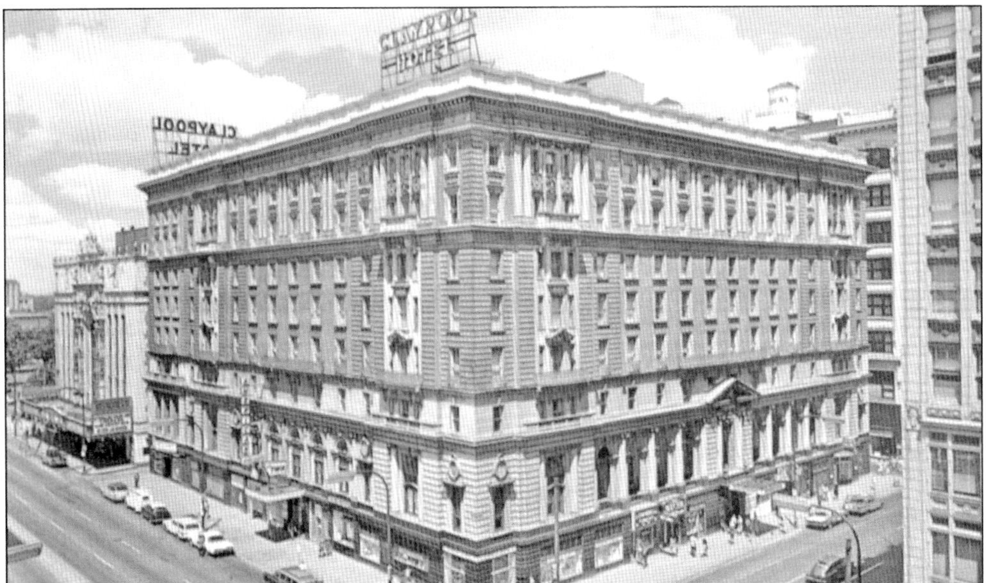

Located at the northwest corner of Washington and Illinois Streets and named in honor of wealthy Connersville businessman Edward Fay Claypool, the Claypool Hotel served as a landmark for many decades. It was a hub for social gatherings and a convention center. Hotel advertisements boasted that it offered more bathtubs than any other hotel in the country and a telephone in every guest room. The lobby was reported to be the largest in the country, and the food and beverage service was legendary. Carl G. Fisher met with W.S. Gilbreath at the Claypool Hotel to plan the Dixie Highway. Fire destroyed the hotel in 1967. (Courtesy Jan Shupert-Arick.)

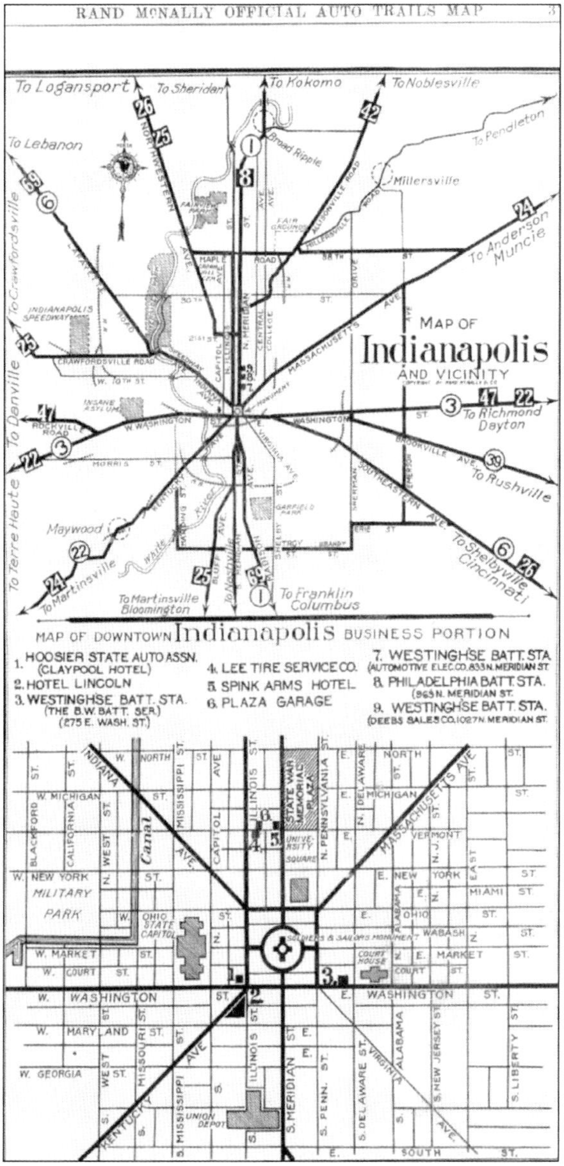

Published in the 1920s, Rand McNally's official automobile trails map shows the main highways leading to downtown Indianapolis. The Dixie is shown as Northwestern Avenue or State Road 25 (now US Route 421) coming into the city center from the northwest to Sixteenth Street and down Meridian Street to Monument Circle. At Sixteenth Street, the Dixie Highway dogleg route from Danville, Illinois, joined the main north-south Indiana Dixie Highway. On the south side of Monument Circle, the Dixie Highway followed Meridian to Bluff Avenue, which was State Road 25 at that time. Today, the highway is known as Bluff Road and becomes State Road 37 near the Marion-Morgan County line. The second map shows the business district near Monument Circle and demonstrates the deliberate design of the city center. The Soldiers' and Sailors' Monument on the circle, the location of the state capitol building, the Union Railroad Depot, the Hoosier State Auto Association at the Claypool Hotel, the Lee Tire Service Company, and the Spink Arms Hotel are listed as major points of interest. The monument is made of Bedford Oolitic Limestone. (Courtesy Russell Rein.)

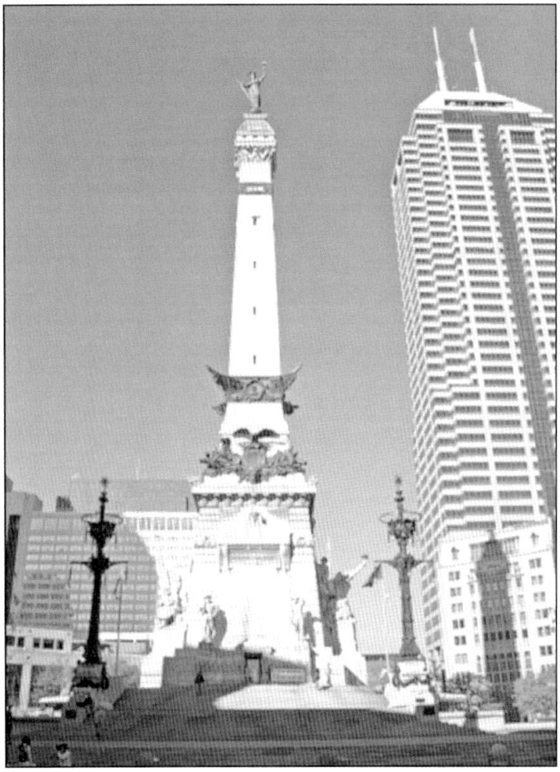

Monument Circle is famous for its statues and figures. The four statues at the corners of the Soldiers' and Sailors' Monument represent the infantry, cavalry, artillery, and navy. Recognized as one of the world's outstanding monuments, the structure symbolizes both the city of Indianapolis and the state of Indiana. The limestone is gray oolitic limestone from the Romona Quarry of Owen County. The monument's central shaft stands at 284 feet. (Courtesy Jan Shupert-Arick.)

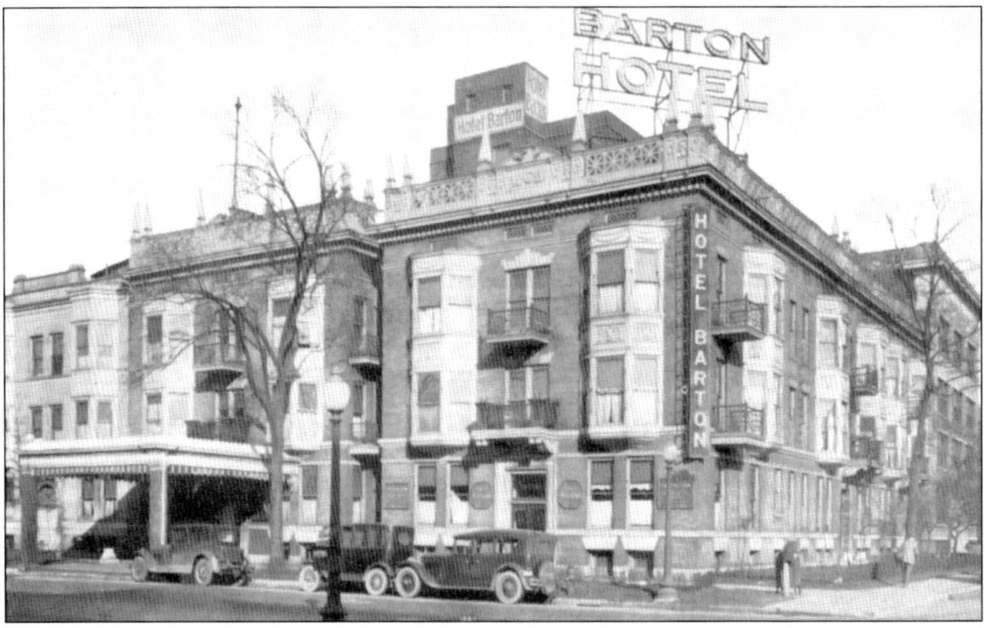

The Barton Building, located at 501–509 North Delaware Street in Indianapolis, was constructed in the Classical Revival–Beaux-Arts style. Designed and built by Lynn B. Millikan and Charles A. Wallingford, it was constructed to be a multifamily residential structure. It was in use as a hotel by the 1920s. Note the elaborate covered entrance, designed to protect automobile travelers from rain and snow. (Courtesy Russell Rein.)

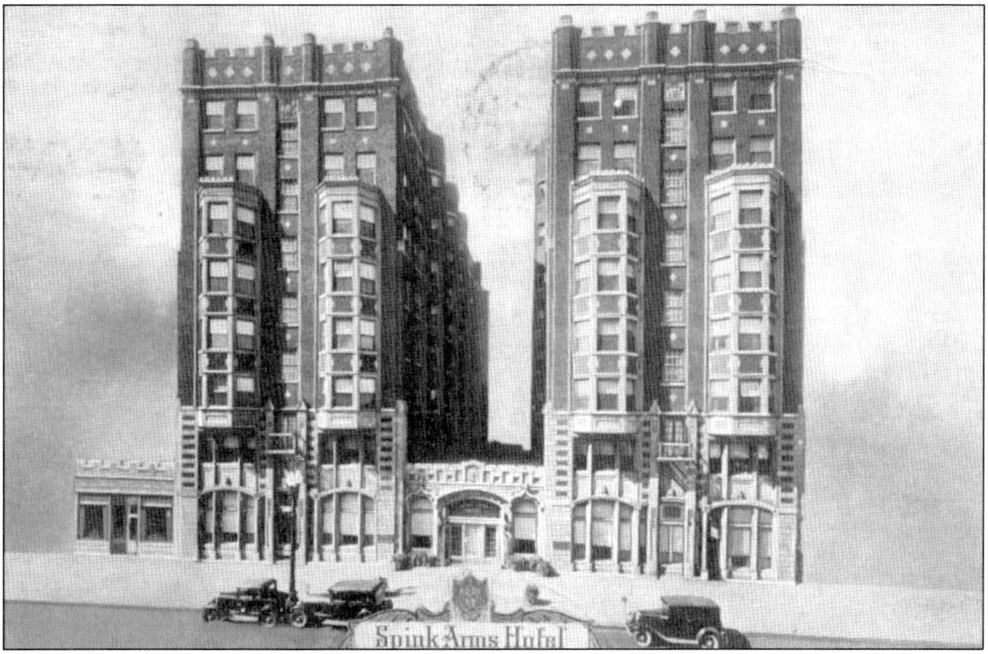

Located at 410 North Meridian Street, the Spink Arms Hotel was built in 1919 in the Tudor Revival architecture style. The building was restored by Van Rooy Properties Company and known as the Continental at Vermont Place; it is advertised as an 89,060-square-foot, multifamily home. Meridian Street is the primary north-south route through Indianapolis. Meridian Street was formerly aligned with US Route 31. Meridian intersects with Monument Circle at Market Street. (Both, courtesy Russell Rein.)

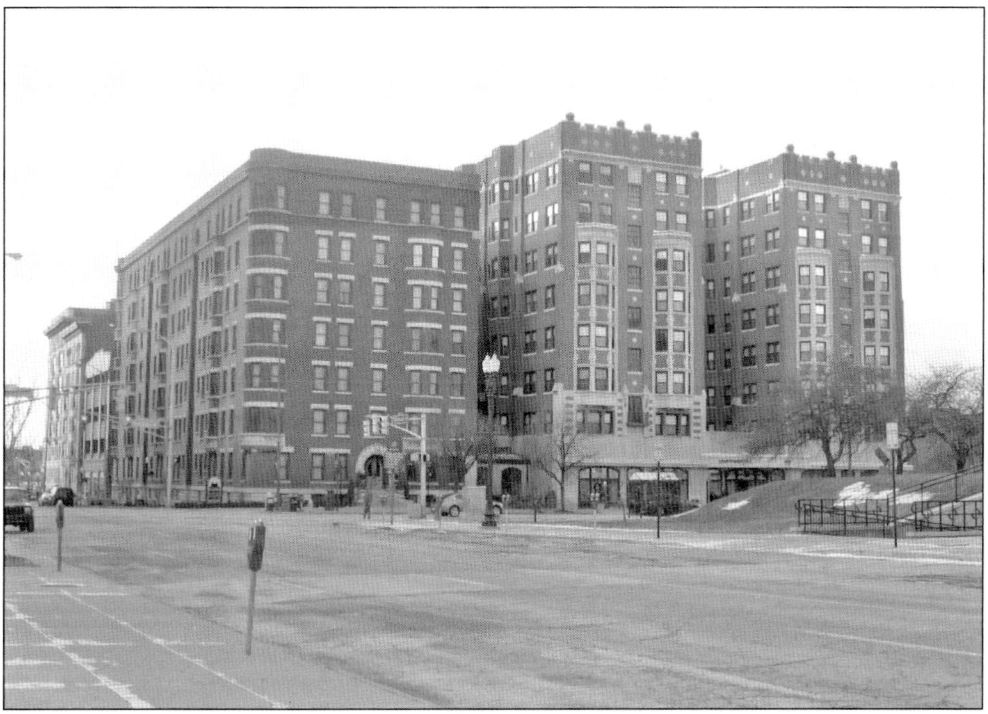

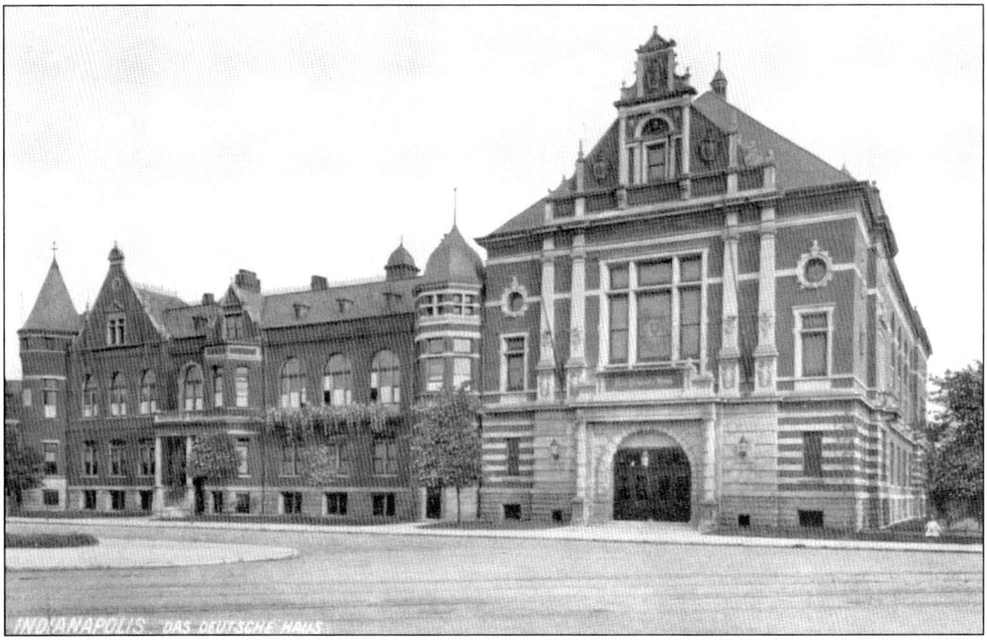

Built in 1894, Das Deutsche Haus, now known as the Athenaeum, was a German social club and German-style restaurant. It was on the southeast corner of Michigan and New Jersey Streets in downtown Indianapolis. Carl G. Fisher and James A. Allison first proposed the Lincoln Highway project at a dinner here on September 10, 1912. The *Indianapolis Star* carried the story. (Courtesy Russell Rein.)

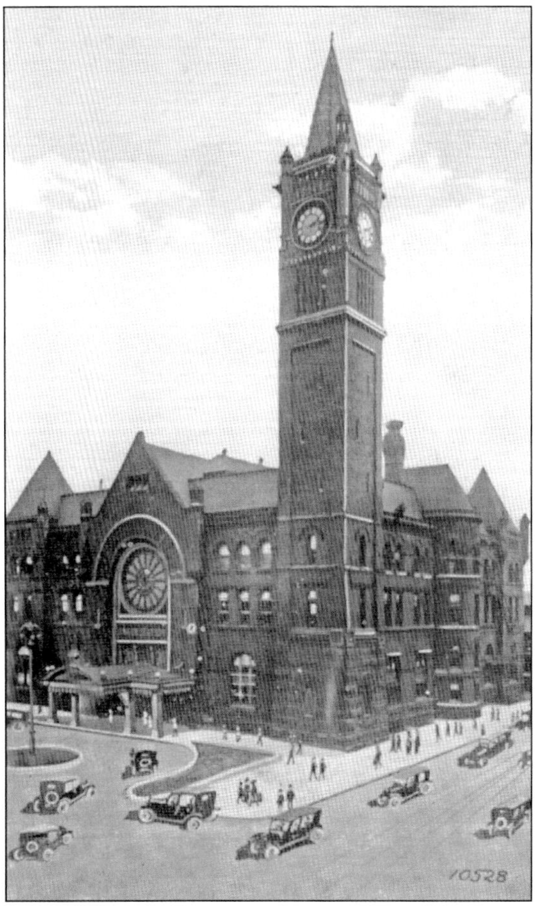

Indianapolis's Union Station—the first union station in the world—opened in 1853. Located at 39 Jackson Place near Meridian Street, it was owned by the Union Railway. In 1888, a larger, more impressive station was built in the Richardsonian Romanesque style. In 1900, over 200 trains a day were serviced; the station had an elevated platform to avoid regular street traffic. Famous for its clock tower, the building is listed in the National Register of Historic Places and is home to the Crowne Plaza Hotel. (Courtesy Russell Rein.)

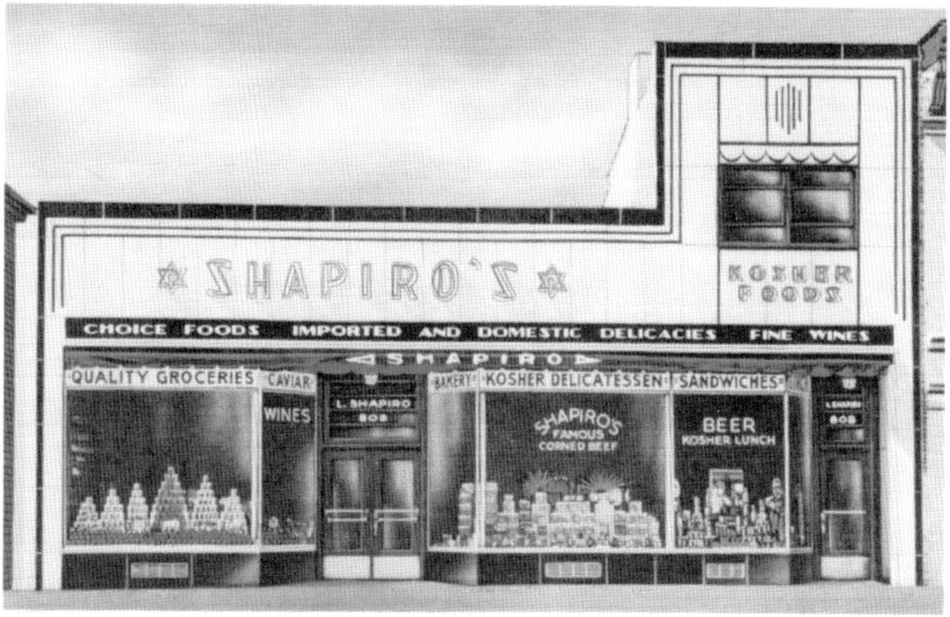

SHAPIRO'S — 808 S. MERIDIAN ST. — INDIANAPOLIS, IND.

In the 1930s, Shapiro's, the famous kosher deli and restaurant, was located at 808 South Meridian Street. Today, Shapiro's has expanded to three locations. The business began as a grocery-deli in 1905. Louis and Rebecca Shapiro came from Russia and lived above the store. It has been in the family since. With brothers Abe, Izzy, and Max taking on several expansions and growth into a full service restaurant, the place is considered a must-see experience by locals and travelers familiar with downtown Indianapolis. (Both, courtesy Brandy Ison.)

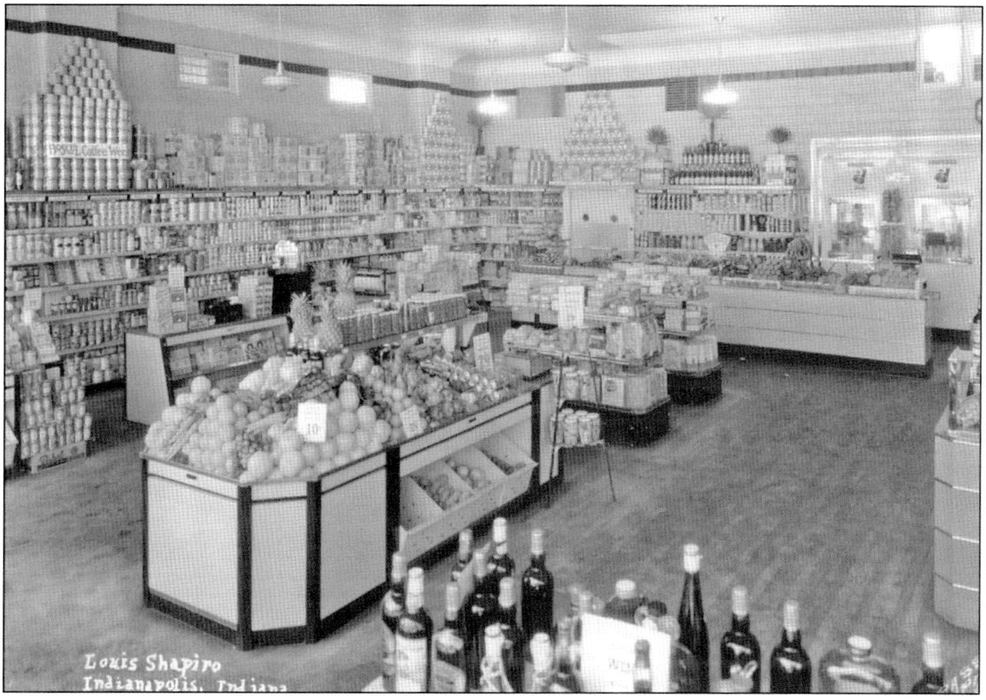

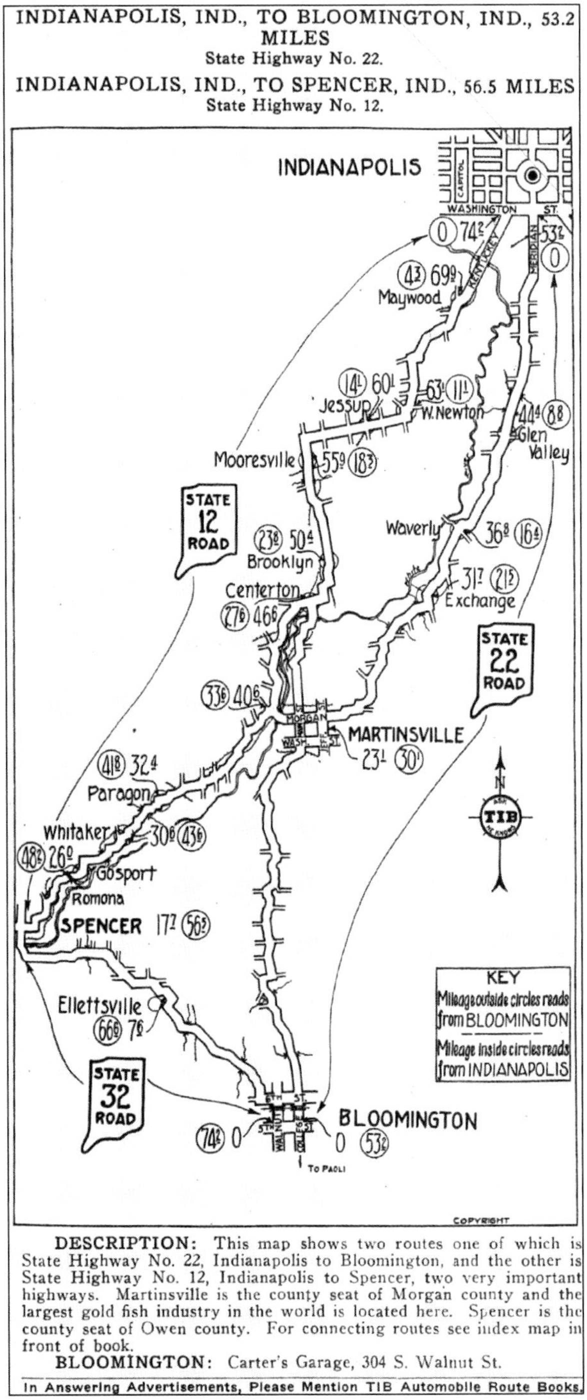

INDIANAPOLIS, IND., TO BLOOMINGTON, IND., 53.2 MILES
State Highway No. 22.
INDIANAPOLIS, IND., TO SPENCER, IND., 56.5 MILES
State Highway No. 12.

DESCRIPTION: This map shows two routes one of which is State Highway No. 22, Indianapolis to Bloomington, and the other is State Highway No. 12, Indianapolis to Spencer, two very important highways. Martinsville is the county seat of Morgan county and the largest gold fish industry in the world is located here. Spencer is the county seat of Owen county. For connecting routes see index map in front of book.

BLOOMINGTON: Carter's Garage, 304 S. Walnut St.

In Answering Advertisements, Please Mention TIB Automobile Route Books.

This early automobile road map published by the TIB Automobile Route Books shows the automobile roads from Indianapolis to Bloomington (the Dixie Highway/State Road 22) and the road from Indianapolis to Spencer (State Route 12). The distance from Indianapolis to Bloomington on State Road 22 was 53.2 miles. Carter's Garage, located at 304 South Walnut Street in Bloomington, advertised in this map. (Courtesy Russell Rein.)

Five

The Dixie Connector

Danville to Indianapolis

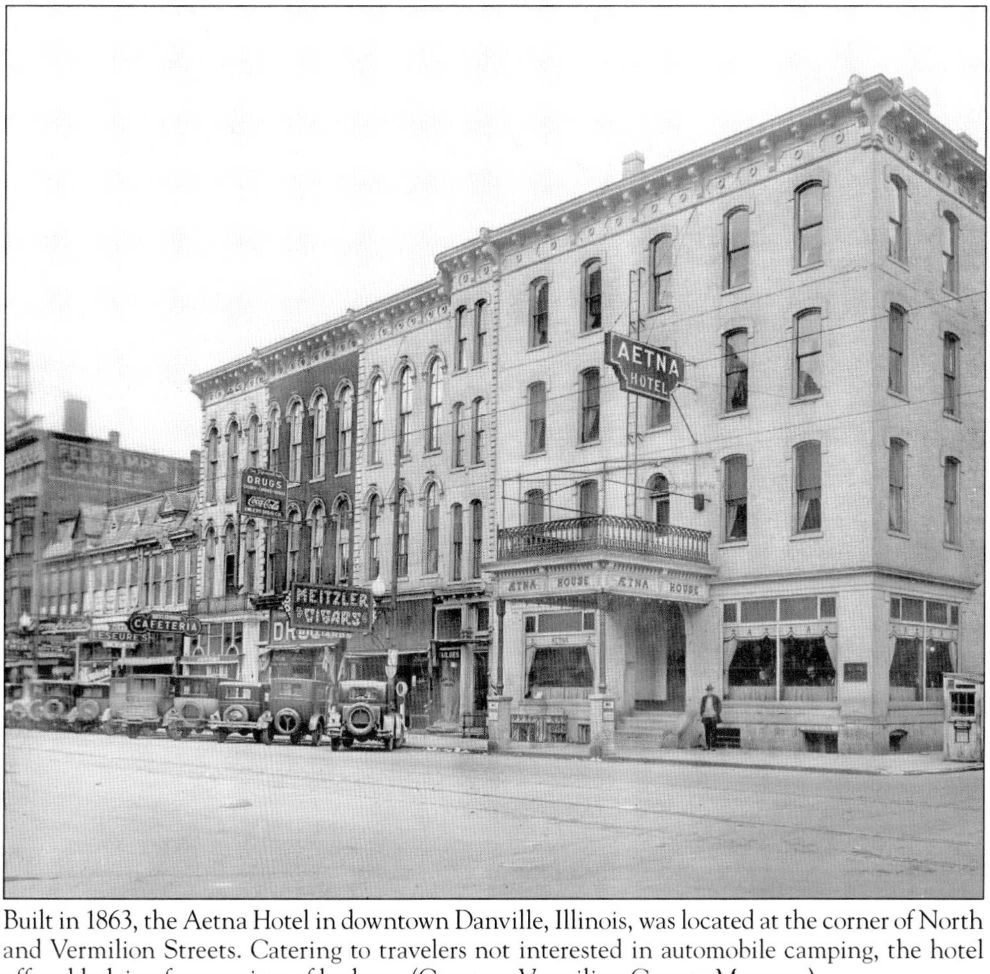

Built in 1863, the Aetna Hotel in downtown Danville, Illinois, was located at the corner of North and Vermilion Streets. Catering to travelers not interested in automobile camping, the hotel offered lodging for a variety of budgets. (Courtesy Vermilion County Museum.)

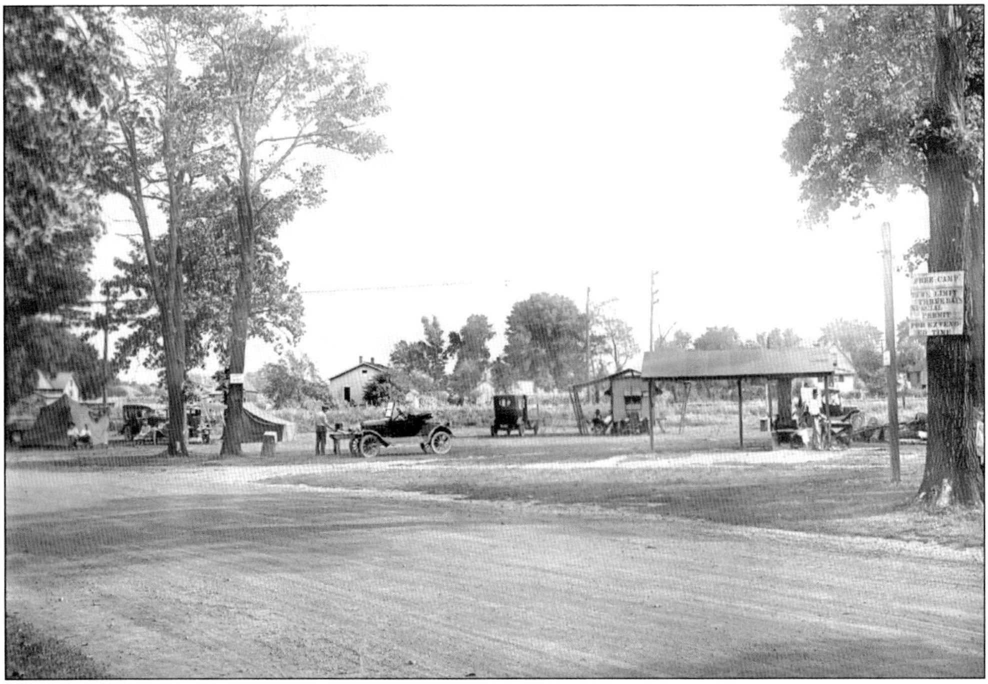

Garfield Park, an automobile camp on North Griffin Street in Danville, Illinois, offered free camping to all travelers. The rules on the sign note a three-day time limit, after which a special extended-stay permit was required. (Courtesy Vermilion County Museum.)

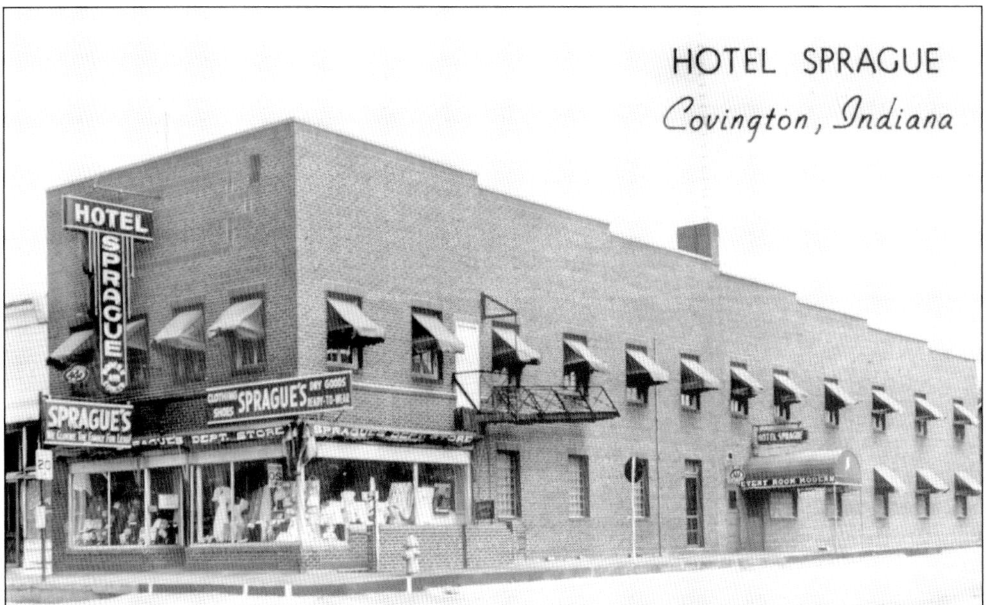

Hotel Sprague in Covington, Indiana, shared the building with the Sprague Dry Goods Department Store. Located in Fountain County, Covington served as the gateway city in Indiana, welcoming Dixie Highway travelers from Chicago. After leaving Chicago, travelers would pass through Vermillion, Warren, and Fountain Counties before reaching the city. (Courtesy Russell Rein.)

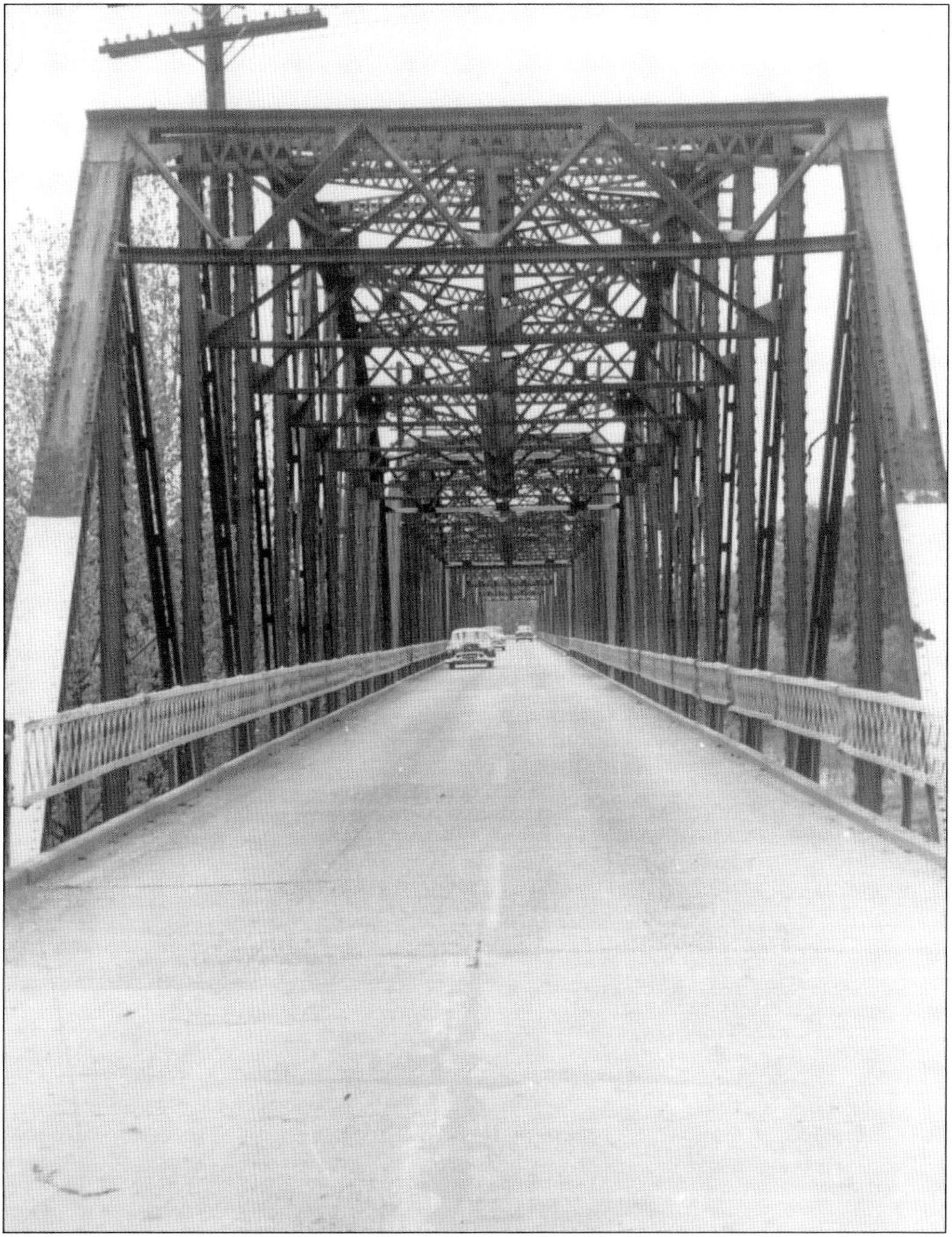

This Pennsylvania-style, metal through-truss bridge was a main gateway into Covington on US Route 136. A wooden covered bridge once crossed the Wabash River at Covington, but it burned in 1916 and was replaced by the six-span bridge pictured. This bridge provided a safe crossing over the Wabash River just west of Covington in Warren County. In 1978, the iron bridge was replaced with a non-distinct concrete slab. (Courtesy Russell Rein.)

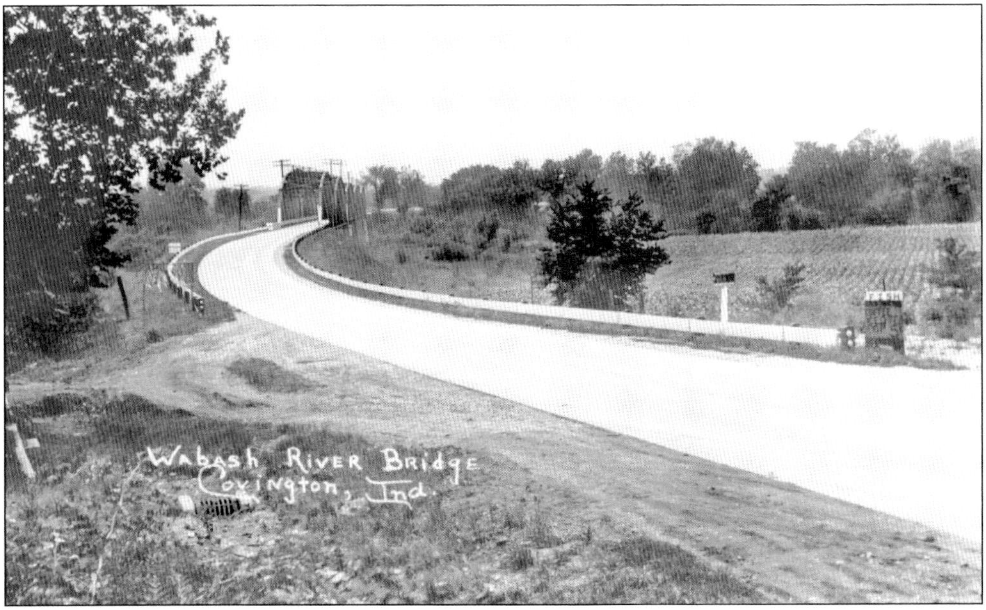

The view of the improved Dixie Highway looking east toward Covington shows the six-span, through-truss bridge over the Wabash River. This photograph appears to have been taken in the 1920s. (Courtesy Russell Rein.)

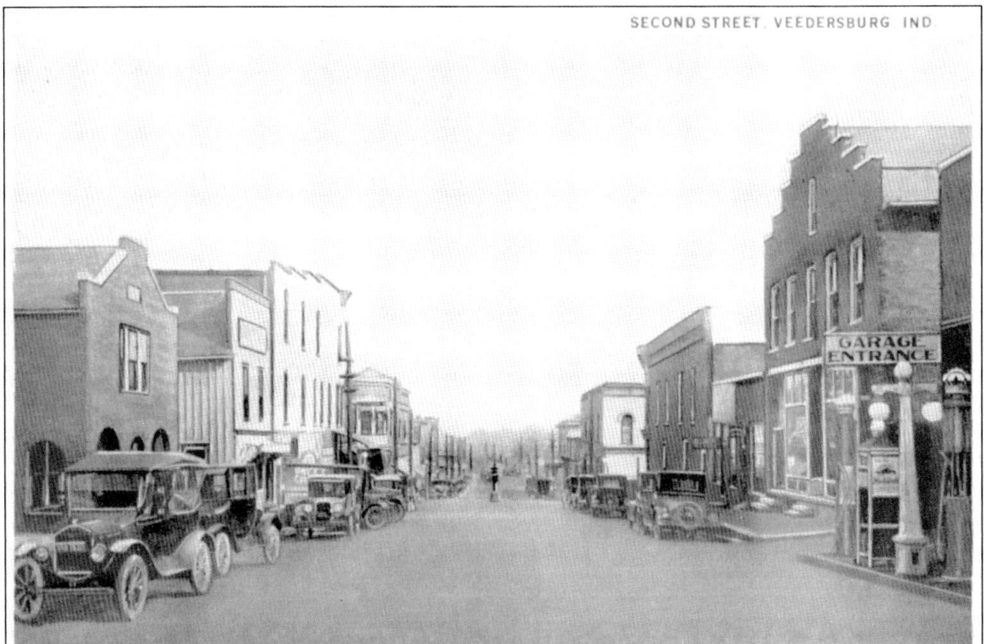

Veedersburg was home to the Veedersburg Paver Company, which produced bricks for over 100 Midwest cities, many of them along the Dixie Highway. Veedersburg is also the home of the Wabash Clay Company, manufacturer of brick pavers for the Indianapolis 500 track in 1909. The company supplied 3.2 million pavers for the project; each paver weighed nine and a half pounds. The garage at left, located on Second Street in Veedersburg, offered pumps on the curb and provided night lighting. (Courtesy Russell Rein.)

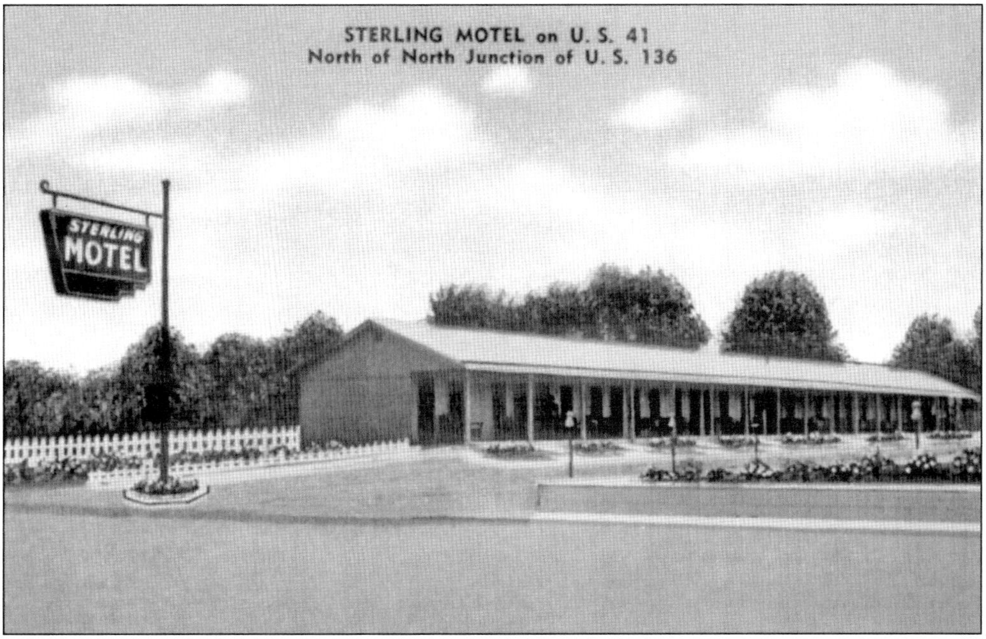

The Sterling Motel was built around 1960 on US Route 41, just three blocks north of the north junction of US Route 136. The motel offered a tidy garden setting with 20 units that featured hot-water heat, forced-air cooling, and individual tile baths. The motel was conveniently located near local restaurants and theaters and was just 20 minutes from Turkey Run and Shades State Parks, both of which were major tourist attractions in the Covington area. (Courtesy Russell Rein.)

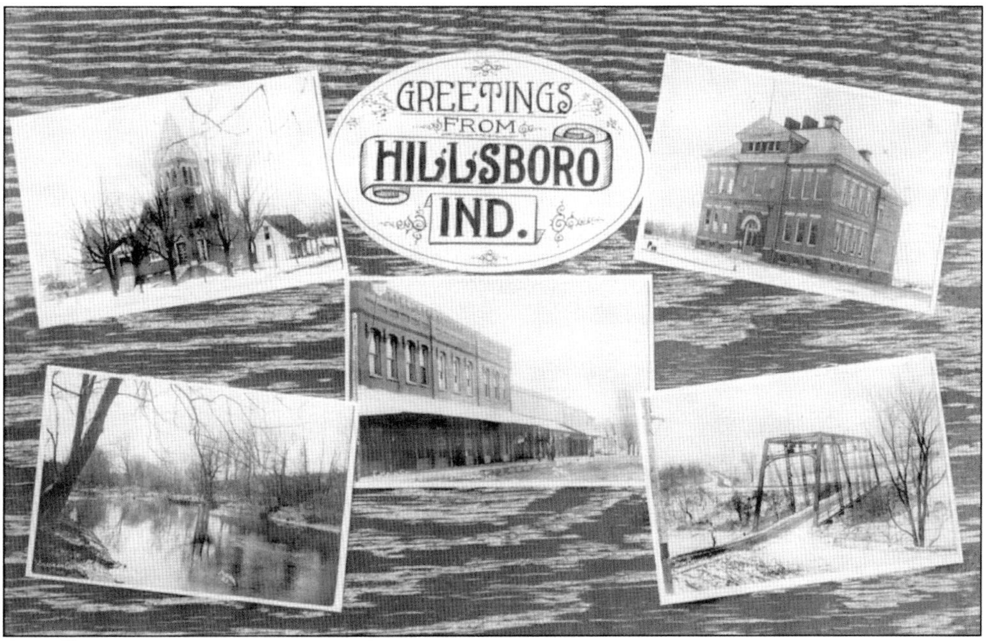

This greetings-style postcard printed for Hillsboro, Indiana, is a collage of local postcards. The images depict a local school, the Hillsboro business district, and an iron through-truss bridge that crossed the river on the south side of town. Hillsboro's Main Street was the Dixie Highway corridor along US Route 136. (Courtesy Russell Rein.)

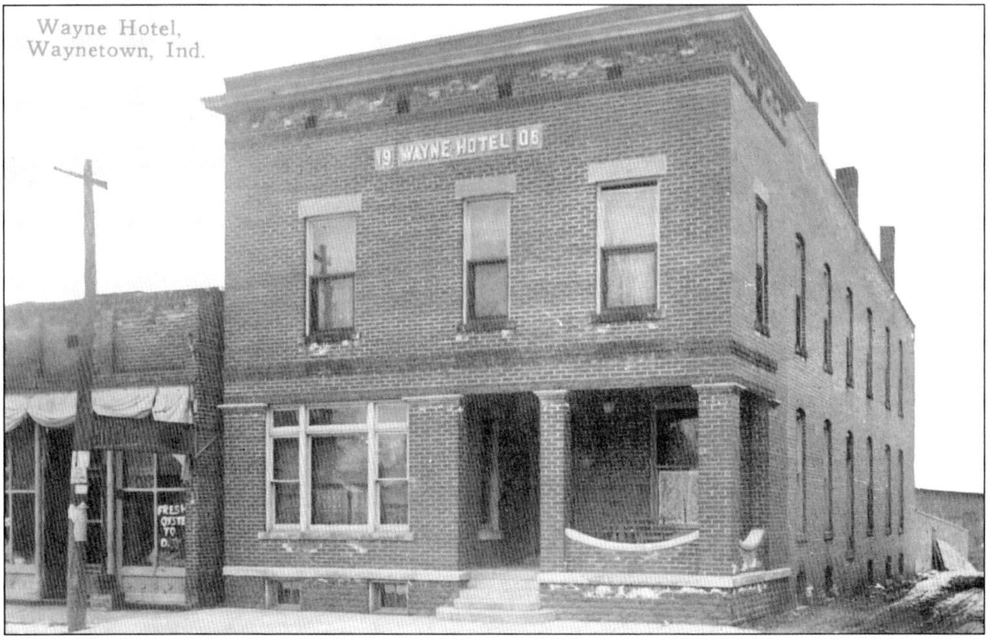

The Wayne Hotel in Waynetown, Indiana, was a small, two-story, brick building that provided meals and a resting place for travelers along the stretch of road between Crawfordsville and Hillsboro. A modest downtown, shown below, provided limited shopping and services to tourists along this quiet section of the Dixie Highway feeding from Danville, Illinois, to Indianapolis. Waynetown was a settled in 1830 by Samuel Mann. William Bratton, a member of the Lewis and Clark Expedition (1804–1806), is buried in Waynetown's Pioneer Cemetery at the intersection of US Route 136 and State Road 25. (Both, courtesy Russell Rein.)

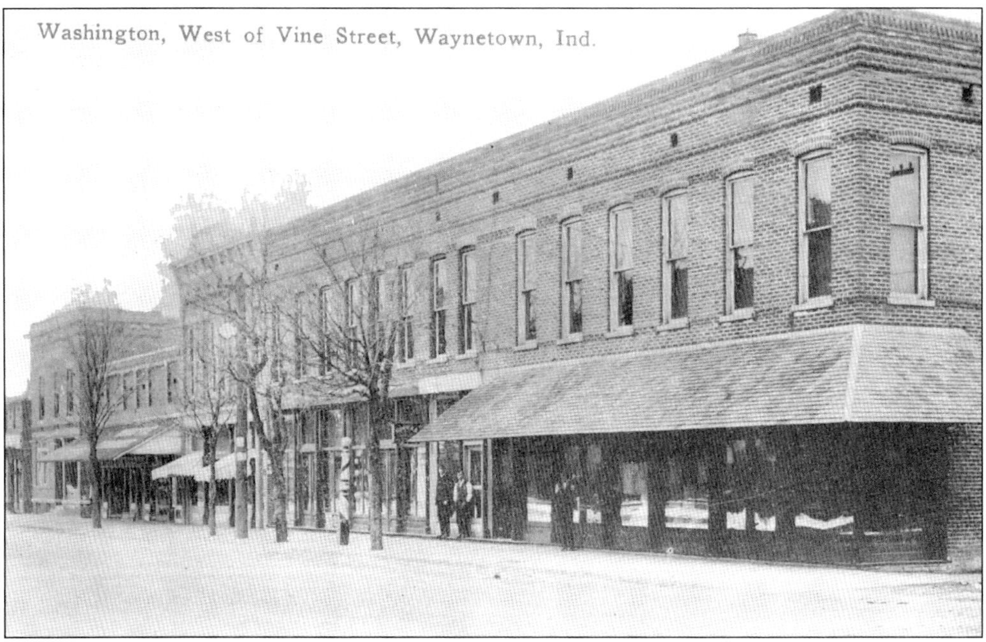

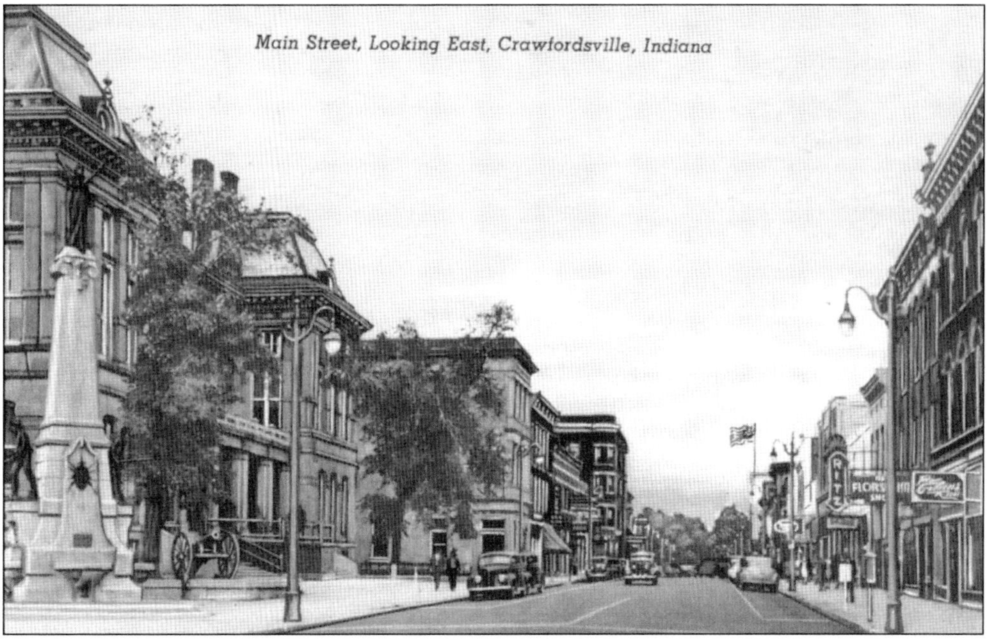

This image captures a thriving downtown Crawfordsville in the 1940s. The downtown area boasted many businesses and city government facilities, including the well-known Montgomery County Jail that today is one of only three such rotary jails still extant in the United States. Notice the designated parking areas along the sidewalks. (Courtesy Russell Rein.)

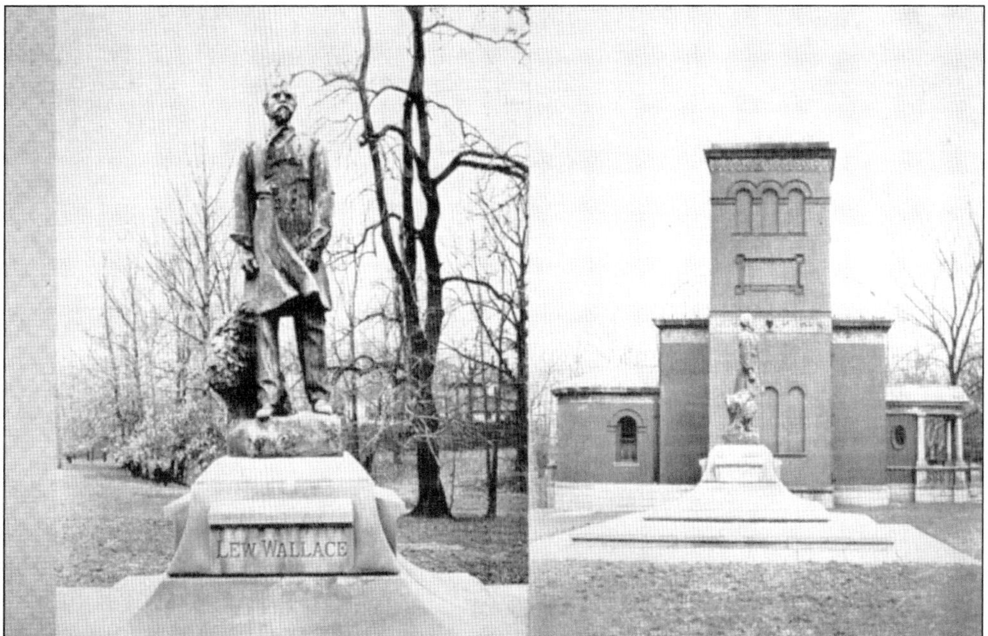

Crawfordsville is the home of the Lew Wallace Statue and Study, a national historic landmark. General Wallace wrote the novel *Ben-Hur: A Tale of the Christ* in his imposing mansion, now a Crawfordsville museum with public tours and a gift shop. (Courtesy Russell Rein.)

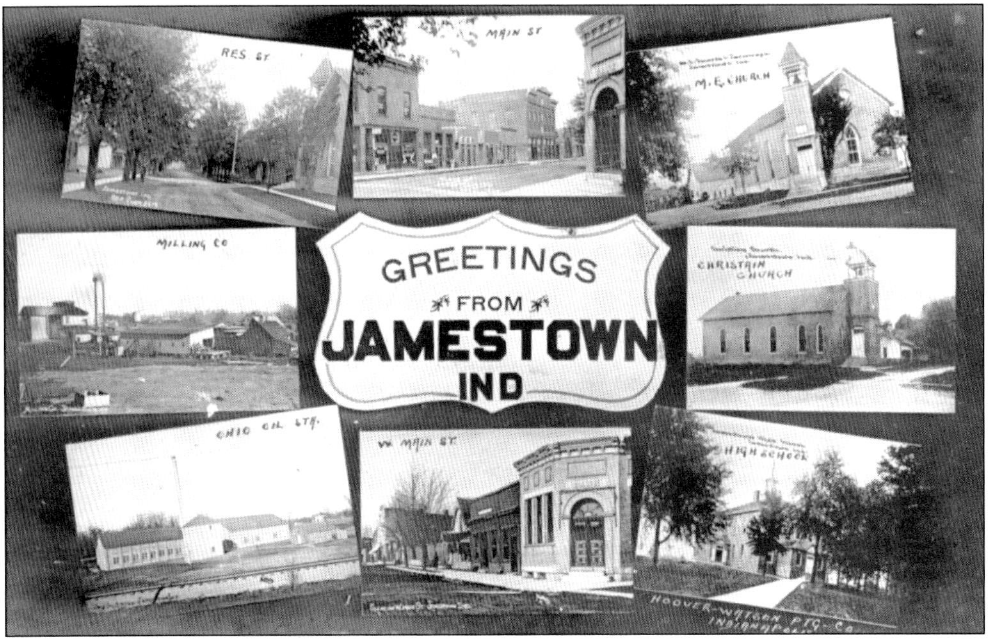

The small towns along the Dixie Highway corridor from Danville to Indianapolis promoted themselves by selling postcards of main buildings, such as churches and schools. Located in Boone County in central Indiana, Jamestown was founded in 1830 and is the oldest community in the county. The Citizens State Bank was organized July 1, 1903, with capital stock of $25,000. In 1904, a bank building (below) was constructed, and the bank was moved to 2 West Main Street, its present location. The first officers were Charles F. Martin, president; Marion Bailey, vice president; George W. Piersol, cashier; and Marion H. Roberts, assistant cashier. Jamestown is located 30 miles west of downtown Indianapolis and 17 miles east of Crawfordsville, Indiana. (Both, courtesy Harley Sheets.)

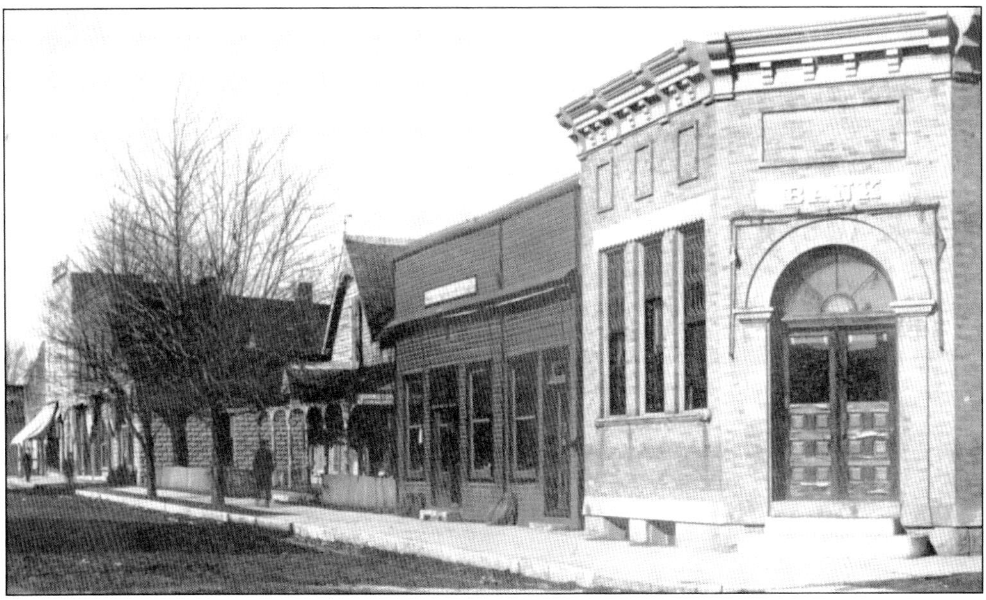

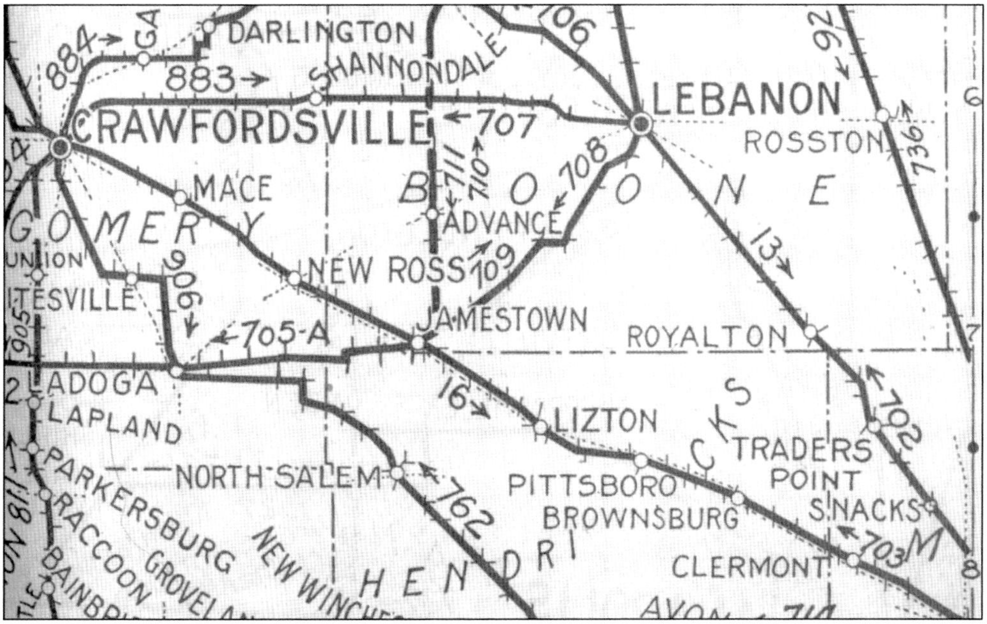

This map shows the Dixie Highway from Crawfordsville through Mace, New Ross, Lizton, Pittsboro, Brownsburg, and Clermont. The small towns offered gas, cafés, and sometimes a hotel. In 1915, the *Jamestown Press* reported that supporters of the Dixie Highway from Indianapolis to Crawfordsville escorted the secretary of the Dixie Highway Association around the area. In 1919, Boone County commissioners granted petitions for the improvement of the portion of the Indianapolis-Crawfordsville road. During the 1920s, the dirt road was transformed to an 18-foot-wide, paved brick thoroughfare. In 1924, the state took over the Dixie Highway between Indianapolis and Crawfordsville, and the road became known as State Road 34. By 1940, the brick surface had become pitted due to heavy traffic, and in October 1940, resurfacing and widening were completed. In July 1951, State Road 34 was renamed US Highway 136. In 1965, heavy traffic was diverted from Highway 136 with the opening of Interstate 74, located one mile north of Jamestown at State Road 75. (Both, courtesy Russell Rein.)

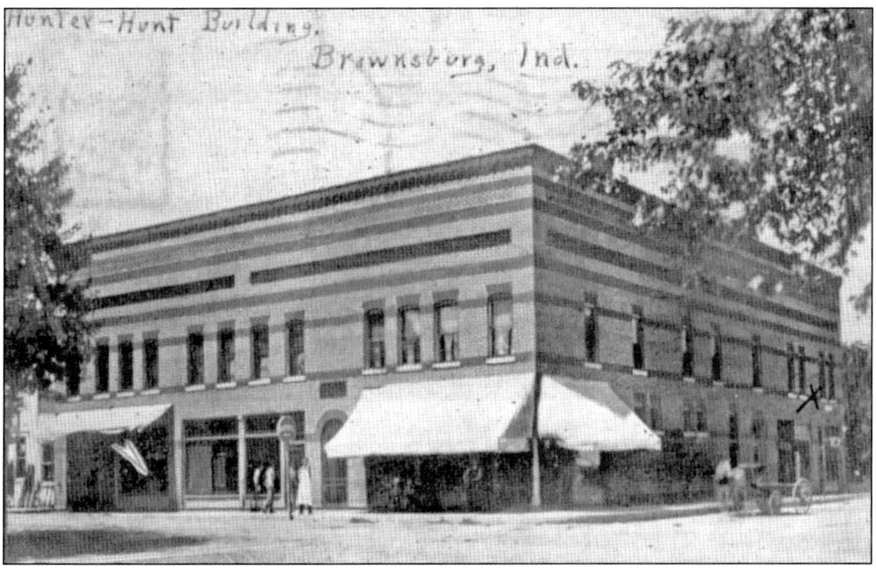

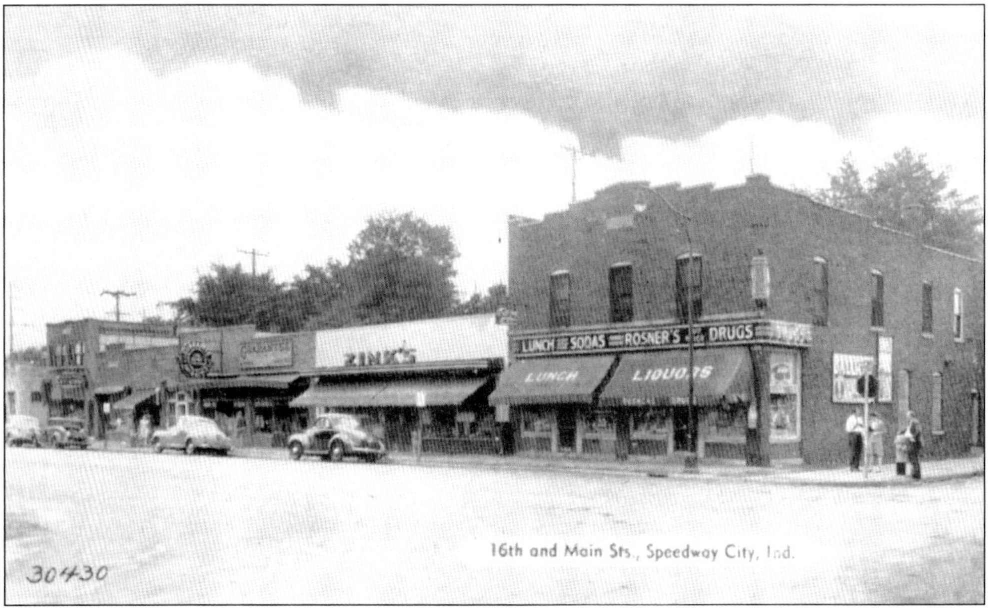

Speedway was platted in 1912. James A. Allison, Frank Wheeler, Arthur Newby, and Carl G. Fisher, the founders of the Indianapolis Motor Speedway, hired realtor Lemon Trotter to purchase the land, plat the area, and sell the lots. Old Speedway City is an early example of a planned residential community. The industrial area was laid out on the east side of Main Street and continued east to the town limits. Above, Main Street businesses grew up to support the community. The residential area was located west of Main Street. The progressive intent of this design was for the residents to walk to work. In 2005, the section of Speedway bordered by Tenth, Winton, Sixteenth, and Main Streets was designated a historic district. Below, pit crews are lined up for an official photograph taken at the Indianapolis Motor Speedway on June 21, 1937. (Both, courtesy Russell Rein.)

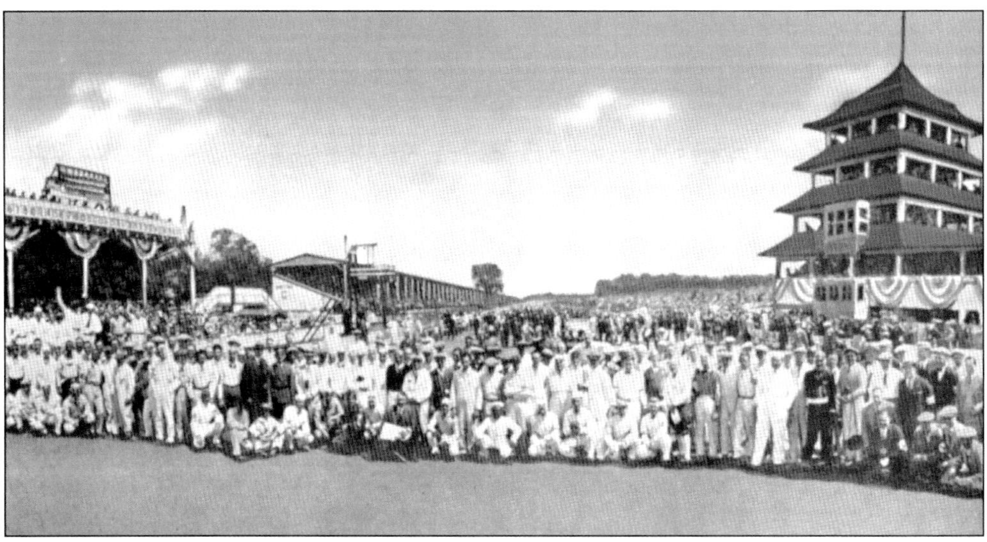

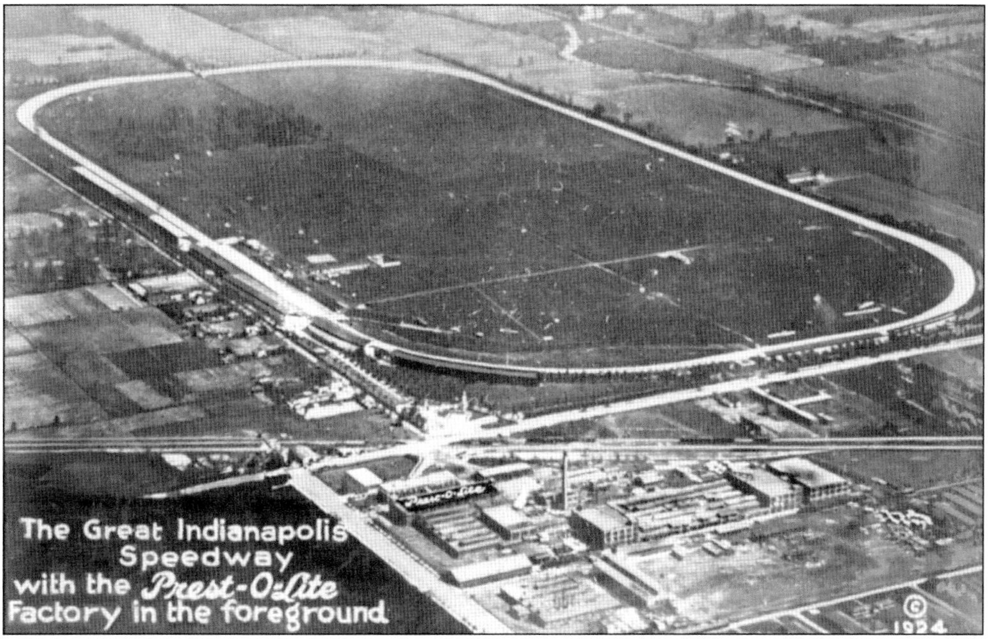

Carl G. Fisher understood that the nation's automobile industry needed to compete with Europe, so he set out to develop a better test track to help deliver higher quality automobiles to consumers. Automobile manufacturers later benefited from the partnership Fisher built with James A. Allison, Arthur Newby, and Frank Wheeler. They purchased farmland outside Indianapolis and incorporated the Indianapolis Motor Speedway Company on March 20, 1909. The first motorsport event at the track was a series of motorcycle races. On August 19, 1909, teams from 15 carmakers arrived at the track for practice. The racetrack soon developed problems, drivers were injured, and Hally Halcomb died when his race car crashed. The owners decided to improve the track by laying brick pavers on the oval. Above, Carl G. Fisher's Prest-O-Lite Company is in the foreground near the speedway track. Below, spectators watch an early race. (Both, courtesy Russell Rein.)

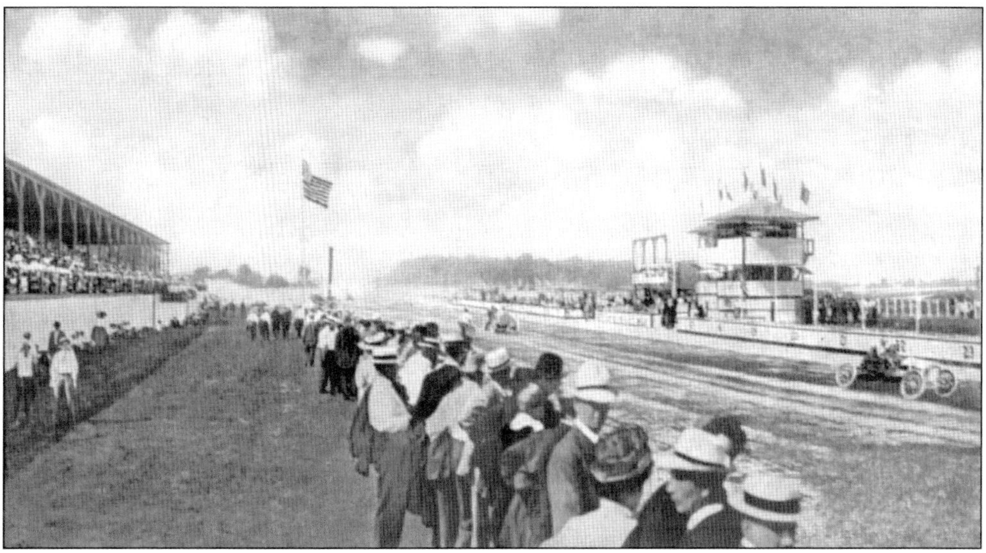

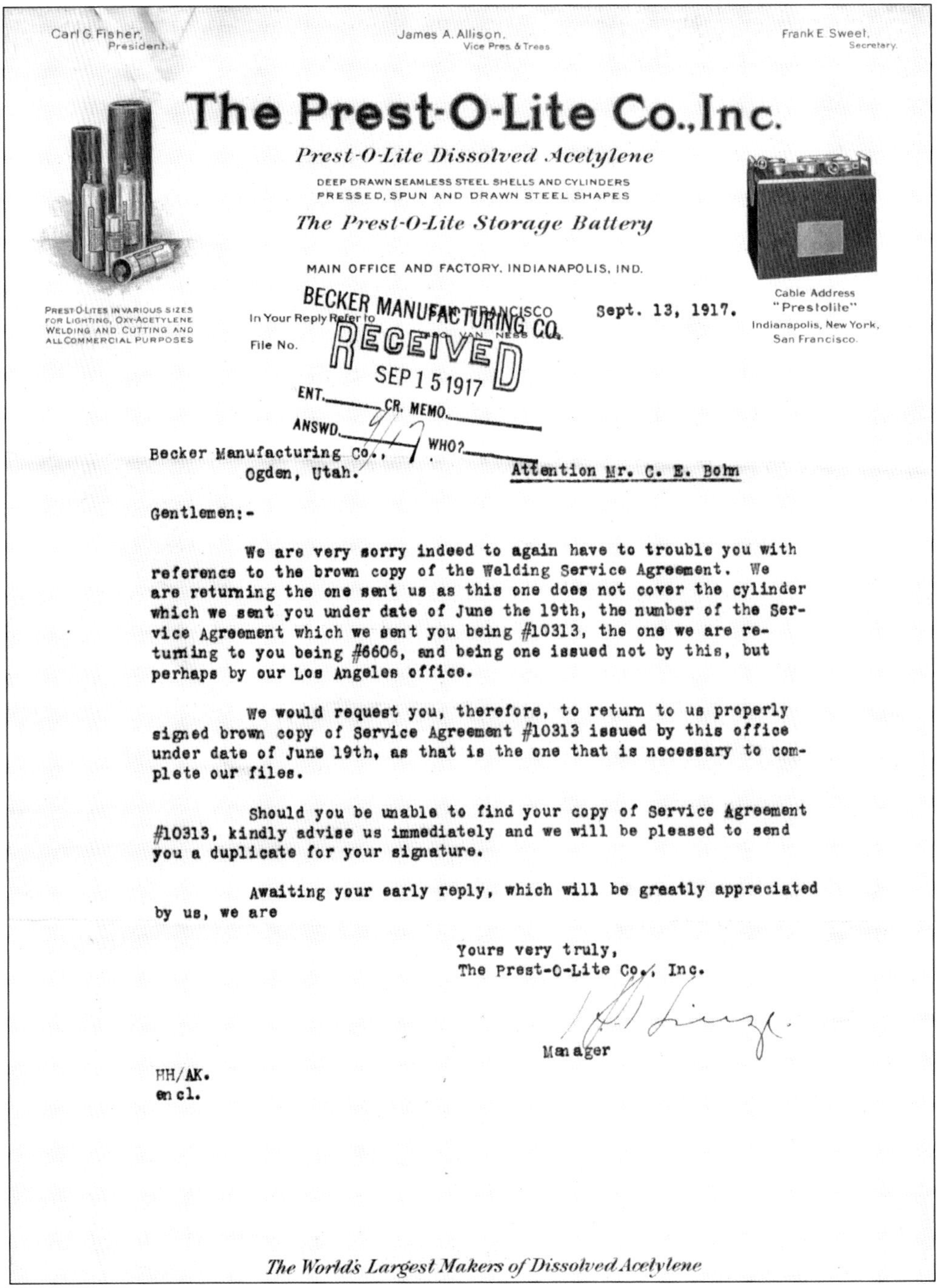

Carl G. Fisher, President. James A. Allison, Vice Pres. & Treas. Frank E. Sweet, Secretary.

The Prest-O-Lite Co., Inc.

Prest-O-Lite Dissolved Acetylene

DEEP DRAWN SEAMLESS STEEL SHELLS AND CYLINDERS
PRESSED, SPUN AND DRAWN STEEL SHAPES

The Prest-O-Lite Storage Battery

MAIN OFFICE AND FACTORY, INDIANAPOLIS, IND.

PREST-O-LITES IN VARIOUS SIZES FOR LIGHTING, OXY-ACETYLENE WELDING AND CUTTING AND ALL COMMERCIAL PURPOSES

Cable Address "Prestolite" Indianapolis, New York, San Francisco.

In Your Reply Refer to
File No.

BECKER MANUFACTURING CO. SAN FRANCISCO
RECEIVED
SEP 15 1917
ENT. CR. MEMO.
ANSWD. 9/17 WHO?

Sept. 13, 1917.

Becker Manufacturing Co.,
Ogden, Utah.

Attention Mr. C. E. Bohn

Gentlemen:-

We are very sorry indeed to again have to trouble you with reference to the brown copy of the Welding Service Agreement. We are returning the one sent us as this one does not cover the cylinder which we sent you under date of June the 19th, the number of the Service Agreement which we sent you being #10313, the one we are returning to you being #6606, and being one issued not by this, but perhaps by our Los Angeles office.

We would request you, therefore, to return to us properly signed brown copy of Service Agreement #10313 issued by this office under date of June 19th, as that is the one that is necessary to complete our files.

Should you be unable to find your copy of Service Agreement #10313, kindly advise us immediately and we will be pleased to send you a duplicate for your signature.

Awaiting your early reply, which will be greatly appreciated by us, we are

Yours very truly,
The Prest-O-Lite Co., Inc.

Manager

HH/AK.
encl.

The World's Largest Makers of Dissolved Acetylene

This letter from the Prest-O-Lite Company in Indianapolis was written on elaborate letterhead and provides evidence of their company's international position as a maker of auto headlights and auto batteries. (Courtesy Russell Rein.)

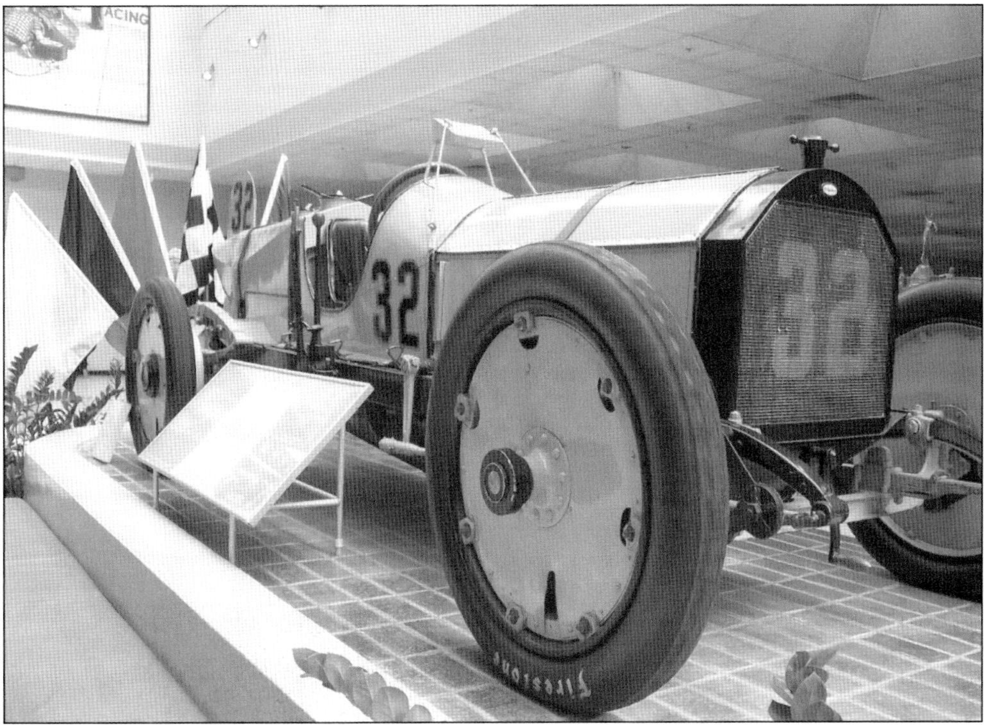

The famous Marmon Wasp is proudly displayed at the Speedway Hall of Fame Museum in Speedway, Indiana. The Model 32 automobile won the first Indianapolis 500 race in 1911. Ray Harroun drove the Wasp to victory with an average of 74.6 miles per hour. The Marmon Auto Company was based in Indianapolis, and the car featured the world's first rearview mirror. Below, an official Indiana Historical Bureau marker stands proudly near the front entrance to the Speedway Hall of Fame. (Above, courtesy Jan Shupert-Arick; below, courtesy Bill Arick.)

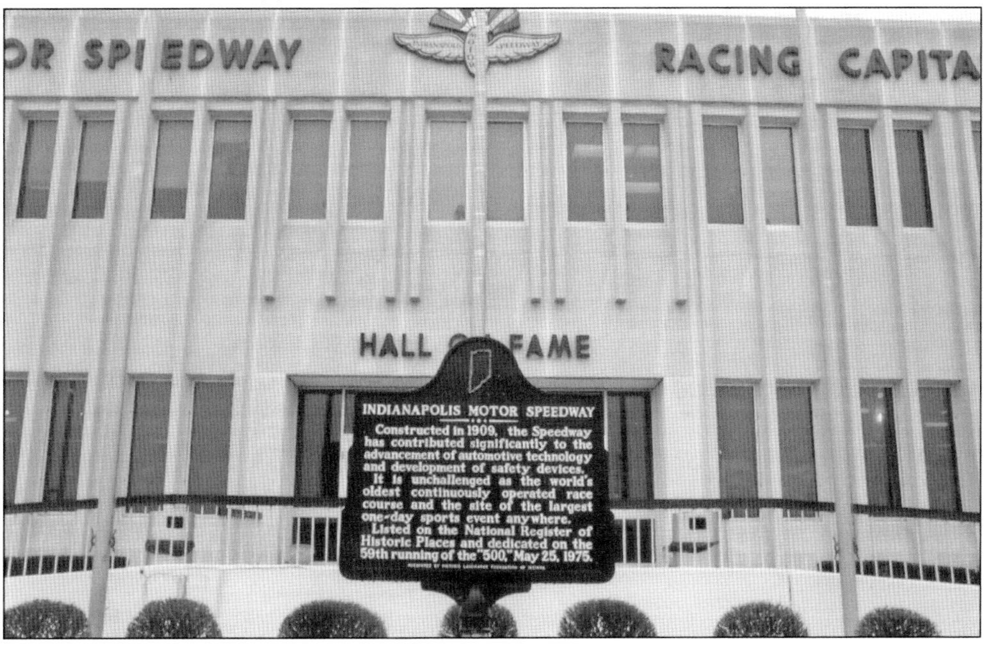

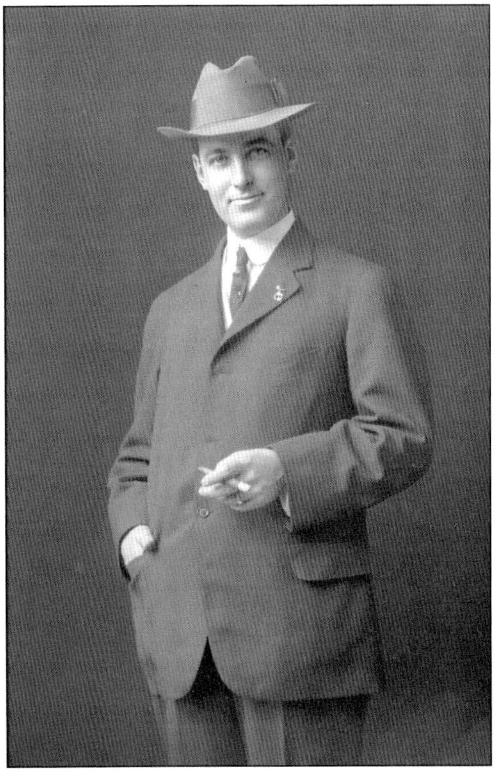

James A. Allison, cofounder of the Prest-O-Lite Company and the Indianapolis Motor Speedway, built a grand home next to the home of Carl F. Fisher. This area became known as Millionaire Row. Named Riverdale, the Allison estate encompassed 64 acres and included gardens, five private lakes, and roads for guests with automobiles. Allison hired architect Herbert Bass of Bass, Knowlton & Company to design his mansion, which included a great hall, a marble aviary, a music room with a two-story pipe organ, and an indoor swimming pool. The grounds and gardens were laid out by noted landscape architect Jens Jensen. James A. Allison also built a house in Miami Beach (the southern terminus of the Dixie Highway) and invested in development there with friend and neighbor Carl G. Fisher. Many years later, the Fisher and Allison mansions became Marian College (now Marian University). The Allison mansion was listed in the National Register of Historic Places in 1971. (Both, courtesy Marian University.)

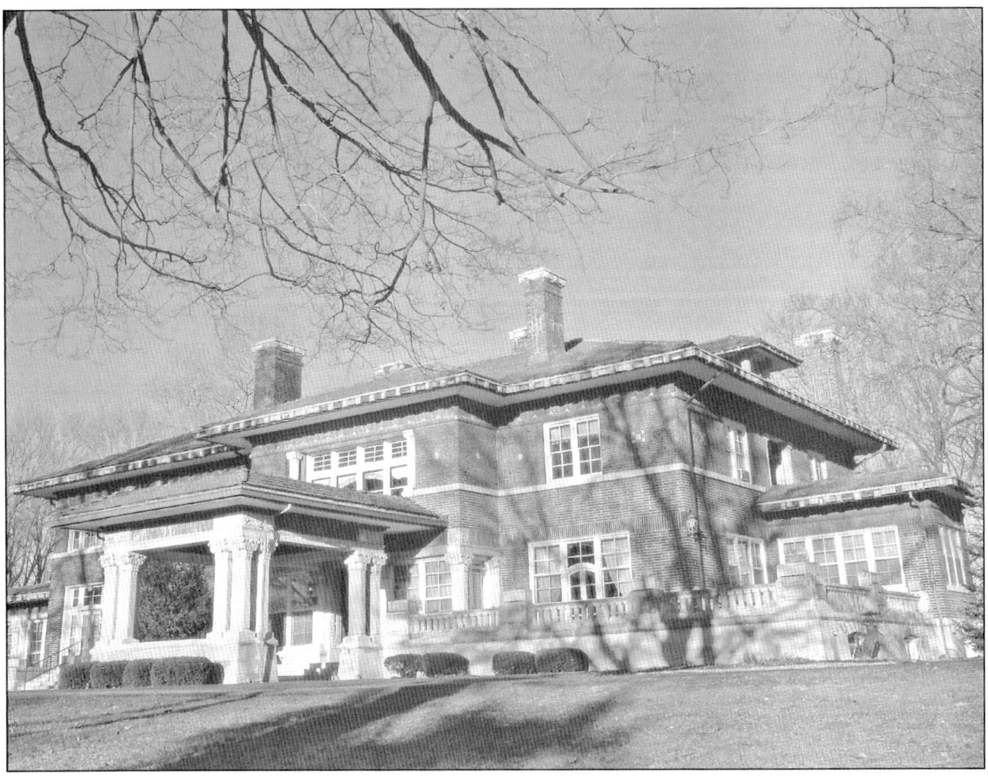

Carl G. Fisher of Indianapolis is considered the father of both the Lincoln Highway and the Dixie Highway—the nation's transcontinental automobile highways. (Courtesy University of Michigan Special Collections Library.)

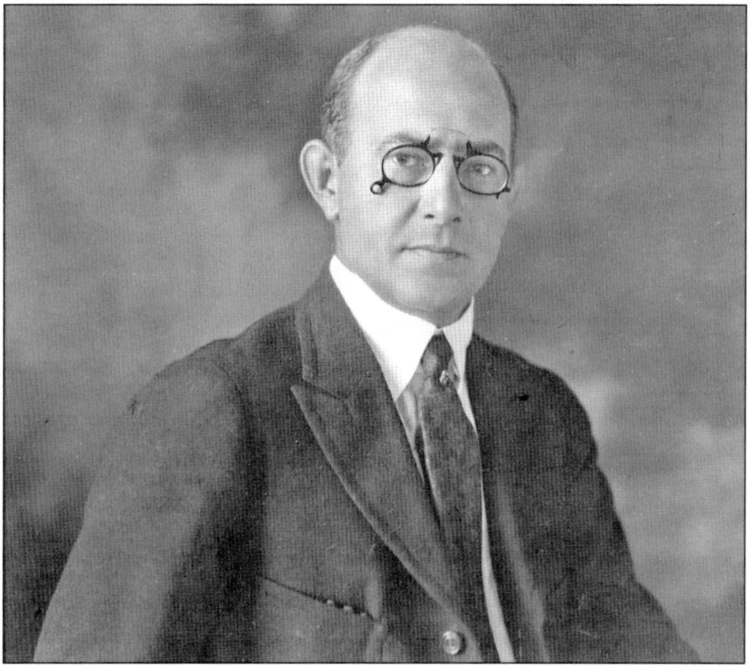

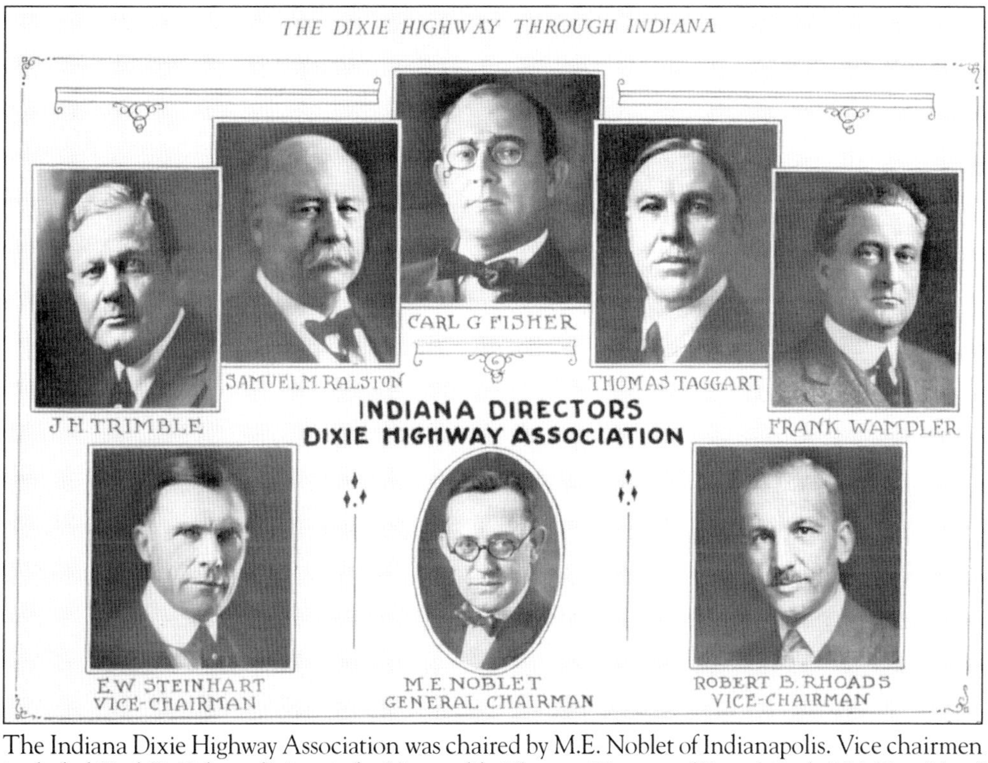

The Indiana Dixie Highway Association was chaired by M.E. Noblet of Indianapolis. Vice chairmen included Carl G. Fisher of Miami, the Honorable Thomas Taggart of French Lick, J.H. Trimble of Indianapolis, Sen. Samuel M. Ralston of Indianapolis, Frank Wampler of Indianapolis, and E.W. Steinhart of Fort Wayne. This committee planned a Dixie Highway celebration for the route's 10th anniversary that took place on October 9–10, 1925. (Courtesy Russell Rein.)

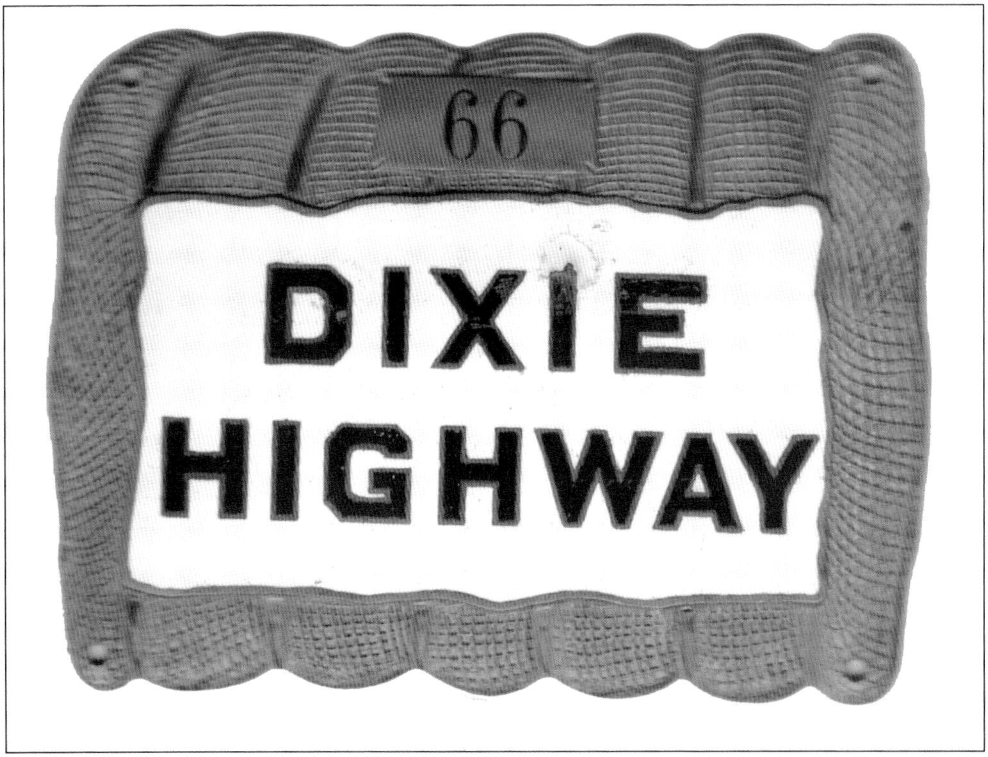

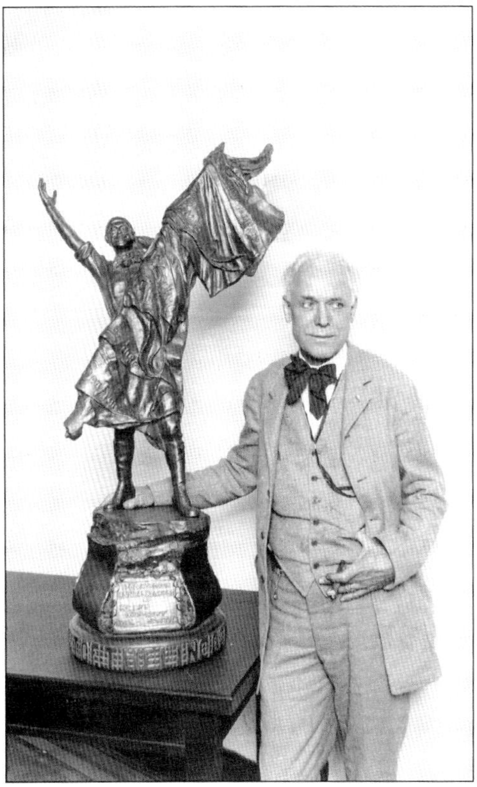

The Dixie Highway was conceived by Carl Fisher as a highway from Indianapolis to Miami. Fisher and his wife, Jane, wintered in Miami and believed other Northerners would want to do the same. With the help of W.S. Gilbreath of the Hoosier Motor Club, Fisher made plans for his second transcontinental road. In 1914, Gilbreath attended the American Road Congress in Atlanta to get approval from the governors of the Dixie Highway states for the new highway. As the Dixie Highway evolved, the dogleg from Chicago to Indianapolis and routes in Michigan from Sault Ste Marie to Indianapolis and Louisville were added. Thus began the "snowbird" phenomena. Shown above is a Dixie Highway radiator badge that was issued for the use of a toll bridge. At left, W.S. Gilbreath, father of the Dixie Highway, stands next to a bronze statue known as the "Spirit of the Lincoln Highway." This was based on a photograph of Gilbreath at the end of the 1913 transcontinental Hoosier Auto Tour. The statue was displayed at the AAA office in downtown Detroit for many years. (Above, courtesy Russell Rein; left, courtesy University of Michigan Special Collections Library.)

Six

The Hoosier Hills

Tooling Down through Martinsville and Bloomington

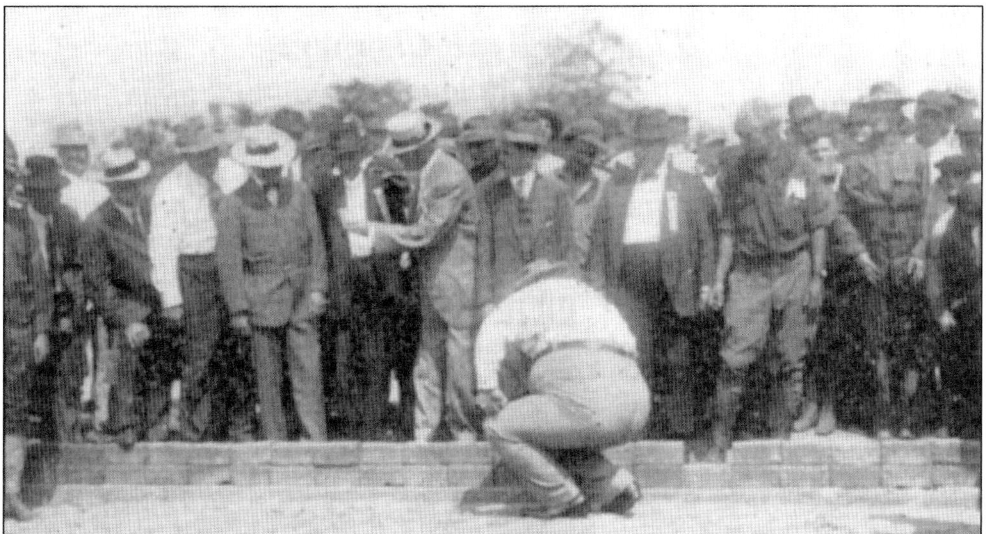

On September 15, 1915, Martinsville residents wanted to bring the Dixie Highway through their city. Tourists came to Martinsville to relax at eight mineral spring resorts, and the community felt a good road would have a positive impact on the tourist industry. Local clay and brick paver companies backed the idea. Here, Indiana's 28th governor, Samuel M. Ralston, lays the first brick in a stretch of pavement in Martinsville, the first official section of the Dixie Highway to be completed. Attending the brick-laying ceremony were Carl G. Fisher, father of the Dixie Highway; Henry Bourne Joy, president of Packard Motor Car Company; and W.S. Gilbreath, Dixie Highway field secretary. (Courtesy Dennis Horvath.)

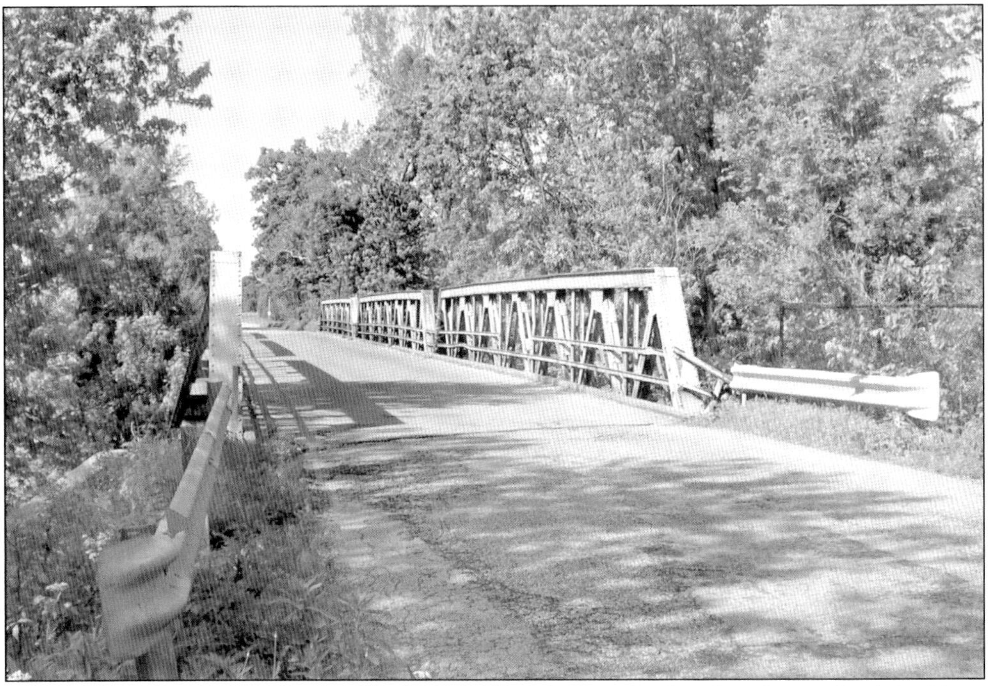

This 19th-century iron pony-truss bridge in Dolan lies on an abandoned stretch of the Dixie Highway just east of State Road 37 and south of Indianapolis. Still in use today, the narrow, one-lane bridge requires a slow, cautious approach. (Courtesy Jan Shupert-Arick.)

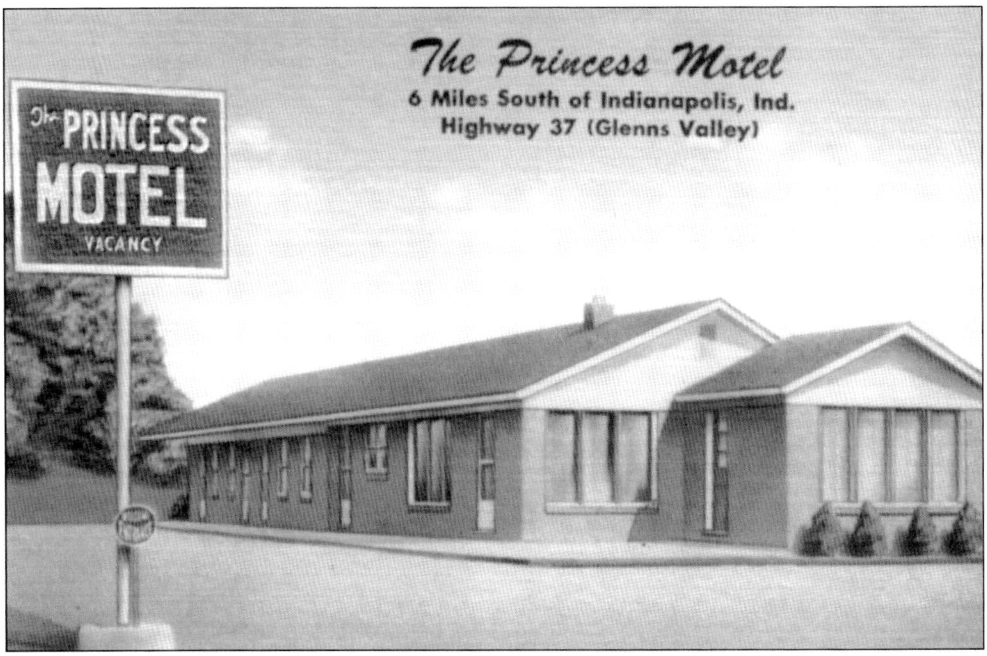

The Princess Motel was built south of Indianapolis in Glenns Valley to serve travelers along this section of the road, which had few other services. (Courtesy Russell Rein.)

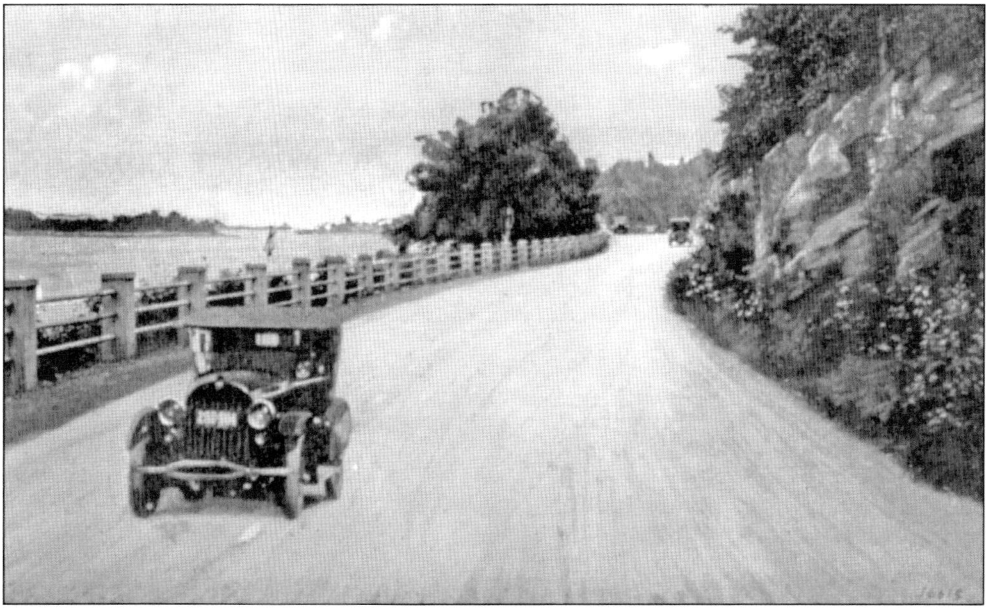

This postcard view captures a drive along the White River into Martinsville, the county seat of Morgan County in the 1920s. Today, Martinsville is accessed by State Roads 37, 39, 252, 44, and 67. In 1899, Eugene Shireman, a Martinsville entrepreneur, turned swampland into the Grassyfork Fisheries. Once dubbed the Goldfish Capital of the World, today, Martinsville fisheries sell fish to many parts of the world. (Courtesy Russell Rein.)

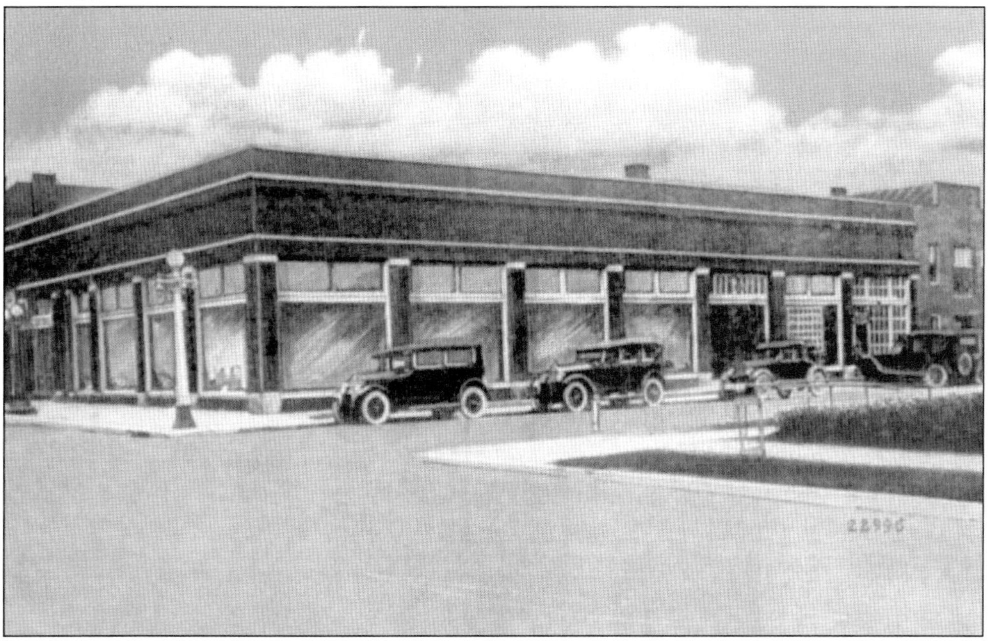

In the 1920s, the Martinsville Motor Company built an impressive showroom and garage. Martinsville is located 30 miles south of Indianapolis and 20 miles north of Bloomington. The southern edge of the Wisconsin Glacier, which smoothed the northern part of the state, bordered what is now Martinsville. Without glacial influence, the rugged hills inspired the nickname, "Gateway to the South." (Courtesy Russell Rein.)

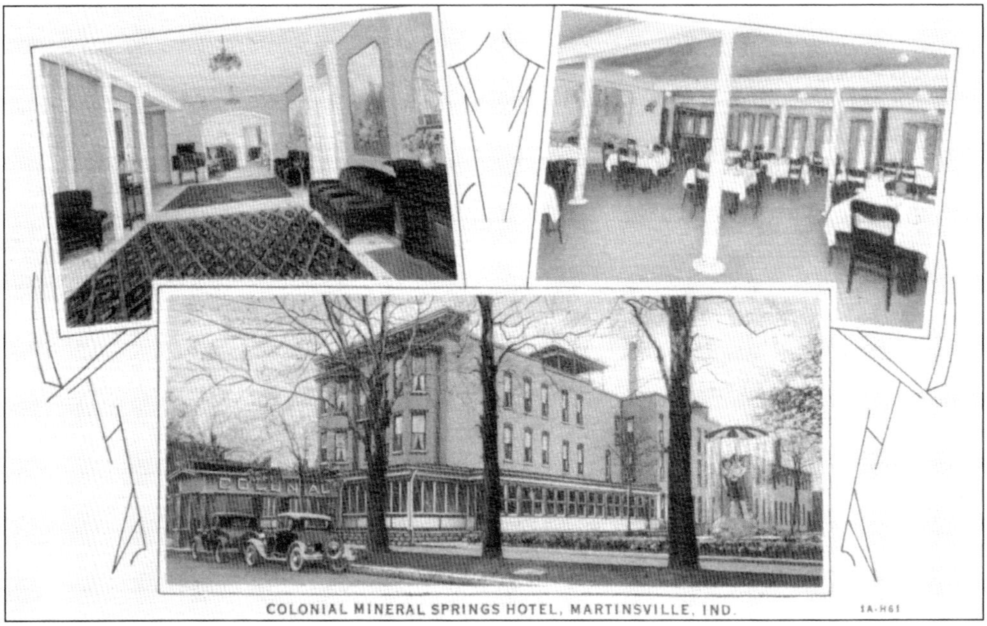

From 1888 until 1968, visitors sought the artesian mineral water health spas of Martinsville. Over the course of nearly 100 years, almost a dozen sanitariums were in operation. Visitors traveled by rail and road to bathe and refresh in the waters. Many dignitaries visited Martinsville in the early 20th century to enjoy the mineral spas for their perceived therapeutic qualities. Topping the former National Sanitarium is a refurbished neon sign that still reads, "Martinsville City of Mineral Water." In the early 20th century, the Colonial Mineral Springs offered an attractive setting and mineral water therapy at a relatively inexpensive price. The sanitarium at West Washington and Mulberry Streets (pictured above) was visible from the town square. In March 1940, Michael and Dolly Cohn purchased the Colonial and renamed it the Cohn-Barnard Sanitarium and Hotel. (Both, courtesy Russell Rein.)

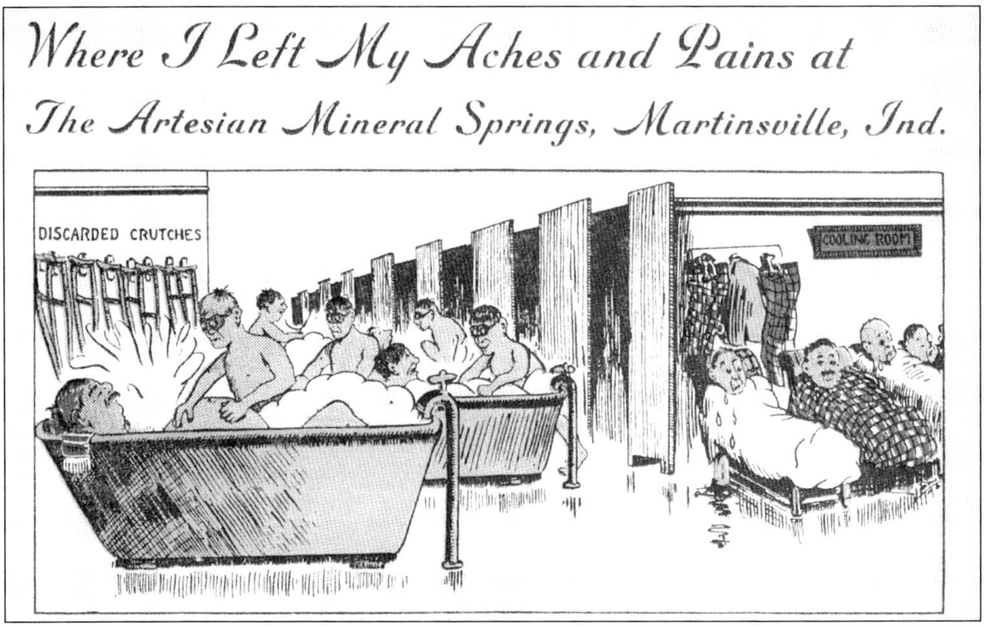

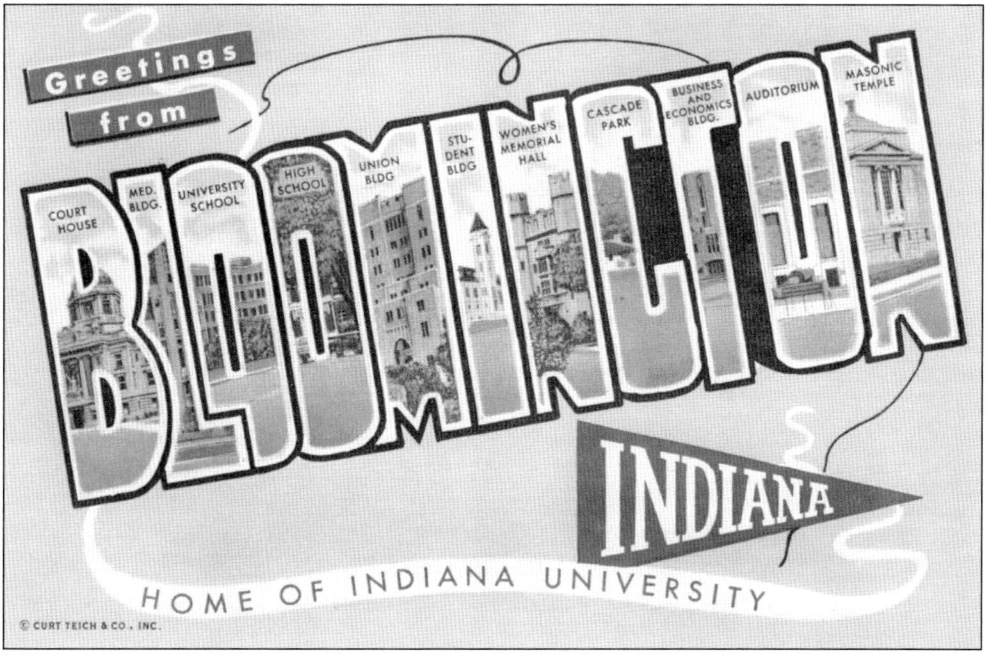

Founded in Bloomington, Indiana, in 1820, Indiana University (IU) has grown along with the city to become one of the nation's great university communities. This postcard brings the school's traditions to life. Indiana University has grown from 10 students and a single professor to a world-class institution of higher learning with over 42,000 students from 145 nations. (Courtesy Jan Shupert-Arick.)

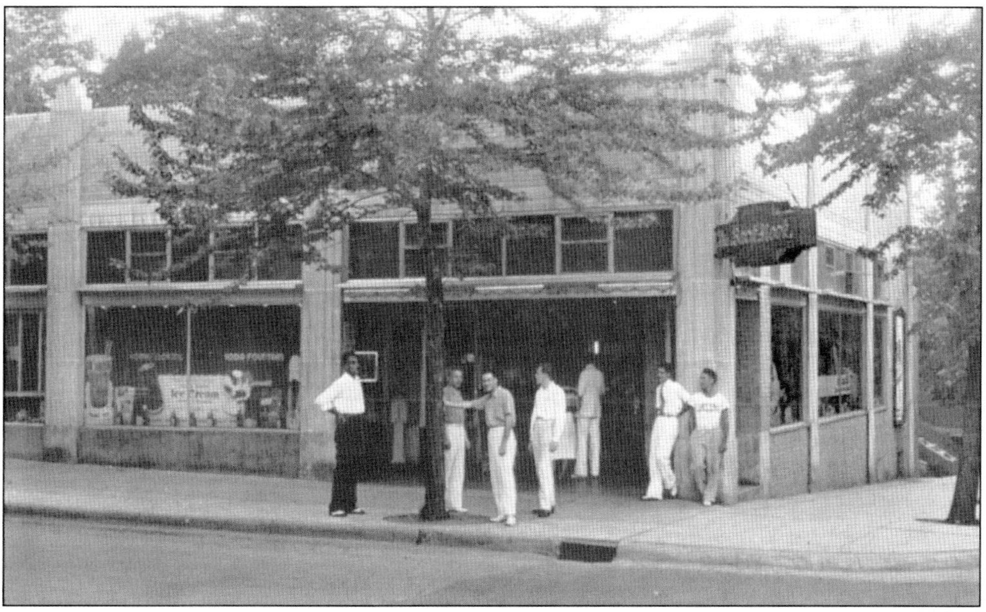

During the first half of the 20th century, the Book Nook was a campus hangout located just across the street from the IU School of Law at Indiana and Kirkwood Avenues in Bloomington. Local folklore purports that Hoagy Carmichael wrote the notes of his famous tune "Stardust" at the Book Nook's piano. (Courtesy Russell Rein.)

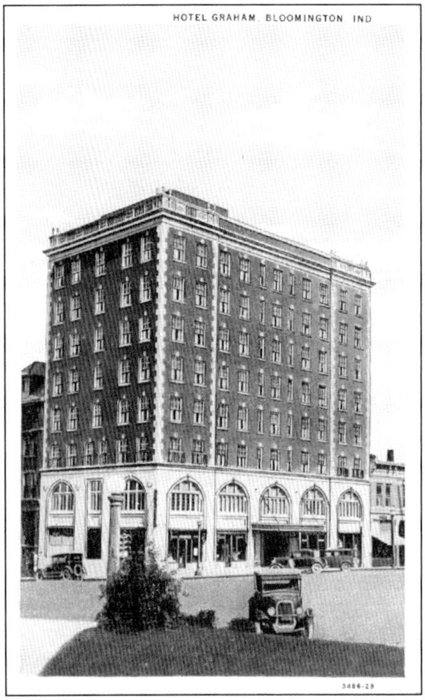

The seven-story brick and limestone Graham Hotel served travelers for decades at the corner of Sixth Street and College Avenue. Ornate windows on the main level created a grand entryway and lounge spaces. Today, the structure is known as Graham Plaza, located in Bloomington's Entertainment & Arts District (BEAD), one of the most intact historic squares in Indiana. (Courtesy Russell Rein.)

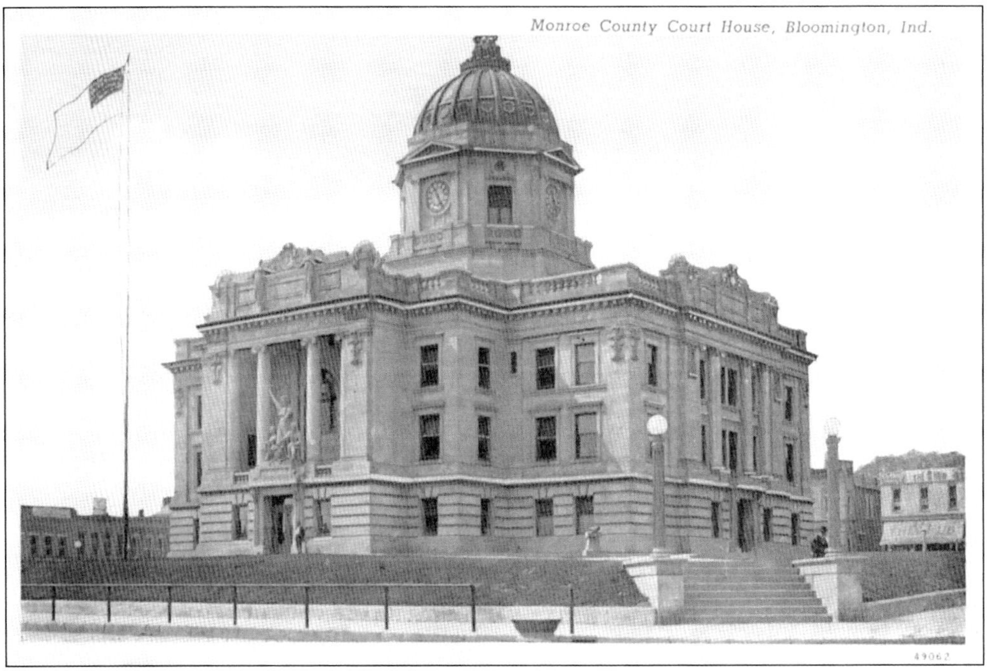

Monroe County constructed a new courthouse in the Beaux-Arts style early in the 20th century. Fortunately for Bloomington, limestone was a building material of choice and the wealth of the community increased dramatically with the national building boom. In 1912, there were 17 limestone quarries, 22 mills, and 15 cut-stone plants operating in Monroe County. Saved from demolition in 1984, the Monroe County Courthouse is a beacon of community pride and commitment to preservation. (Courtesy Russell Rein.)

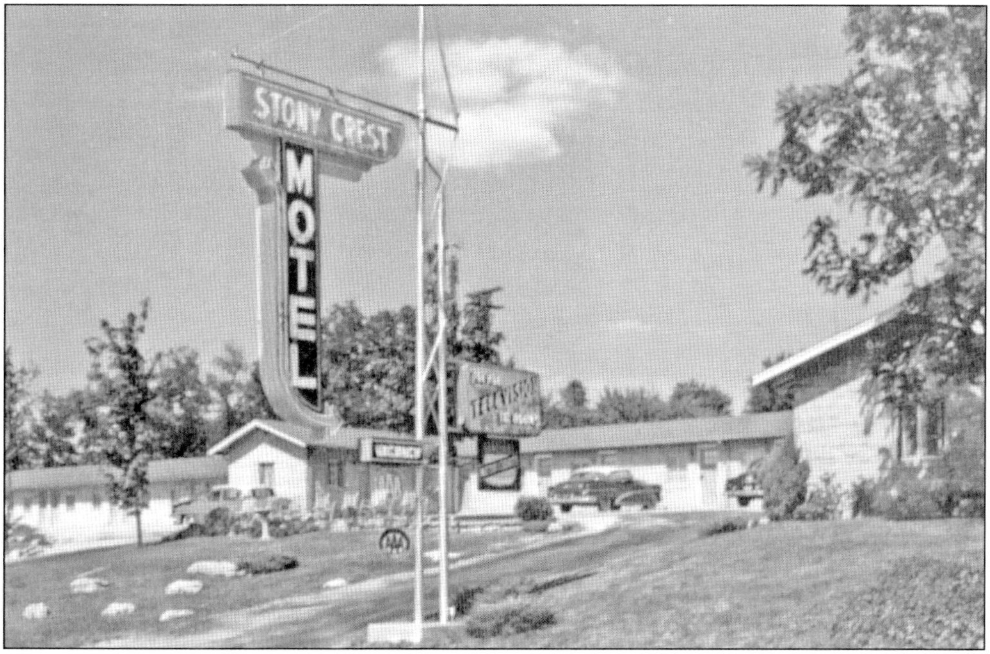

The two-story Stony Crest Motel at 1300 North Walnut Street in Bloomington was built in the 1950s. Its large neon sign indicated vacancies or no vacancies. Later postcards printed in the 1960s show that the motel featured some patio-level rooms with pine paneling and trim interiors and access to an outdoor pool. Motel guests could park their cars near their rooms in an adjacent parking lot, which was AAA approved. (Courtesy Russell Rein.)

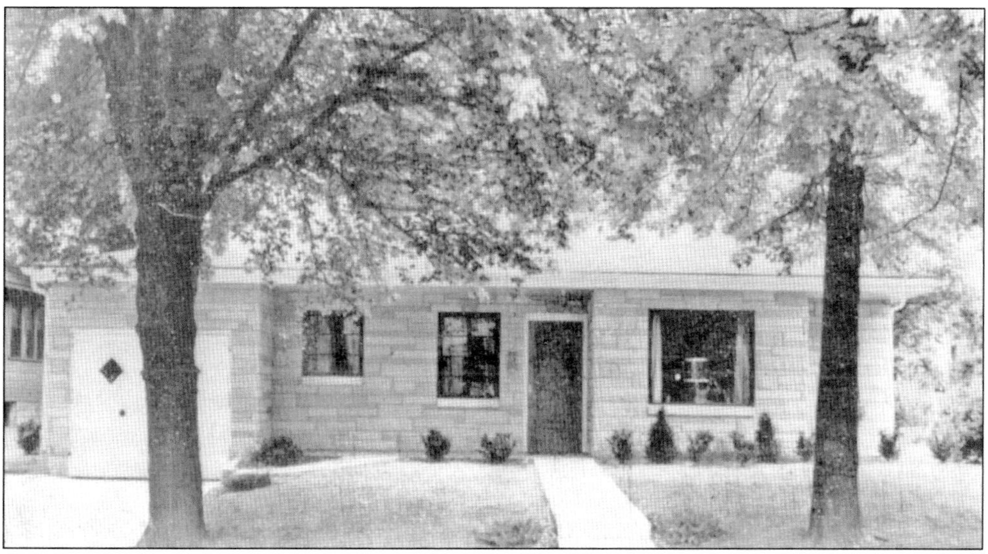

The Joe Solomito Stone Company of Bloomington created a flat style of limestone used for constructing buildings. This became a very popular house style in the early 1960s. The limestone was machine-split. According to the information printed on the back of the promotional postcard, the split-stone veneer for the exterior of this three-bedroom home cost $800. (Courtesy Russell Rein.)

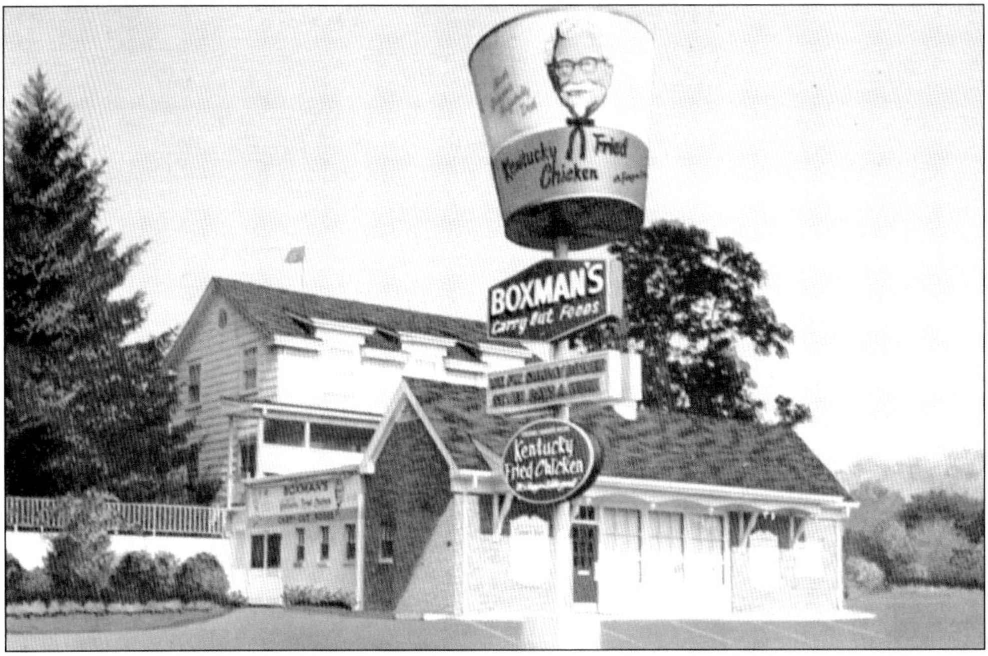

Henry F. Boxman, a Bloomington-area entrepreneur, bought the Dew Drop Inn at 422 South Walnut Street and turned it into the Boxman's Kentucky Fried Chicken Carry Out Restaurant, which became well known for its Dutch apple pie. (Courtesy Russell Rein.)

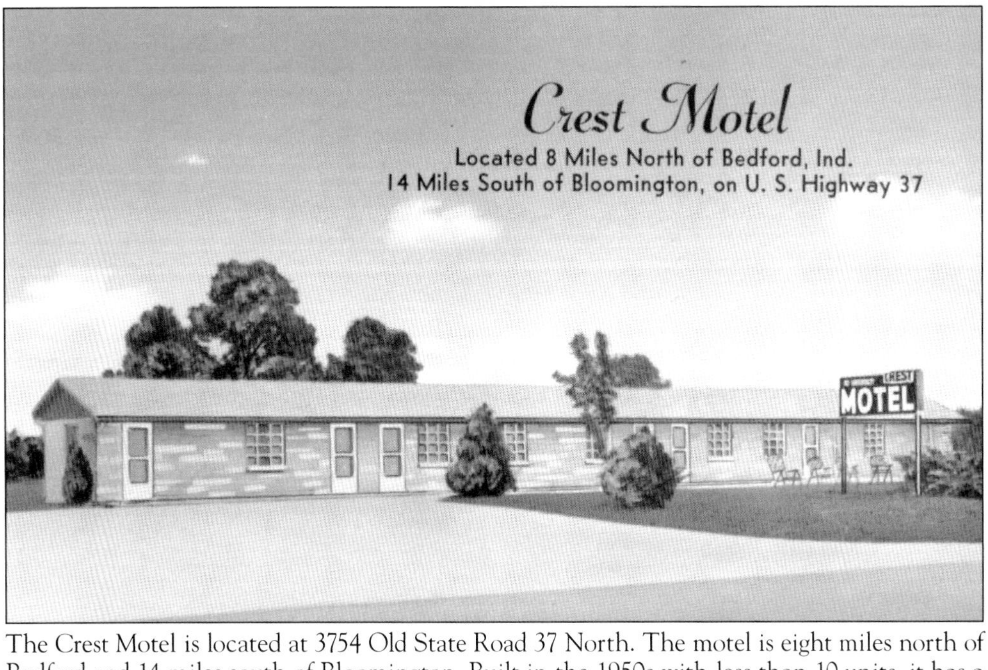

The Crest Motel is located at 3754 Old State Road 37 North. The motel is eight miles north of Bedford and 14 miles south of Bloomington. Built in the 1950s with less than 10 units, it has a second building and now offers 15 rooms. The motel was built with a limestone facade. (Courtesy Russell Rein.)

Seven

Bedrock
Through Oolitic, Bedford, and Mitchell

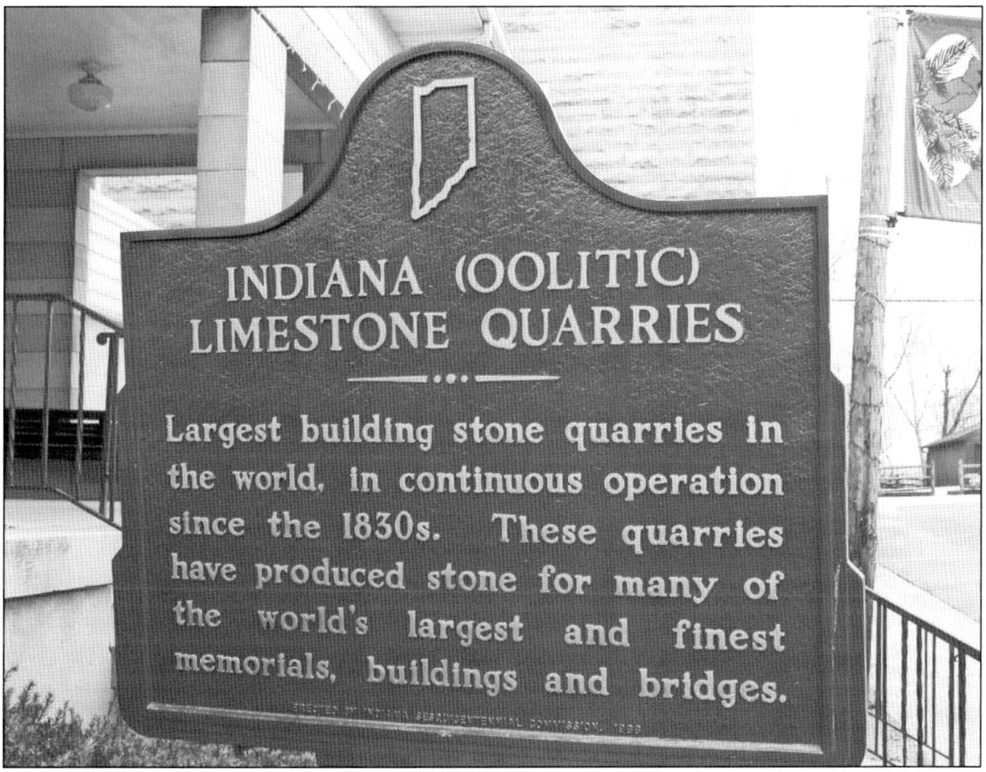

By the mid-1960s there was a move to make State Road 37 a four-lane highway through southern Indiana. The historic marker in this photograph stands near the Oolitic Post Office and honors the significance of local limestone quarries. The original Dixie Highway was truncated at Oolitic so the area could be mined. A large gap now breaches what was once the Dixie Highway north of Oolitic. (Courtesy Jan Shupert-Arick.)

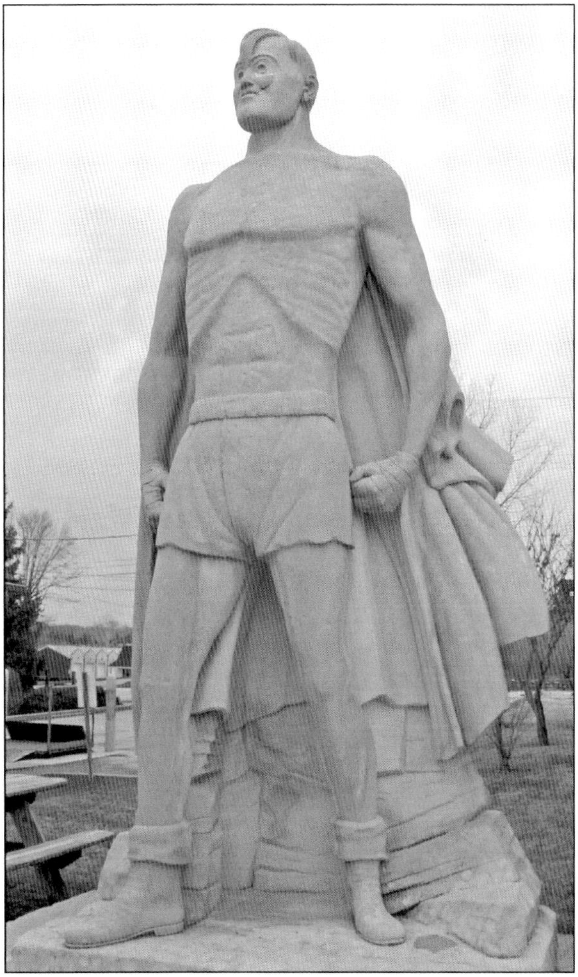

Between the post office and town hall is good-hearted boxer Joe Palooka, the title character of a comic strip. When the Indiana Limestone industry carved a likeness of Palooka into a 10-foot, 20,000-pound piece of limestone, 4,500 people gathered for the dedication of the statue in Bedford in 1948. The statue later became a target for vandals and was moved to a local park, then to a limestone mill, and then to another park. Finally in 1984 (the year the comic strip was cancelled), the statue was given to the town of Oolitic to stand on Main Street. (Courtesy Jan Shupert-Arick.)

Limestone was used in great quantities through the 1920s. This period saw technological advances in quarrying and fabrication, enabling the Indiana Limestone Company to maintain an edge over newer, man-made product companies. Here, a section of limestone is turned on a lathe to create a massive column. (Courtesy Russell Rein.)

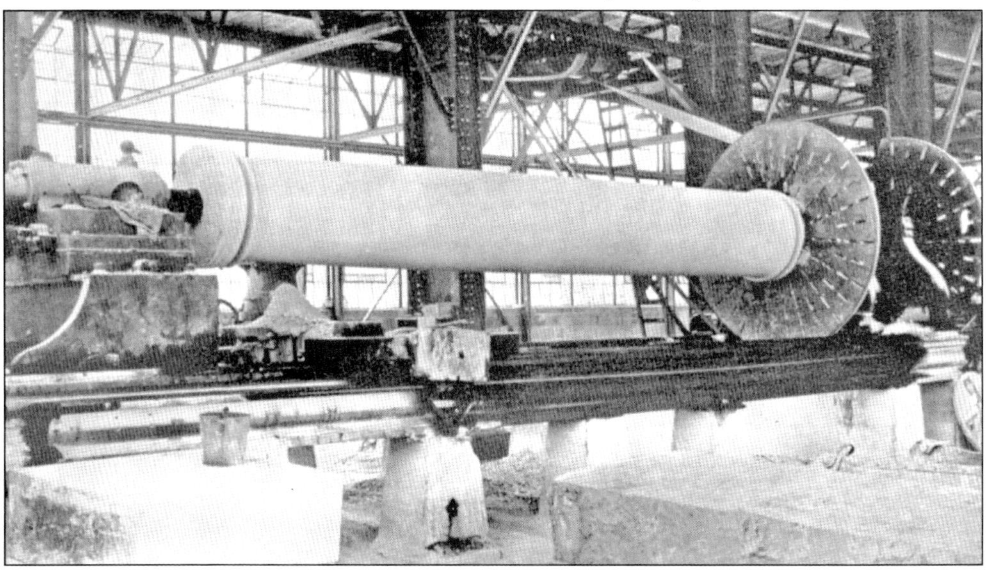

PAOLI, IND., TO BLOOMINGTON, IND., 46.6 MILES
State Highway No. 22.

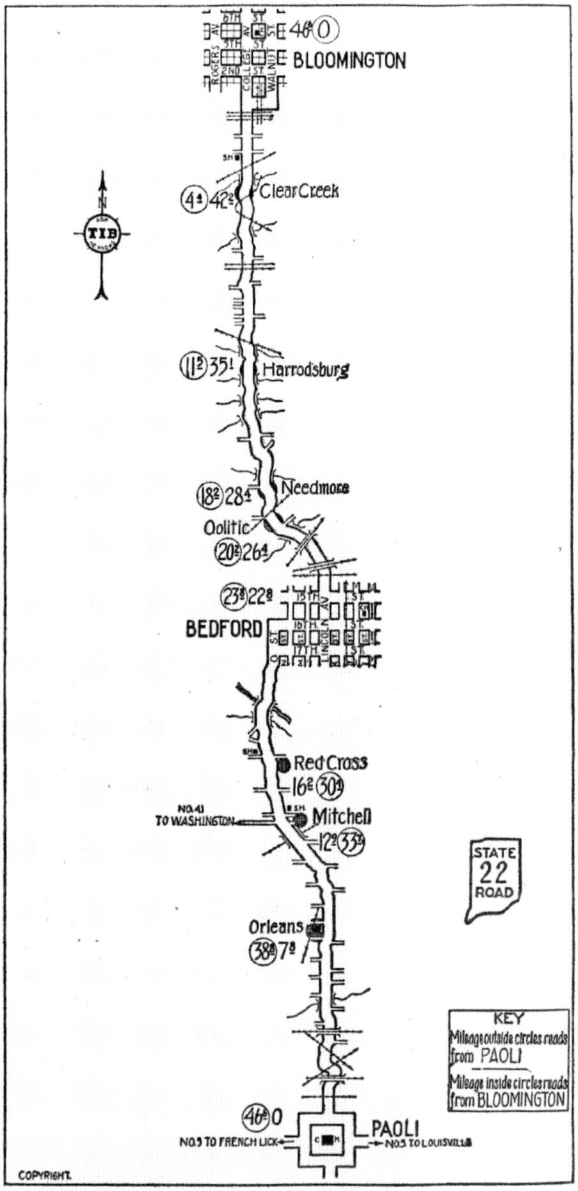

DESCRIPTION: Very good road consisting of gravel and paving. Bloomington is the home of Indiana State University. Bedford is famous for its lime stone quarries which is used throughout the country for building constructions. Bedford is the county seat of Lawrence county; Paoli is the county seat of Orange county. Connections are made at Paoli for Louisville. For connecting routes see index map in front of book.

BLOOMINGTON: Carter's Garage, 304 S. Walnut St.

This Dixie Highway strip map shows State Road 22 (now SR 37) from Bloomington to Paoli. This section of the historic road ran through Clear Creek, Harrodsburg, Bedford, Red Cross, Mitchell, Orleans, and Paoli. The road surface was comprised of gravel and some pavement. (Courtesy Russell Rein.)

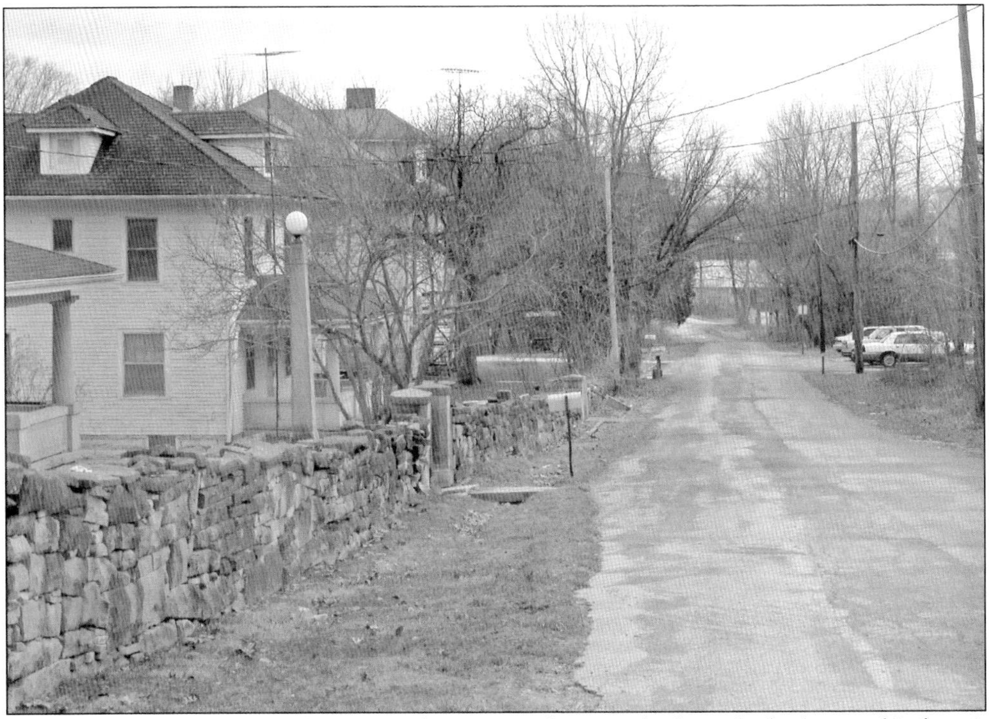

A trip along parts of the old Dixie Highway in Oolitic winds through the heart of Indiana's limestone country. The roads pass outcroppings of limestone, old quarries now used as swimming holes, caves, and sinkholes. The photograph above shows a portion of the highway that is still in use but has been cut off by the quarry to the north. Once a prominent section of the road, large homes with limestone-capped stone fences are common. Limestone pillars held electric lights. Front porches, pillars, steps, and decorative architectural elements were all made from local limestone. A great amount of wealth was created by the limestone industry, but most of it has faded over the last half century. The photograph below shows an abandoned portion of the original Dixie Highway north of Oolitic. An abandoned park and other structures are located along the road, which is now private property. (Both, courtesy Jan Shupert-Arick.)

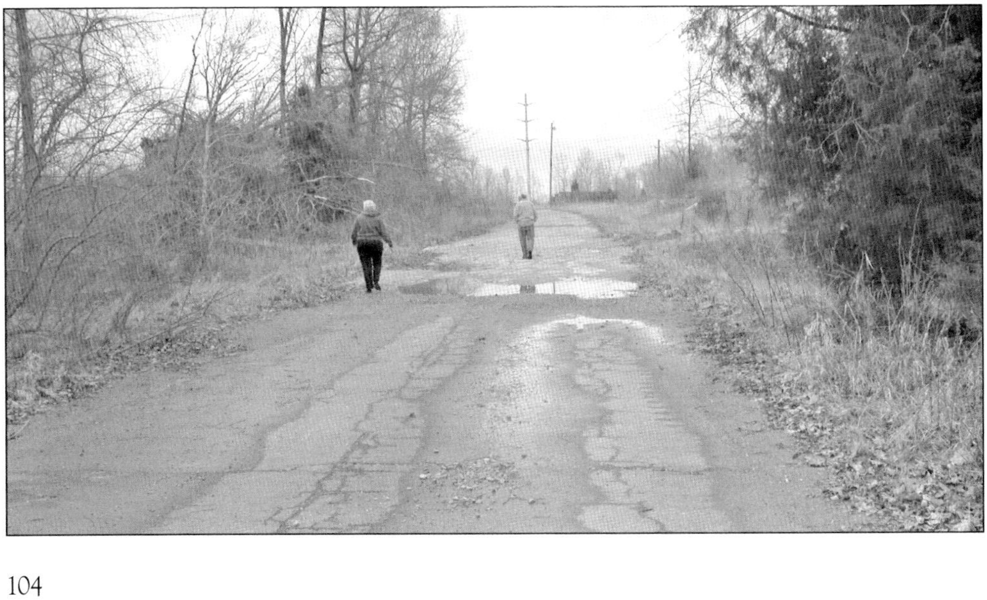

Charlie Pace stands in front of an abandoned section of the Dixie Highway on the north edge of Oolitic. Local residents share stories about the changes over the last 50 years; a proud heritage remains. Limestone from this area has been used in buildings in the state's capital, in the nation's capital, and in other cities throughout the United States, including in the National Cathedral, the Waldorf Astoria, the Biltmore, the Empire State Building, and New York's Grand Central Station. Recently, Indiana Limestone was used to restore and rebuild the Pentagon following the attack on September 11, 2001. (Courtesy Jan Shupert-Arick.)

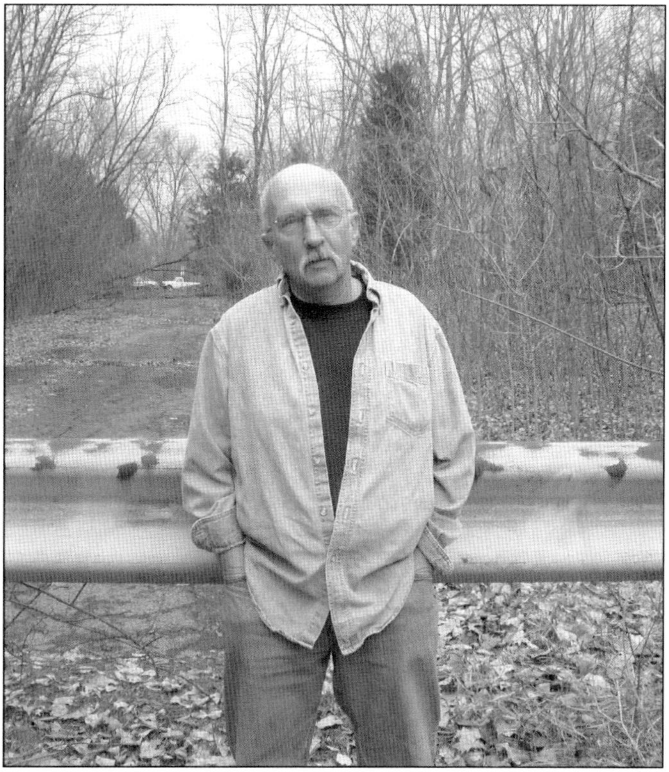

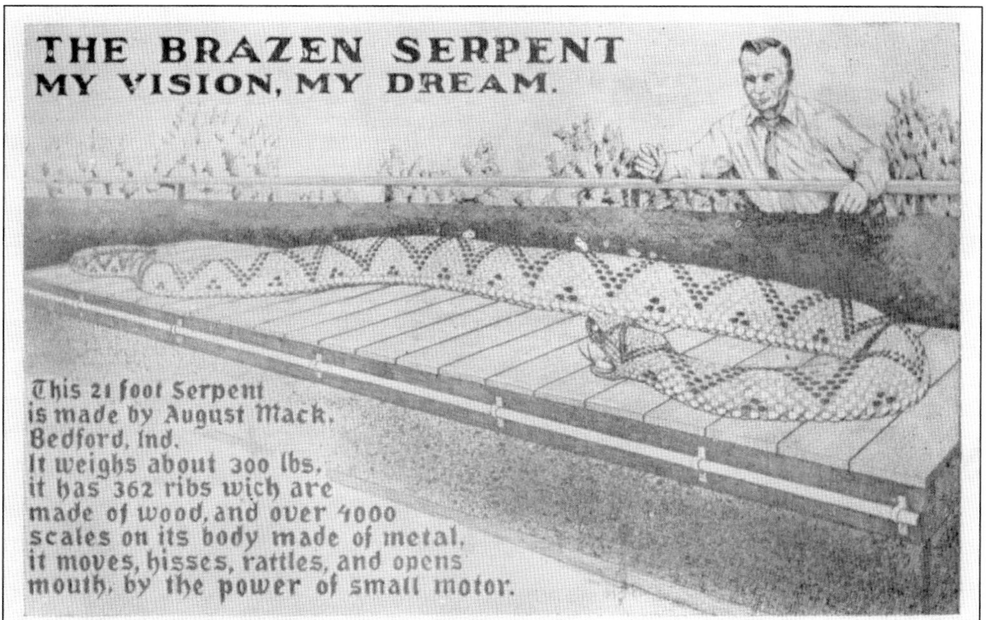

August Mack from Bedford built a local tourist attraction to lure in travelers from the Dixie Highway. This postcard reads, "The Brazen Serpent—My vision, My dream." The 21-foot serpent weighed 300 pounds and had 362 ribs made of wood. It moved, hissed, and rattled. (Courtesy Russell Rein.)

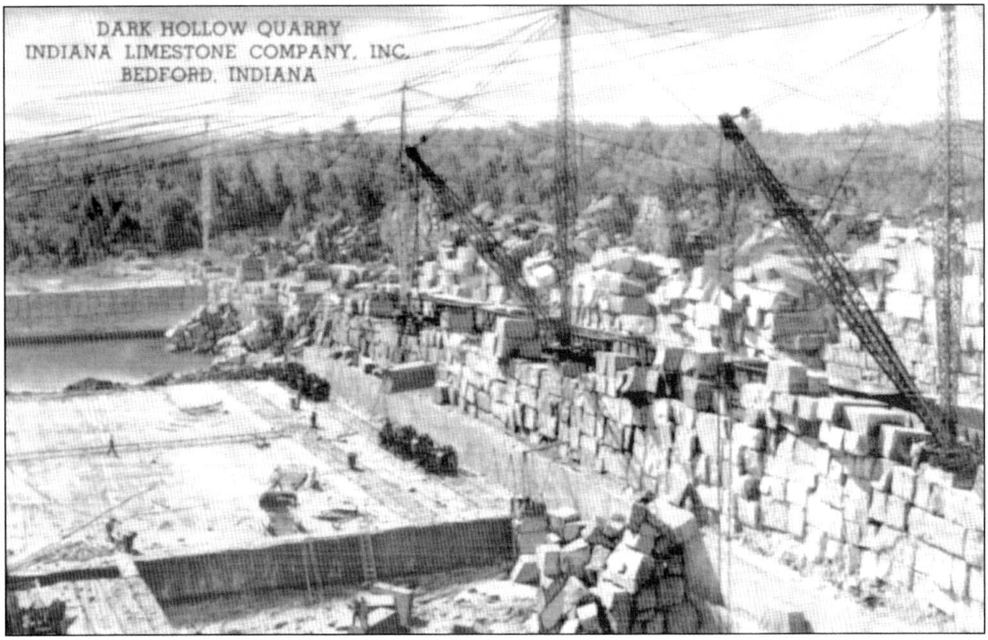

The Dark Hollow Quarry, later known as the Elliott Stone Company, was located in Bedford. The Bedford and Bloomington Branch of the Monon Railroad served the Dark Hollow Quarry. Limestone from Indiana is divided into three types: oolitic (composed of fine-grained, round particles), crystalline (composed of interlocking grains), and flagstone (occurring in thin slabs). Indiana Limestone is the commercial name for dimension stone produced from the oolitic rock formation known to geologists as the Salem outcrop. During the Mississippian era about 340 million years ago, Salem limestone was deposited in a shallow sea that covered much of what is now the middle of the United States. In Indiana, the greatest production of limestone occurs in a stone belt that is approximately two miles wide and 30 miles long. (Both, courtesy Russell Rein.)

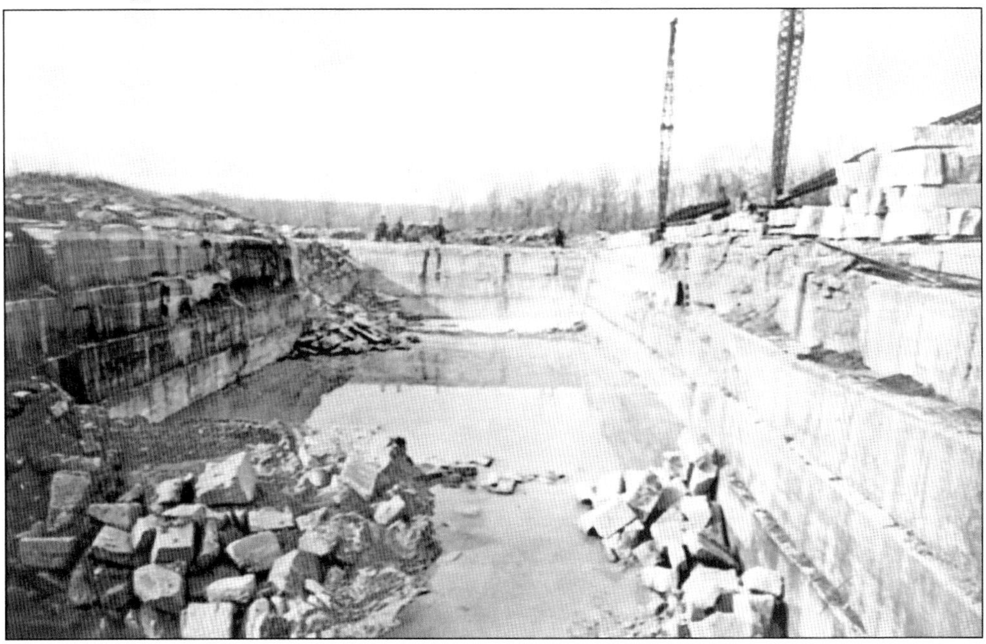

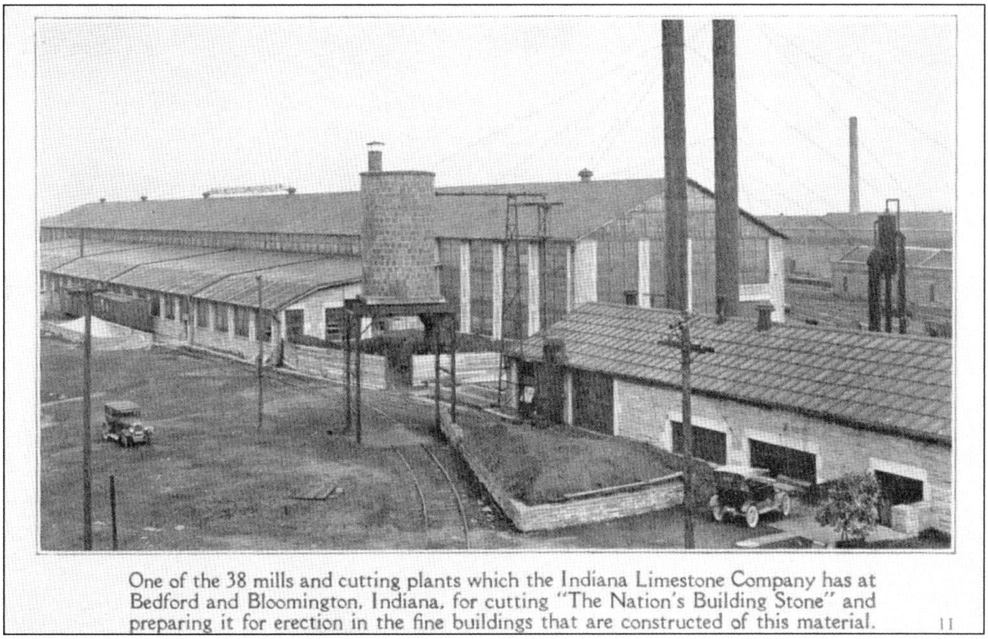

This image shows one of the 38 mills and cutting plants that the Indiana Limestone Company owned at Bedford. (Courtesy Russell Rein.)

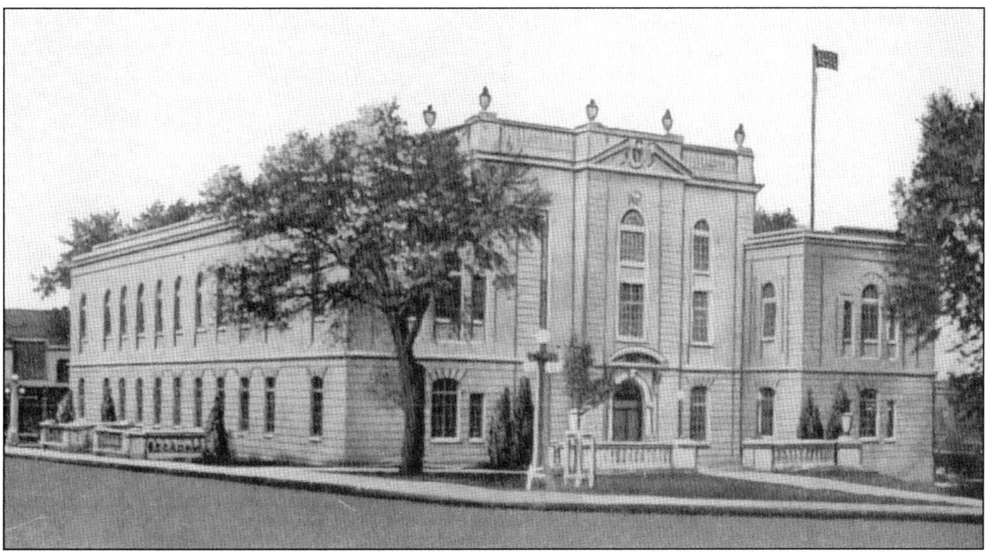

The Lawrence County Courthouse was built in the 1870s and remodeled in the 1930s. Bedford was founded as a town and the county seat in 1825 and received a charter in 1889, named Bedford at the suggestion of businessman Joseph Rawlins, who relocated to the area from Bedford County, Tennessee. The original county seat was Palestine, four miles to the south near the White River; it was moved by the legislature when the original location was deemed unhealthy because of malarial mosquitoes. (Courtesy Russell Rein.)

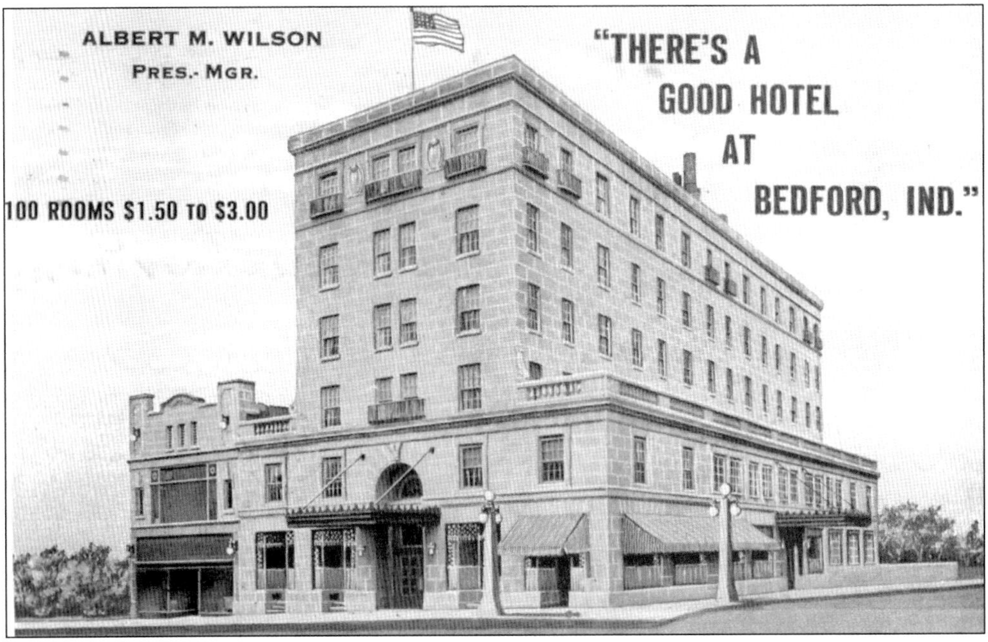

The Greystone Hotel was built in 1923 on the public square in Bedford. Constructed of Indiana Limestone, the six-story hotel was managed by Albert M. Wilson. It featured 100 rooms that cost between $1.50 and $3 per night. A large neon sign was added to the building around 1940. In its heyday, the hotel was advertised as one of the best in the nation. The hotel graced the downtown for 71 years. It burned twice and was finally torn down and replaced with a modern building. Businesses on the square by the mid-20th century included Woolworth's Department Store, Montgomery Ward, the Singer Sewing Store, and a Franklin's Drug Store. (Above, courtesy Russell Rein; below, courtesy Linda McIver.)

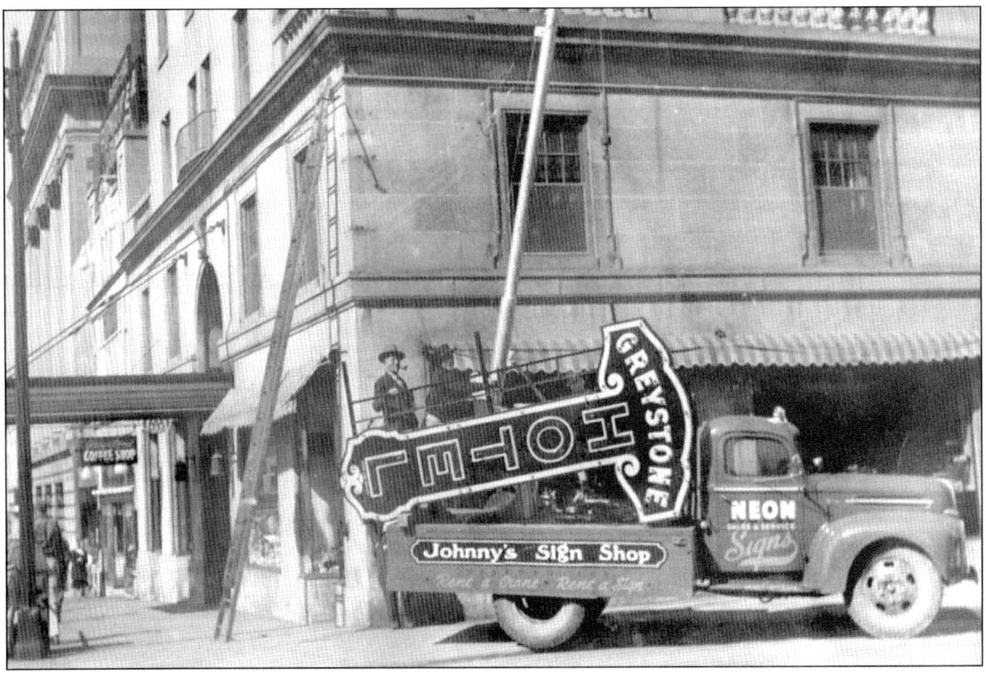

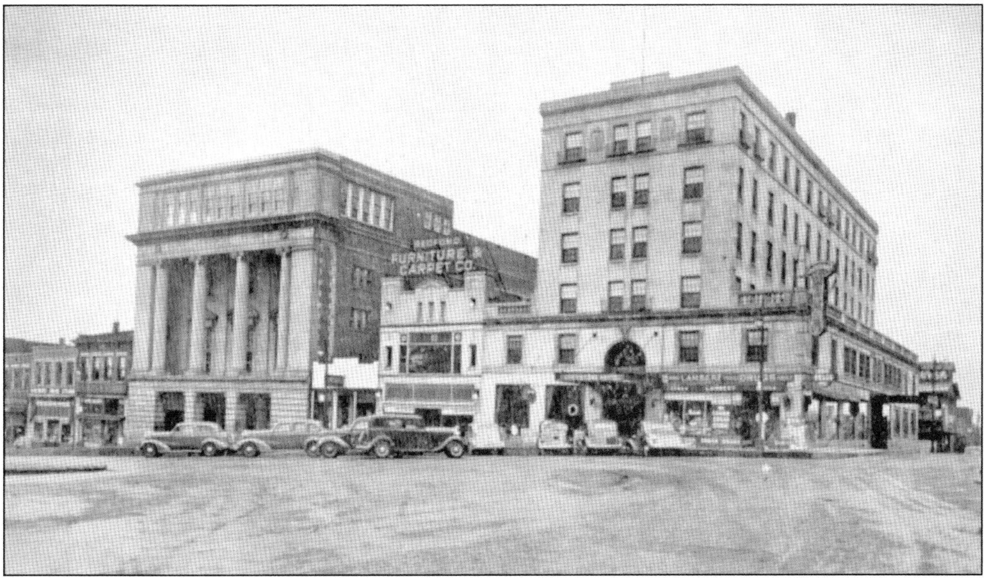

The north side of the public square in Bedford includes a large Masonic temple, the Greystone Hotel, and a furniture and carpet company. The Buck Lemon building to the left is now the home of the Lawrence County Historical Museum. This photograph was taken in the late 1930s from the parking lot on the east side of the Lawrence County Courthouse. (Courtesy Russell Rein.)

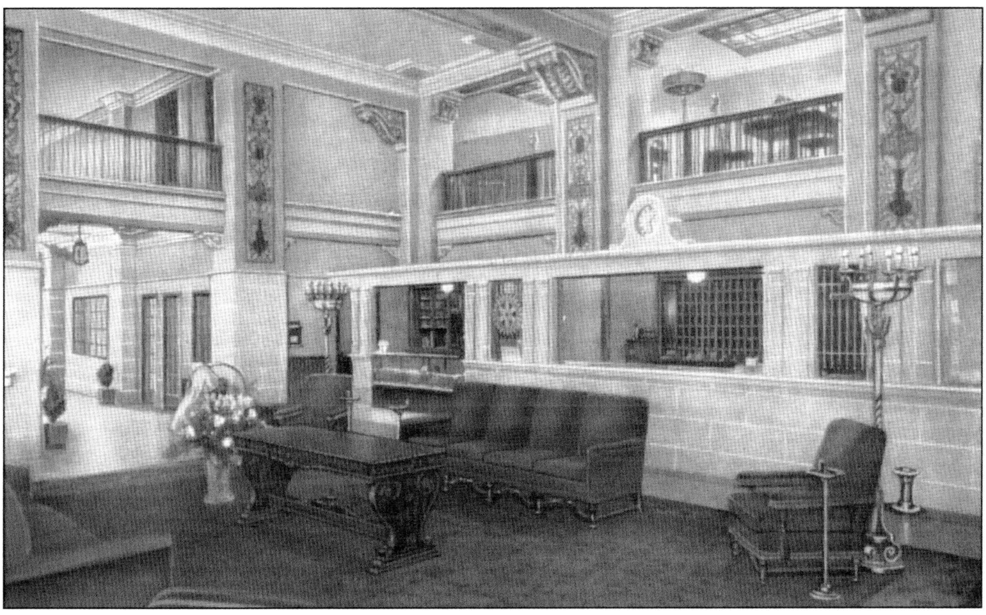

Shown is the grandly decorated interior of the Greystone Hotel in Bedford. The hotel registration desk, a comfortable lounge with a smoking stand, elegant lamps, and a mezzanine café provided services and comfort to hotel guests. The hotel was built in 1923 at a cost of $300,000. To finance the construction, local residents purchased subscriptions. (Courtesy Russell Rein.)

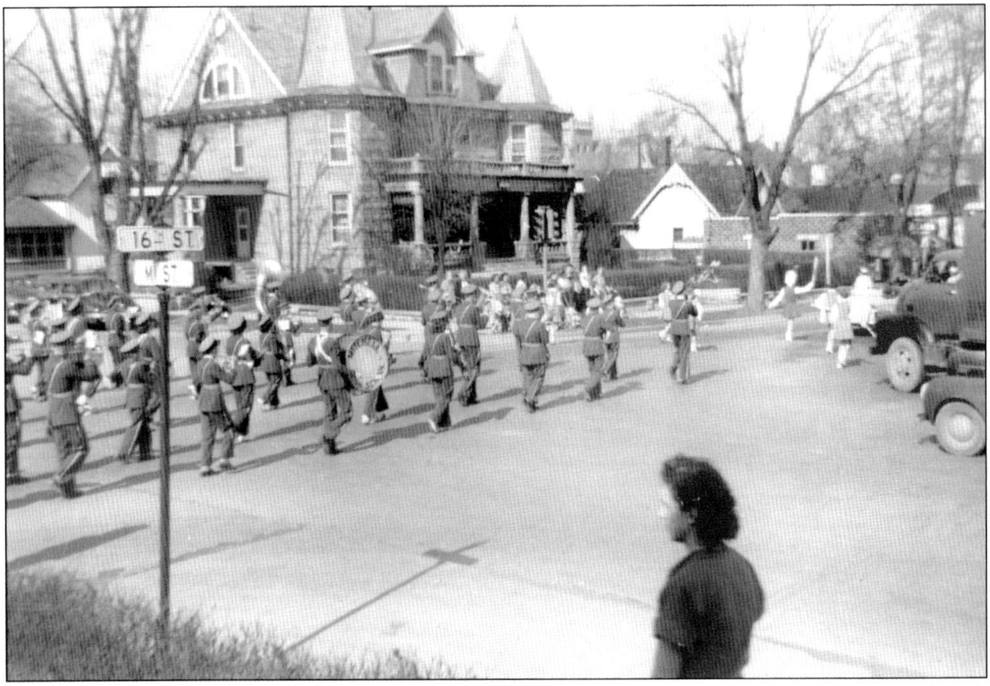

Hoosier communities have a long tradition of Fourth of July parades on main streets lined with parade watchers. Many parades host competitions for marching bands that play well-rehearsed music in hopes of winning trophies and cash prizes. This photograph shows the Mitchell High School marching band in Bedford, Indiana. The parade was held along the Dixie Highway at Sixteenth and M Streets. (Courtesy Linda McIver.)

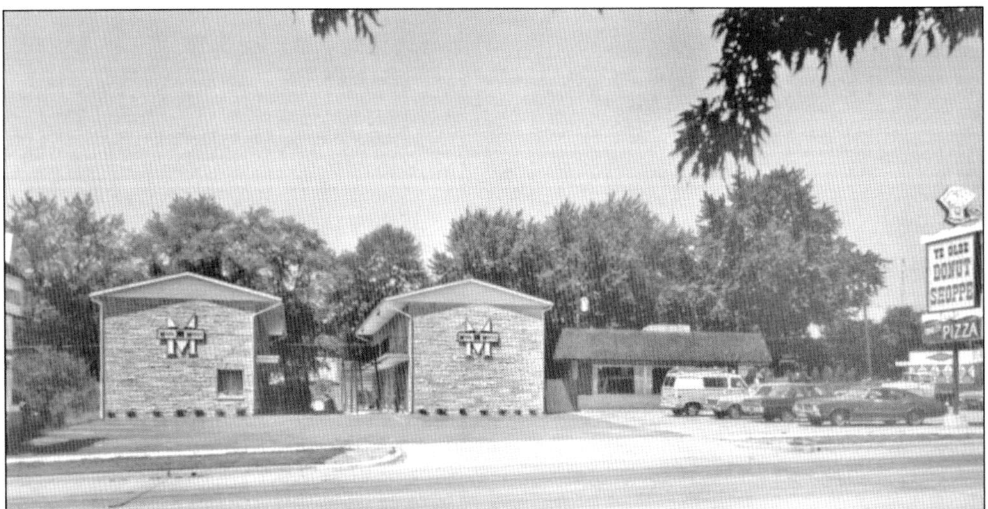

Built in the 1950s, the Mark III Motel in Bedford at 1709 M Street (State Road 37 and US Route 50) has a front facade made of limestone. Today, the two-story motel offers an economical and friendly stay with free wireless Internet, cable television, and other amenities. The 21-room motel is a 30-minute drive from the Indiana University in Bloomington. (Courtesy Russell Rein.)

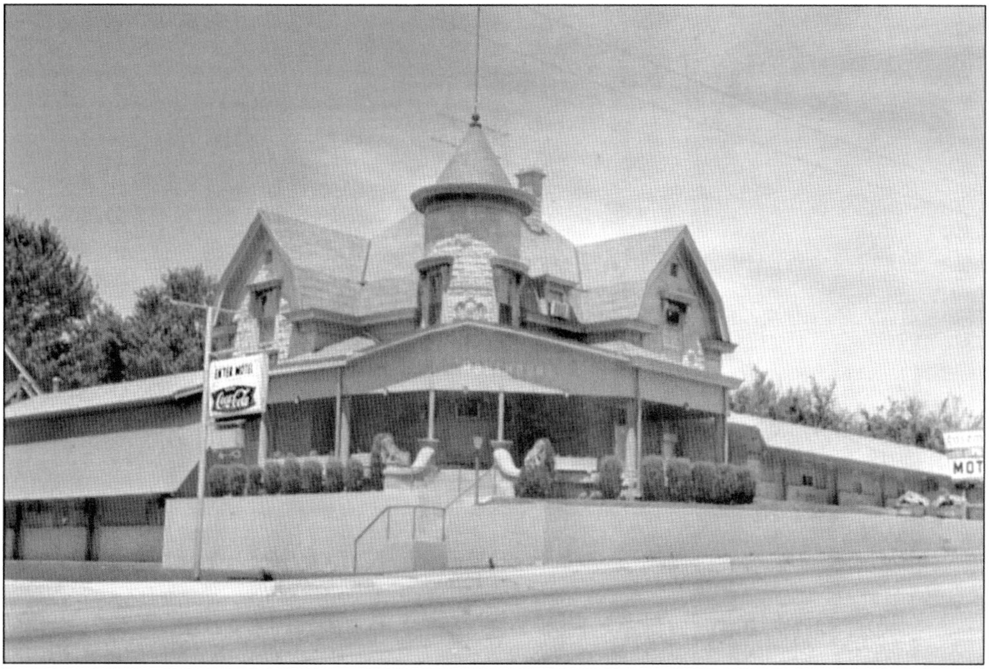

Built in 1906 at 1923 M Street just a short distance from downtown Bedford, the historic portion of this motel is actually a grand home constructed on the south side of Bedford across from the city cemetery. These views of the Rosemont Motel in Bedford show how little it has changed since the 1950s. The motel wings were added to the two-story mansion. Guests today may rent rooms in the added wings or in the historic portion of the motel. Motel amenities include air-conditioning, complimentary coffee, computer and fax services, microwaves, cable television, and free movies. (Above, courtesy Russell Rein; below, courtesy Jan Shupert-Arick.)

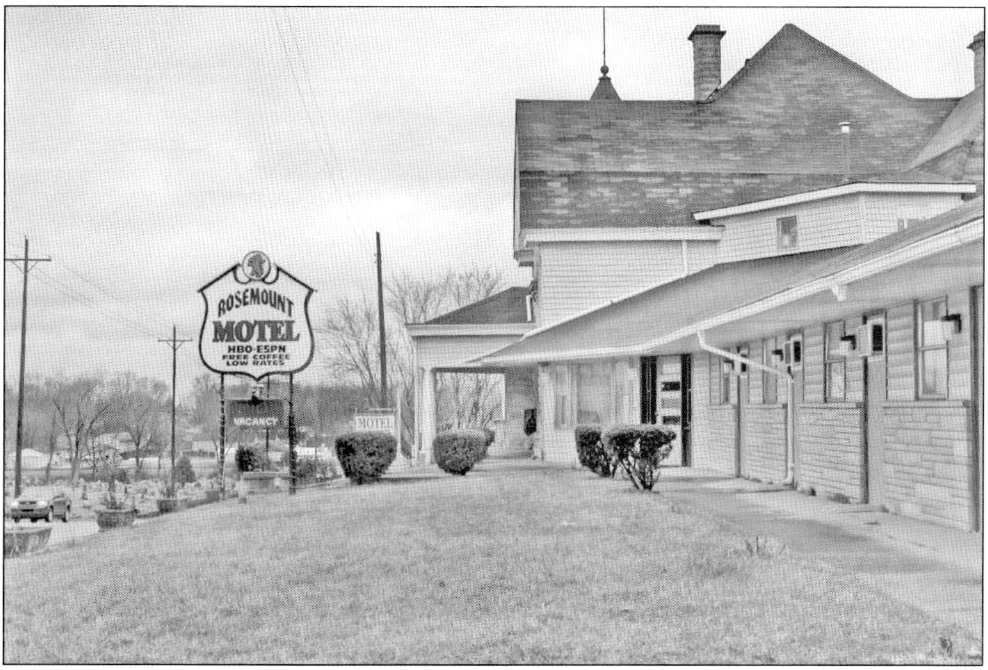

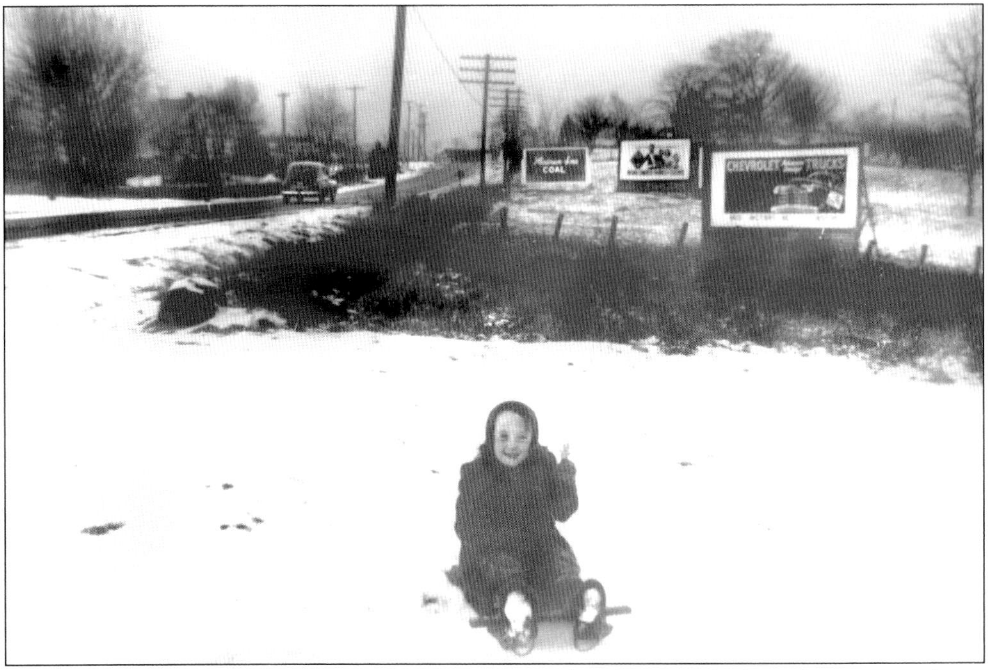

Linda Pace McIver was a child when her mother took this photograph along the Dixie Highway in Bedford, Indiana. Notice the road and the billboard advertising along this section in the 1940s. (Courtesy Linda McIver.)

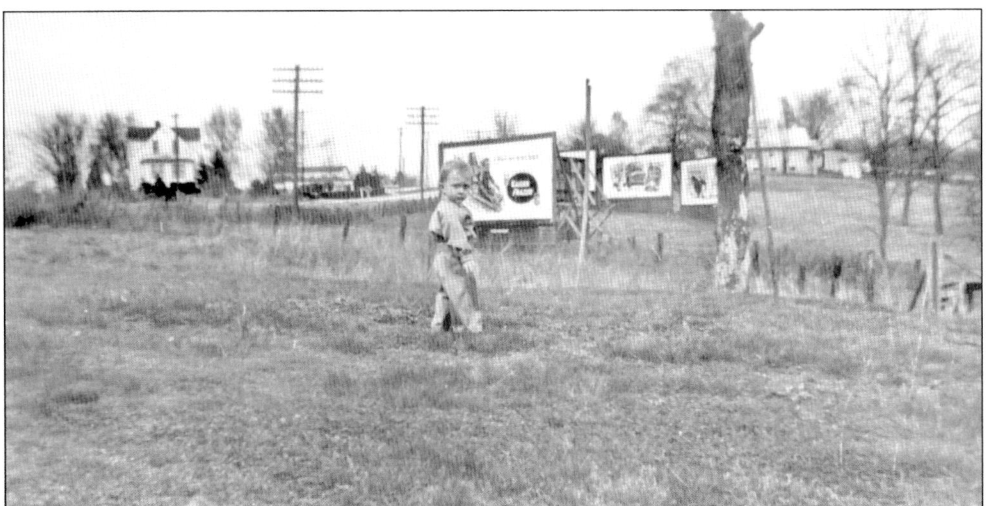

Charles Pace poses along the Dixie Highway on the south end of Bedford during his playtime in the 1940s. The billboards advertise local businesses to automobile travelers. The airport was just down the road and provided hangers and a landing strip for small aircraft. (Courtesy Linda McIver.)

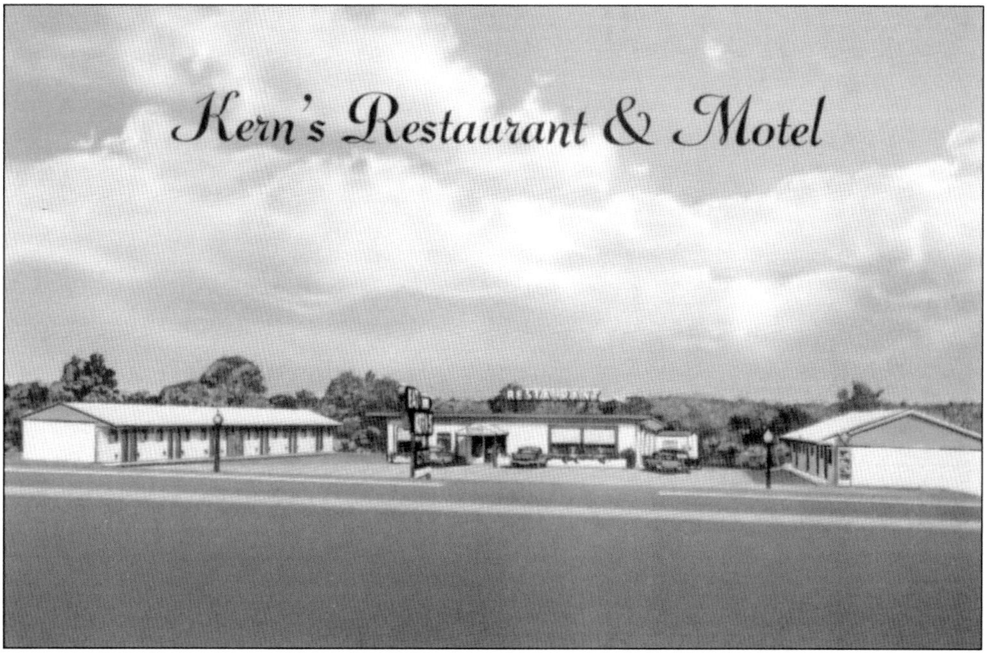

Kern's Restaurant & Motel was located a half mile south of Bedford. The motel was constructed in the 1950s and included three separate buildings. The annexes on either side of the main building each contained 10 units. The central building housed the motel office and the restaurant. (Courtesy Russell Rein.)

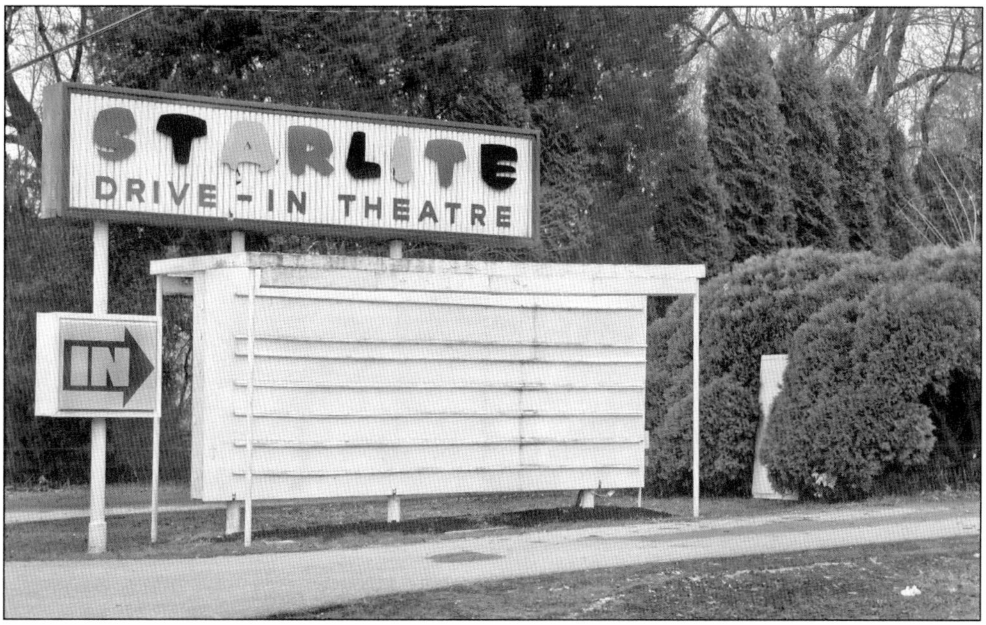

The Starlite Drive-In Theatre at 7630 South Old State Road 37 between Bloomington and Bedford is tree-lined with one main building and one screen. The car capacity is 418. The Starlite Drive-In has been serving the area for decades and has been named the number one entertainment business in Bloomington. The drive-in was started in the backyard of the previous owners and offers a full concession selection and great movies. (Courtesy Jan Shupert-Arick.)

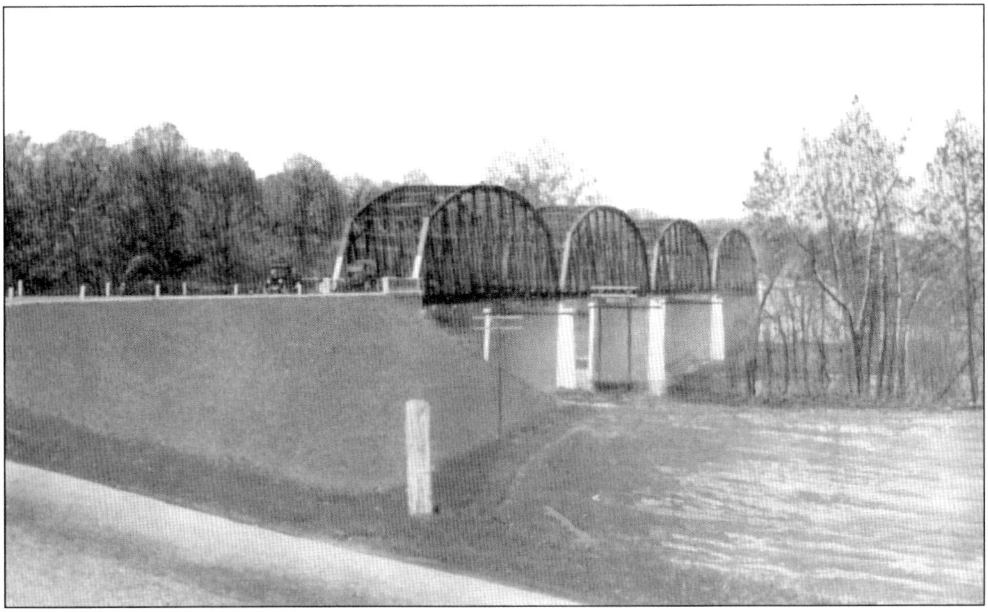

The east fork of the White River intersects State Road 37 south of Bedford. This four-span iron bridge has been replaced with a modern concrete bridge. The Dixie Highway (Old State Road 37) from Bedford to Indianapolis has been bypassed by a modern highway. (Courtesy Russell Rein.)

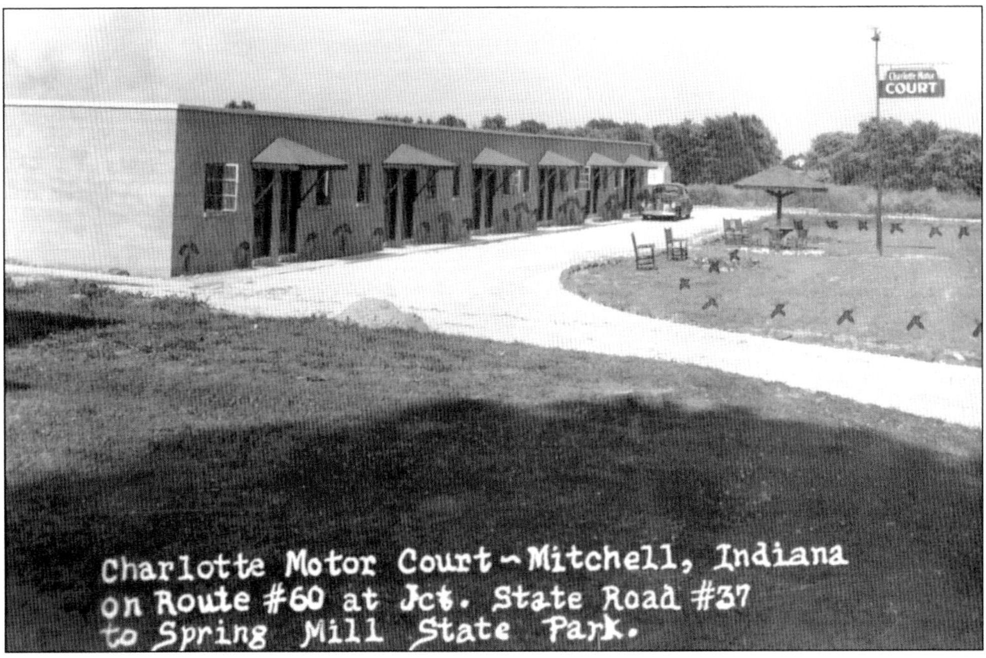

The Charlotte Motor Court in Mitchell was located on State Road 60 at the junction of State Road 37 near Spring Mill State Park. A neon sign and light advertised the motel to nighttime travelers. The business included 12 simple units, a gazebo, and hickory furniture made by local folk artists. (Courtesy Russell Rein.)

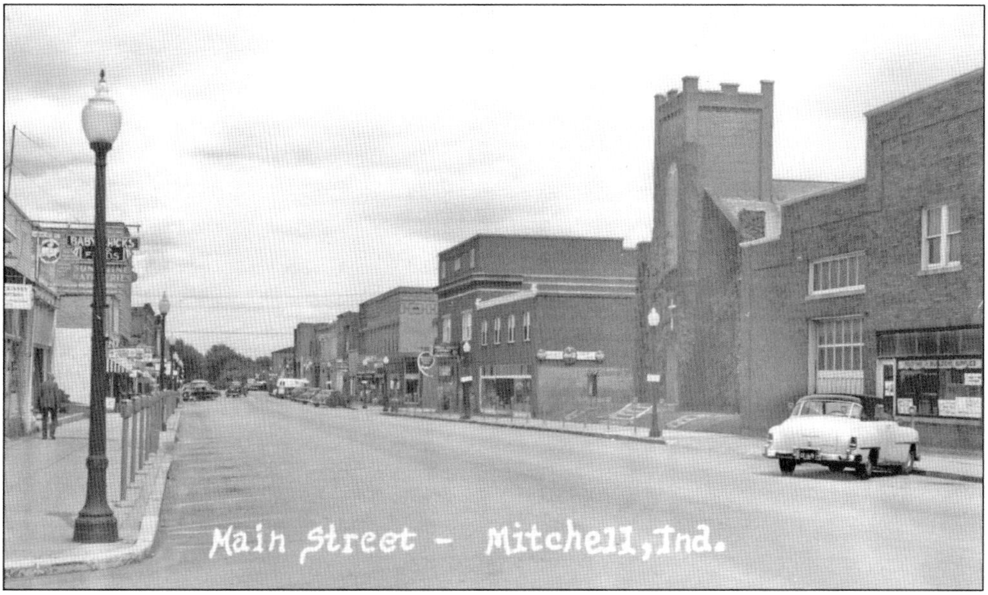

This image shows a peaceful Main Street in Mitchell, Indiana. The Lawrence County town was formed in the mid-19th century as a railroad town. Gus Grissom, the second American in space, was born here. Grissom flew on *Liberty Bell 7* and *Gemini 3*, and he died in a launch-pad fire at Kennedy Space Center in 1967. A memorial in his honor is located in nearby Spring Mill State Park. (Courtesy Russell Rein.)

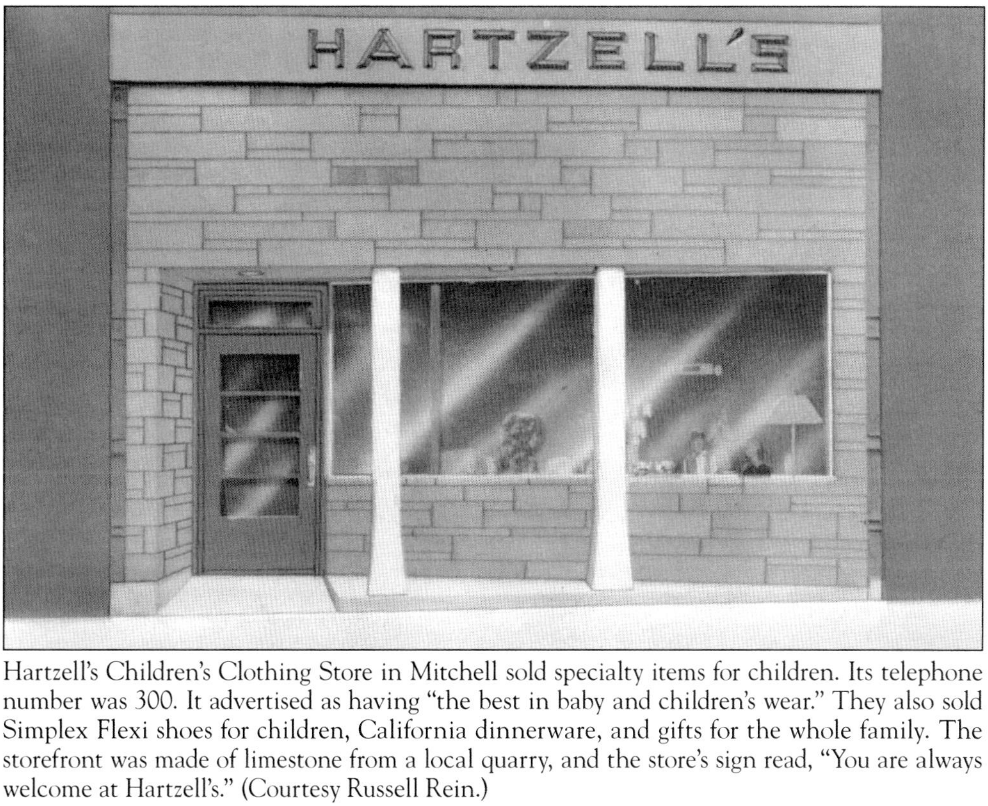

Hartzell's Children's Clothing Store in Mitchell sold specialty items for children. Its telephone number was 300. It advertised as having "the best in baby and children's wear." They also sold Simplex Flexi shoes for children, California dinnerware, and gifts for the whole family. The storefront was made of limestone from a local quarry, and the store's sign read, "You are always welcome at Hartzell's." (Courtesy Russell Rein.)

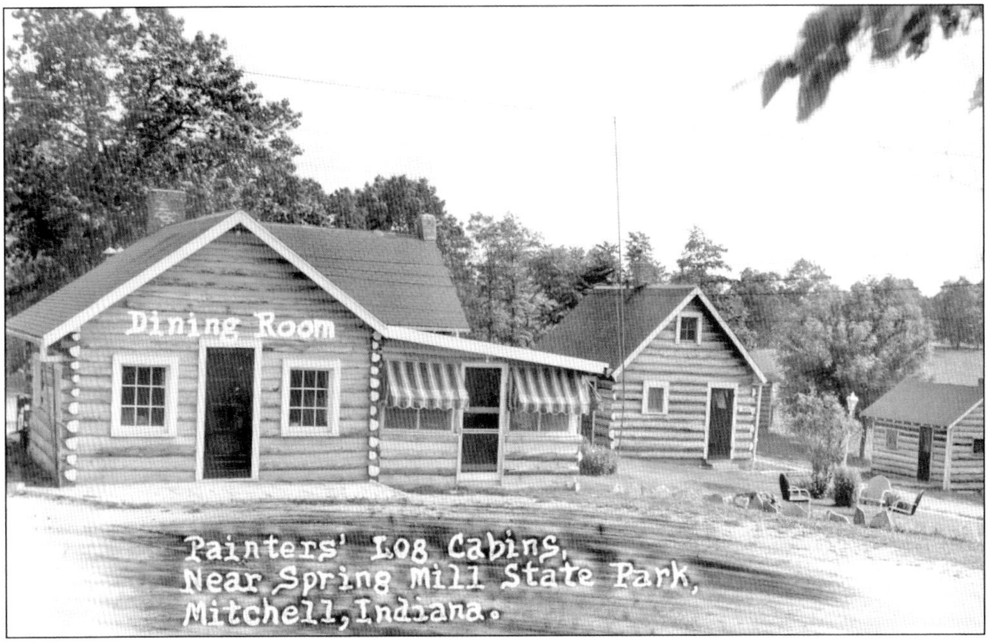

Painters' Log Cabins were a picturesque stop on the Dixie Highway near Mitchell. The business offered dining, well-lit walkways, and gathering spots for weary travelers seeking the quiet of the countryside. The Mitchell area drew many tourists on their way south, but local Spring Mill State Park was also a famous destination that featured the historic 19th-century Hamer Mill and Hamer Cemetery. (Courtesy Russell Rein.)

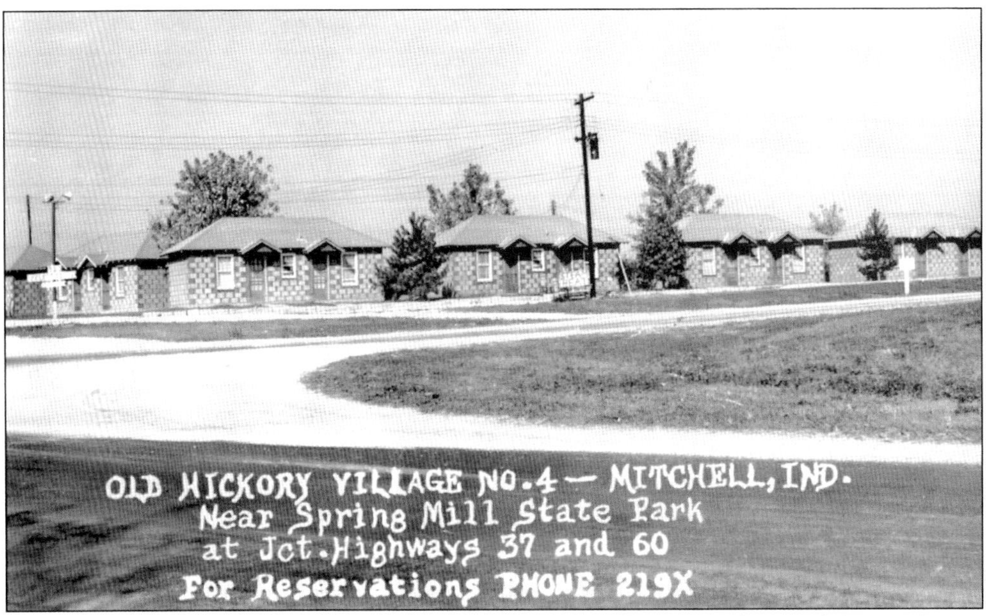

The Old Hickory Village No. 4 was located at the junction of State Roads 37 and 60 near Spring Mill State Park. The Old Hickory Village tourist camps were part of the franchise. (Courtesy Russell Rein.)

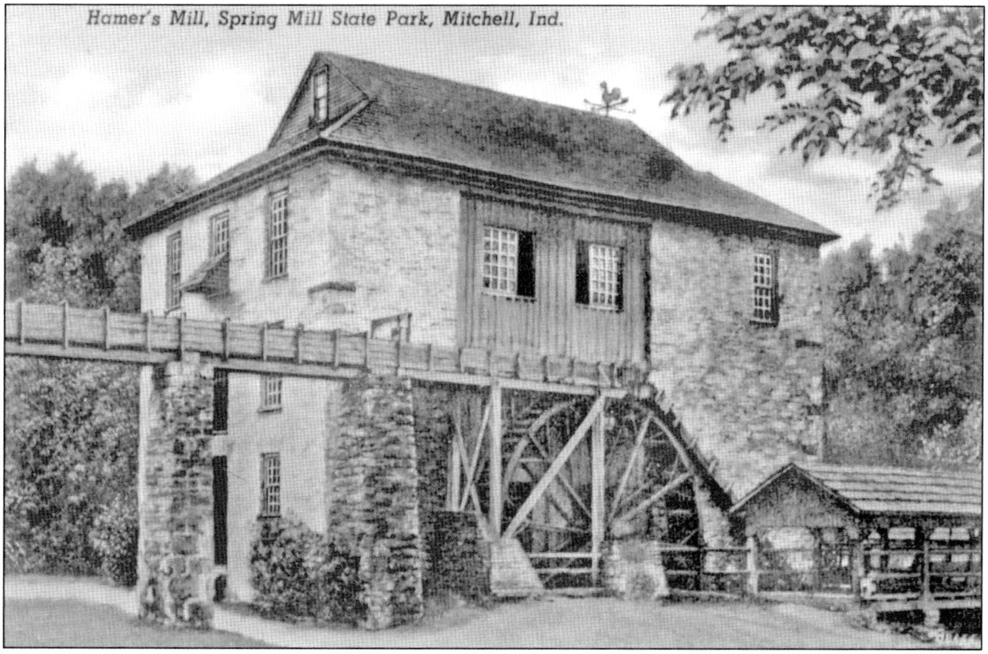

The historic water-powered grain mill and sawmill known as the Hamer Mill is located in Spring Mill State Park east of Mitchell, Indiana. Today, the park offers lodging at its inn, exhibits at the Virgil I. "Gus" Grissom Memorial Museum, dining, picnic areas, a pioneer village, the gristmill and sawmill, mountain bike rentals and trails, fishing and swimming, cave tours, camping, hiking, and a nature center. (Courtesy Jan Shupert-Arick.)

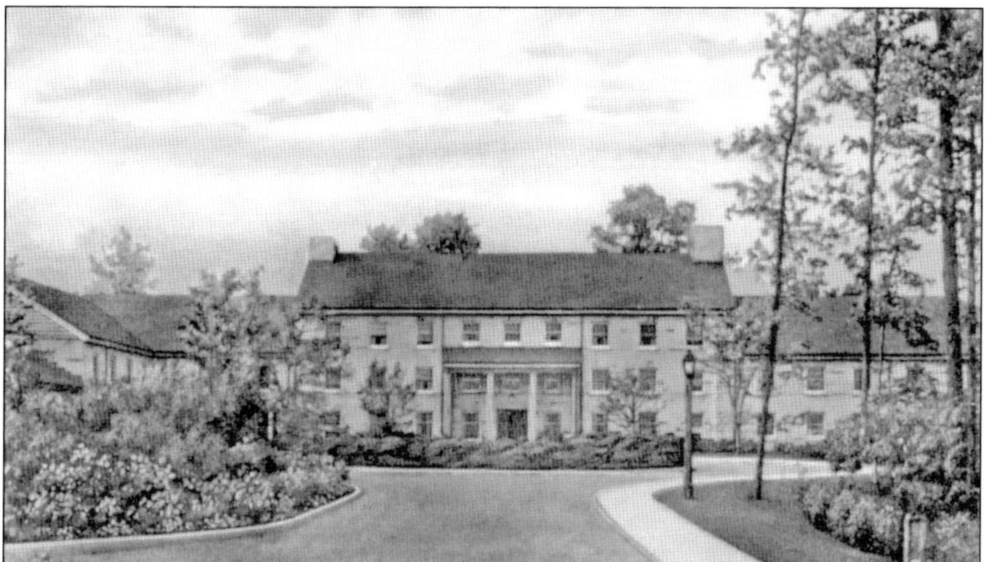

Spring Mill State Park and the Spring Mill Inn have long served as a destination off the Dixie Highway on State Road 60 just east of Mitchell, Indiana. (Courtesy Jan Shupert-Arick.)

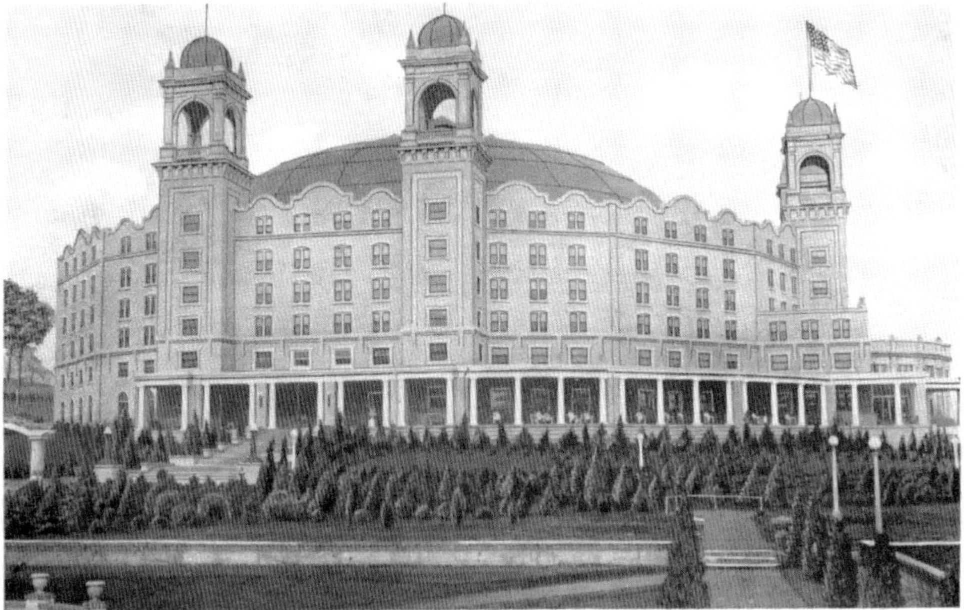

FRONT VIEW OF WEST BADEN SPRINGS HOTEL, WEST BADEN, IND. 86773

The West Baden Hotel (above) and French Lick Resort (below) are located west of Paoli off US Route 150. One of the earliest outposts in the Midwestern wilderness and first settled more than 200 years ago by French traders, rich mineral springs attracted animals to lick the waters and wet rocks and the valley became known as the Lick. In 1832, Dr. William Bowles opened the first French Lick Springs Hotel, a ramshackle, three-story frame building. It was a success. People flocked to partake of the so-called miracle waters. In 1901, the property was purchased by the French Lick Springs Hotel Company, headed by Thomas Taggart, an Irish immigrant and the mayor of Indianapolis. Under Taggart's rule, French Lick Springs gained international prominence. He modernized the resort and began bottling Pluto Water. French Lick Springs became equally known for its resort and casino facilities. Taggart served as a director of the Indiana Dixie Highway Association. (Both, courtesy Russell Rein.)

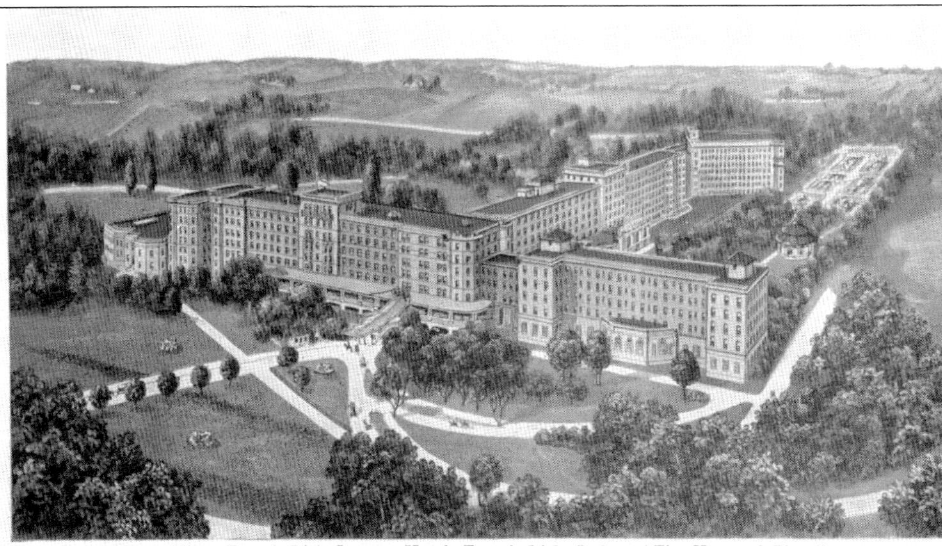

Bird's-eye View, French Lick Springs Hotel, French Lick, Ind. "The Home of Pluto"

Eight

On to the Ohio River
Orleans, Paoli, and New Albany

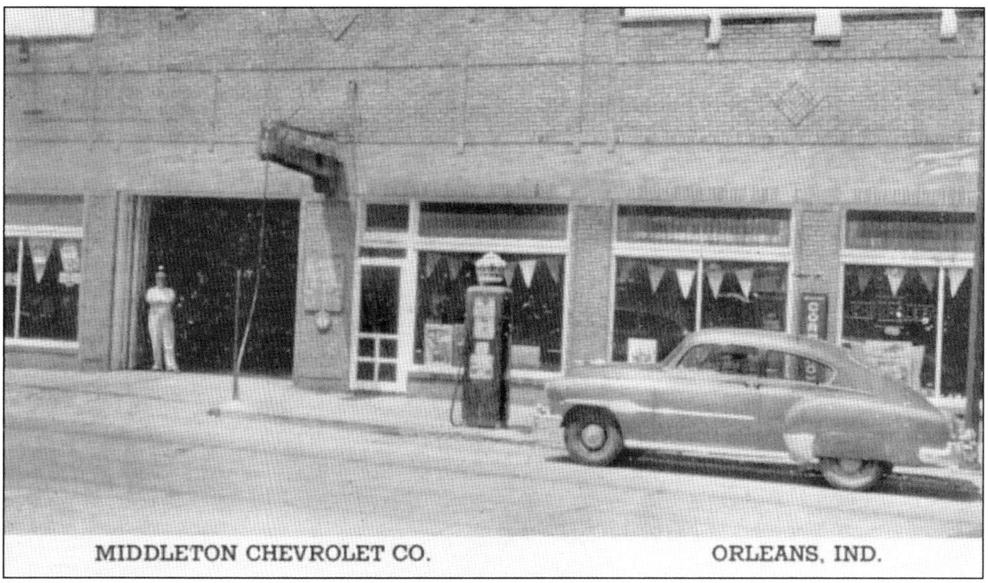

This photograph shows the Orleans Middleton Chevrolet Company with a 1949 two-door Chevy coupe parked in front with a Royal Crown gas pump at the curb. Located in Orange County, Orleans was platted in 1815 and is the oldest town in the county. Founded two months after Andrew Jackson's victory over the British at New Orleans, the settlers named their new town to honor this event. Local residents planted dogwood trees along the Dixie Highway through Orleans, which is now the dogwood capital of the Indiana. (Courtesy Russell Rein.)

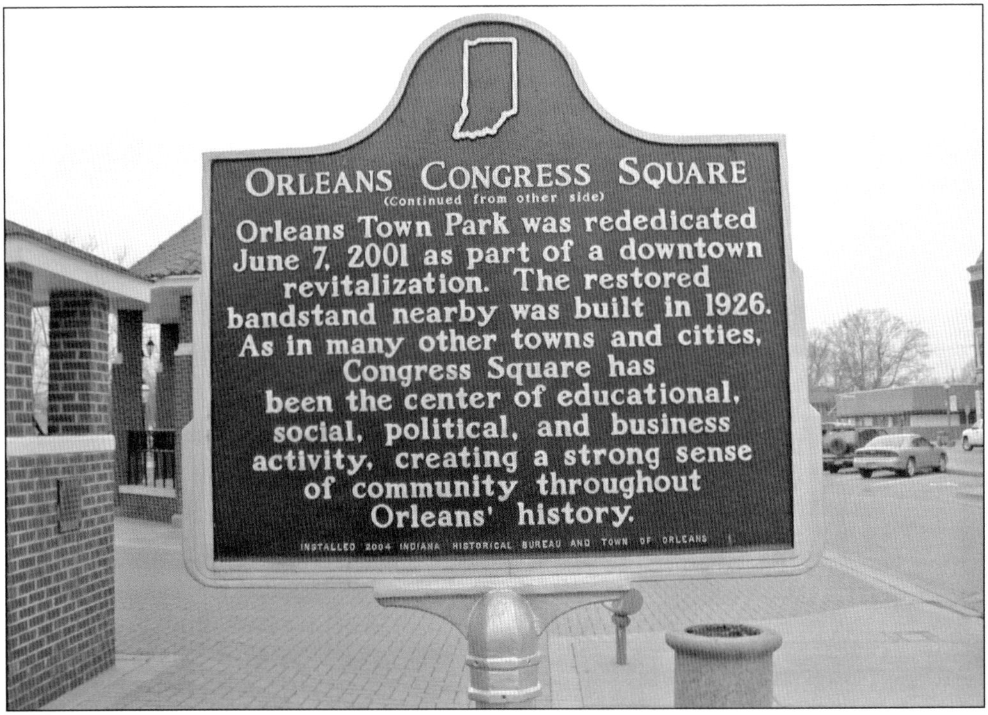

This Indiana Historical Bureau marker was placed at the Orleans Congress Square to mark the restoration of the community's bandstand that was built in 1926. (Courtesy Jan Shupert-Arick.)

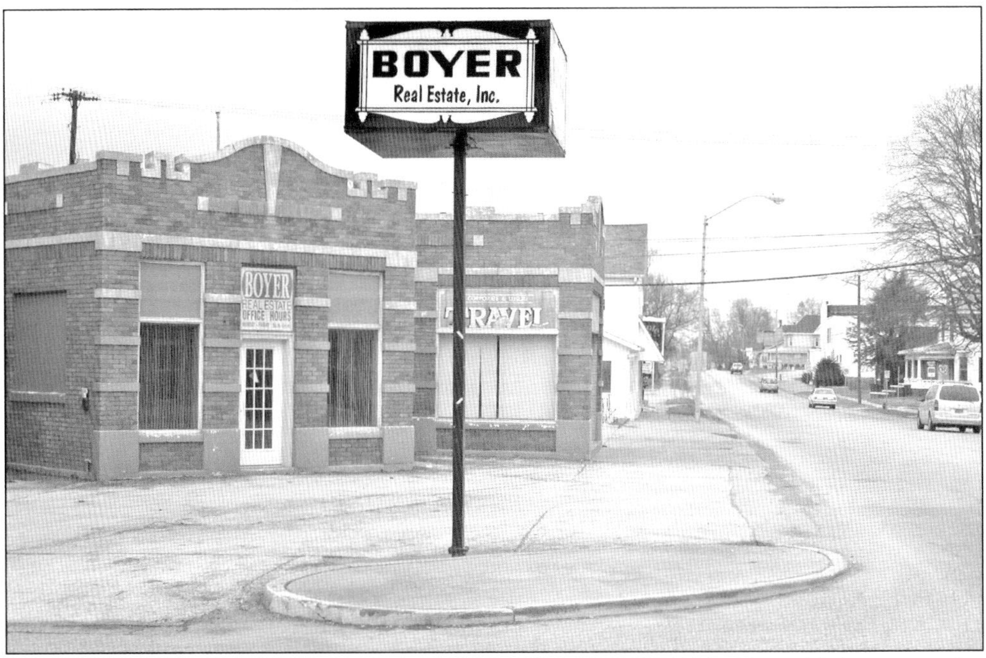

Boyer Real Estate at 141 North Maple Street in Orleans stands on the Dixie Highway corridor running through Main Street and past the town square. The real estate business is located in a former gas station building constructed on an angle to provide easy access to gas pumps from either street. (Courtesy Jan Shupert-Arick.)

LOUISVILLE, IND., TO PAOLI, IND., 47.3 MILES
State Highway No. 5.

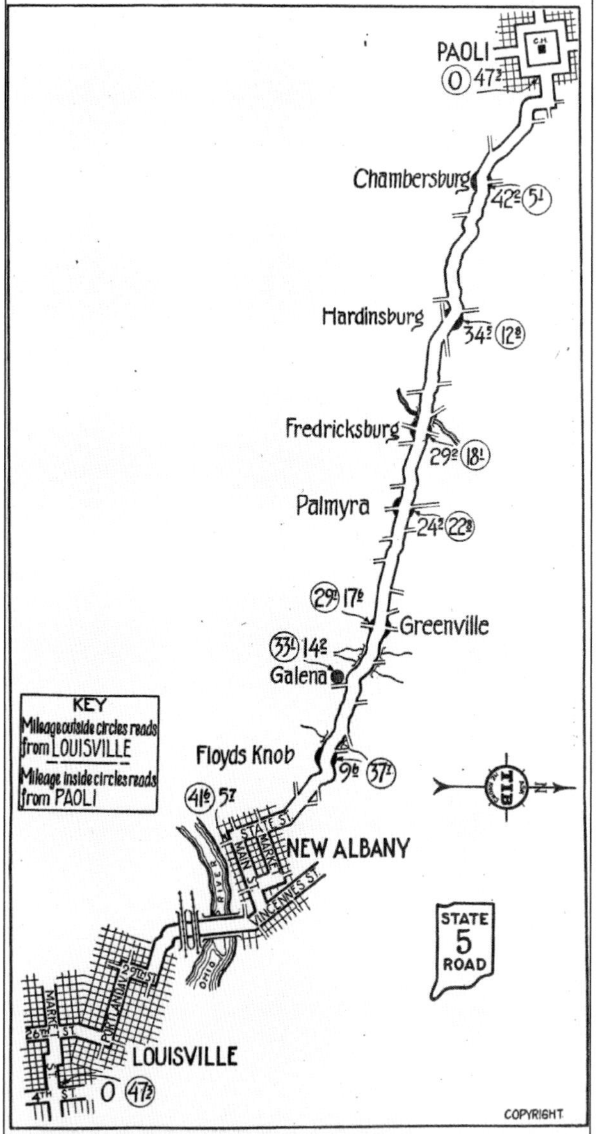

DESCRIPTION: This road is about 50 per cent paved with balance good gravel. Very good road. Louisville is the principal town in Kentucky and is famed for its derby which is held every year in May. This route is part of State Highway No. 5 from Louisville to Vincennes although the section between Paoli and Shoals is not completed and it is necessary to go north to Mitchell thence west to Vincennes. For connecting routes see index map in front of book.

This Dixie Highway strip map from Paoli to New Albany was published in the TIB Automobile Route Books in the early 1920s. The map shows State Road 5 (the Dixie Highway) from Paoli to New Albany. Along this route, travelers would pass through Chambersburg, Hardinsburg, Fredericksburg, Palmyra, Greenville, Galena, and Floyd's Knob. (Courtesy Russell Rein.)

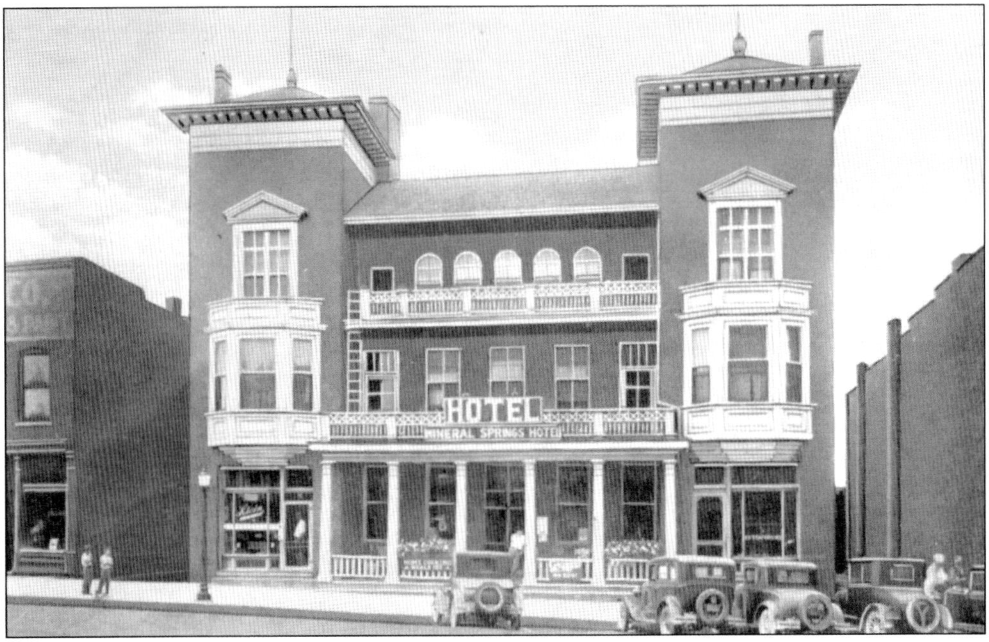

The Mineral Springs Hotel opened in 1896 and still stands on the public square in Paoli. The facade remains nearly the same as when it was built. The King Tailor Shop was located on the main level. The hotel competed with mineral spas in French Lick, West Baden, and Martinsville. Today, a ghost sign under the twin tower spells "HOTEL." (Courtesy Russell Rein.)

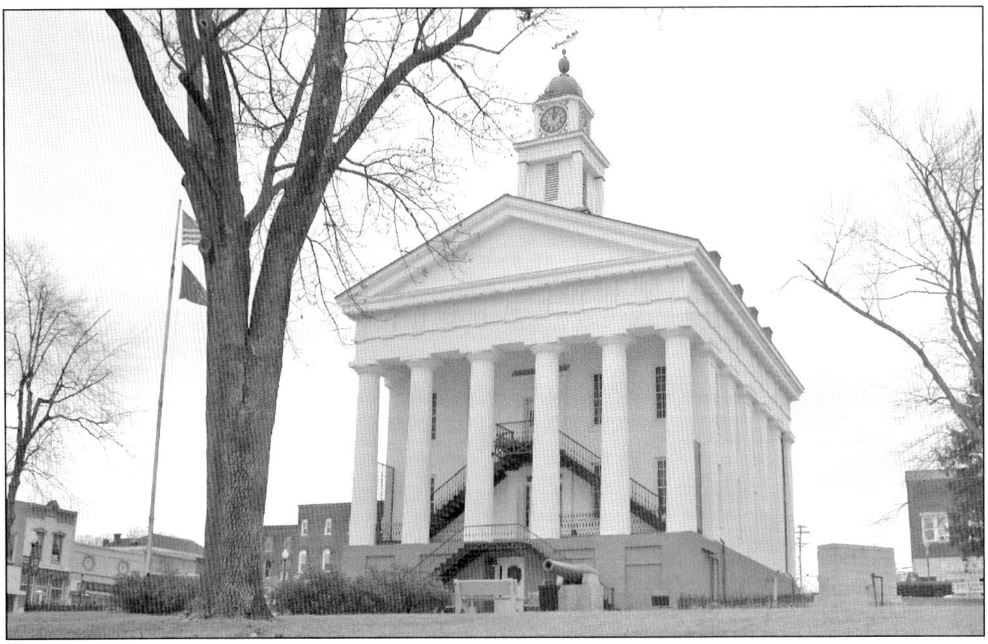

The Orange County Courthouse was built in Paoli between 1848 and 1850—one of the oldest in Indiana still serving as a seat of government; the courtroom ceiling is 26 feet high. The Greek Revival–style building stands on the square at the intersection of State Roads 37 and 156. The building was listed in the National Register of Historic Places in 1976, and its restoration was celebrated in 2009. (Courtesy Jan Shupert-Arick.)

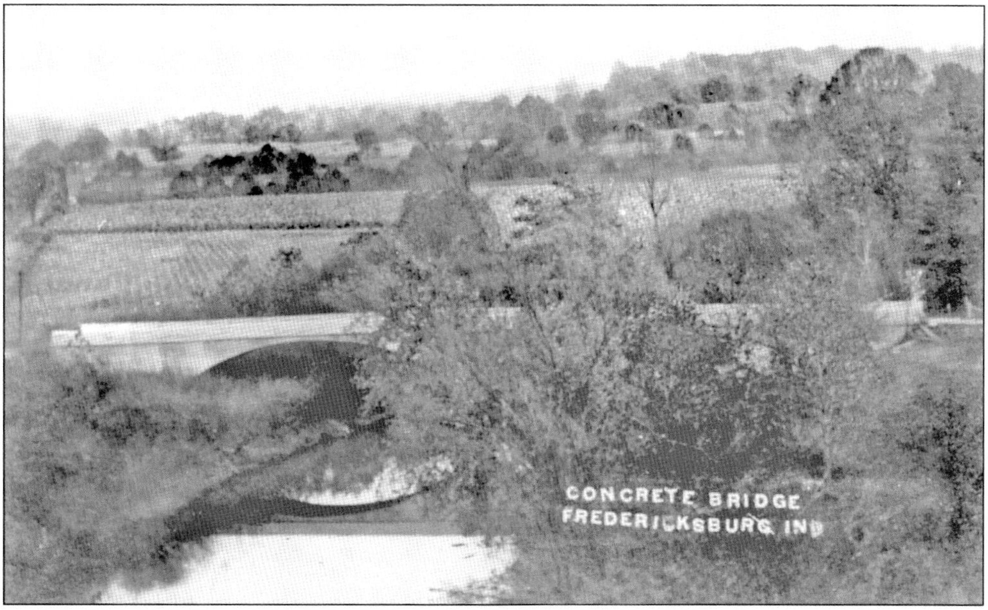

The Blue River Bridge, a concrete span near Fredericksburg, was 26 miles northwest of Louisville on the Paoli Pike Road (the Dixie Highway). Fruit orchards and farm fields lined this stretch of the road. (Courtesy Russell Rein.)

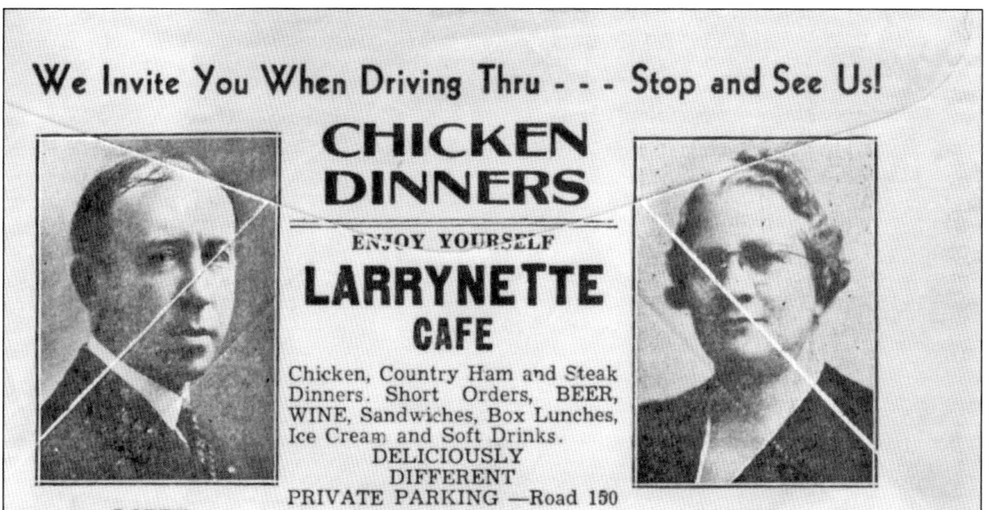

The Larrynette Café printed this advertisement on the backs of their business envelopes. (Courtesy Russell Rein.)

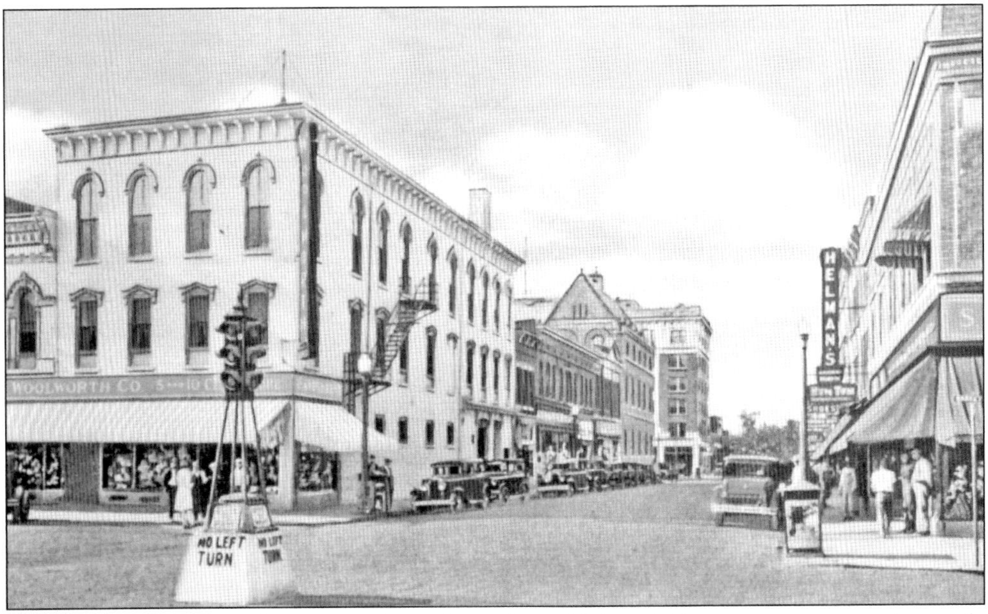

This 1920s image of Pearl Street in New Albany shows Helman's Department Store and an early electric traffic light in the center of the intersection. New Albany is located in Floyd County. The county courthouse was built of Bedford Oolitic Limestone quarried at Bedford. (Courtesy Russell Rein.)

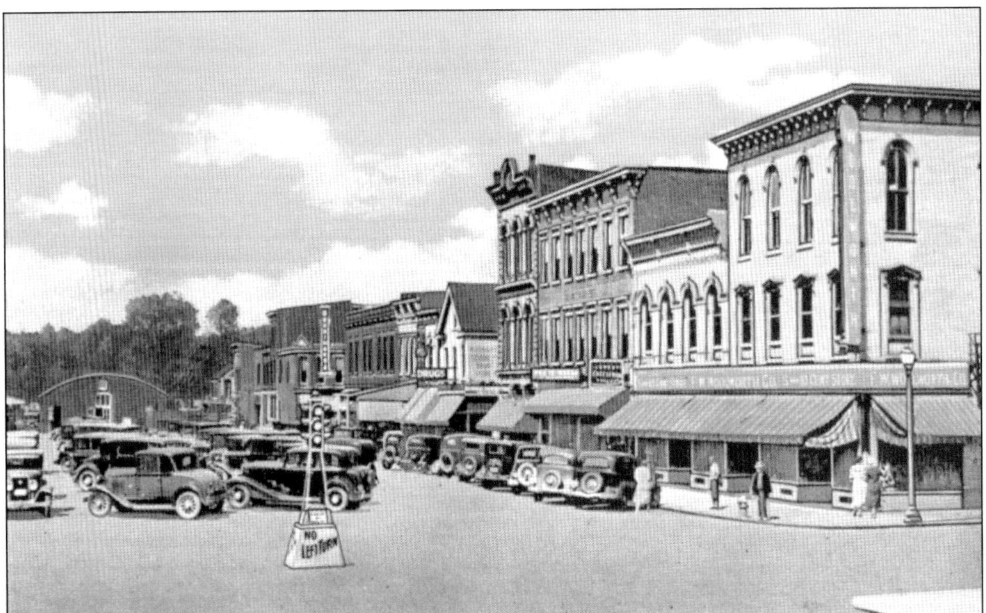

Woolworth's Plaza in New Albany was a popular shopping area in the 1920s and 1930s. The F.W. Woolworth building is included in the modern New Albany Historic District. The three-story Italianate building displayed merchandise in storefront windows and had colorful fabric awnings that attracted customers. (Courtesy Russell Rein.)

Best's Motel and Tourist Home in New Albany consisted of a 1920s-style home and a new two-story motel building, both constructed of redbrick. The motel's doorways were painted bright green. Located at 1939 State Street on US Route 150 just north of the city limits, the business offered 13 units with combination shower-baths, central forced heat, television, and fans. A neon sign in the front lawn promoted the business to travelers. (Courtesy Russell Rein.)

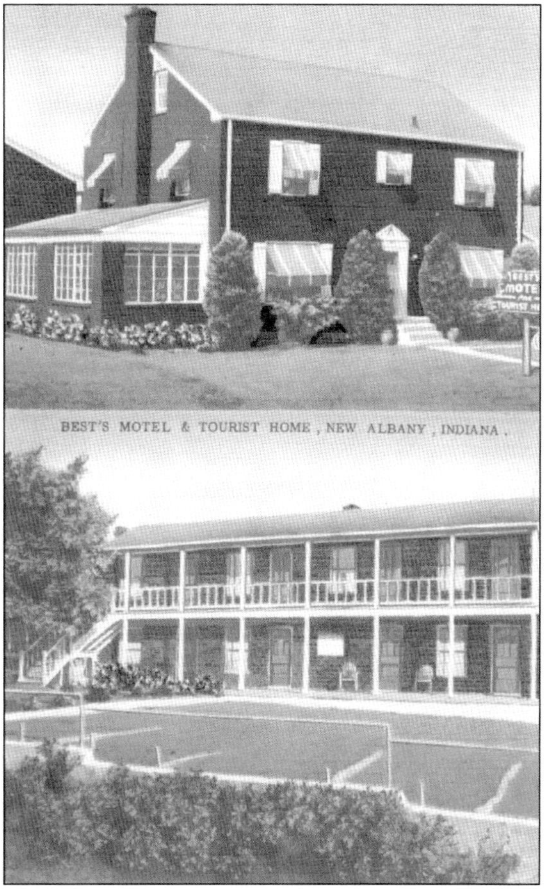

A lighted sign hangs on the corner of the historic Italianate-style New Albany Inn in the early 1960s. Traveling on the Dixie Highway, it is approximately 290 miles from the Michigan-Indiana line to New Albany. The trip is divided almost equally on either side of Indianapolis. (Courtesy Russell Rein.)

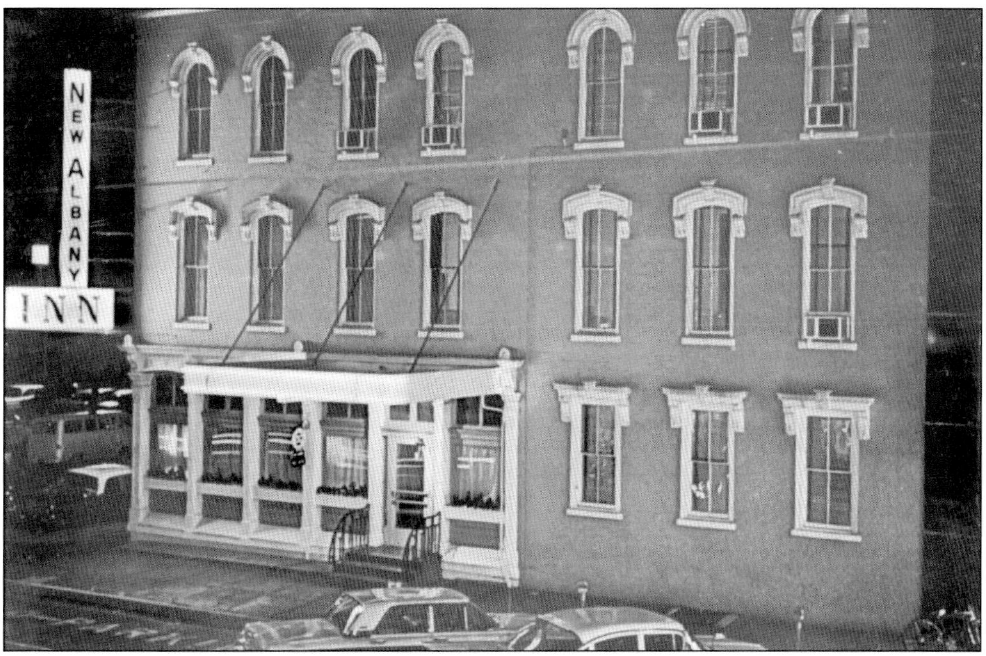

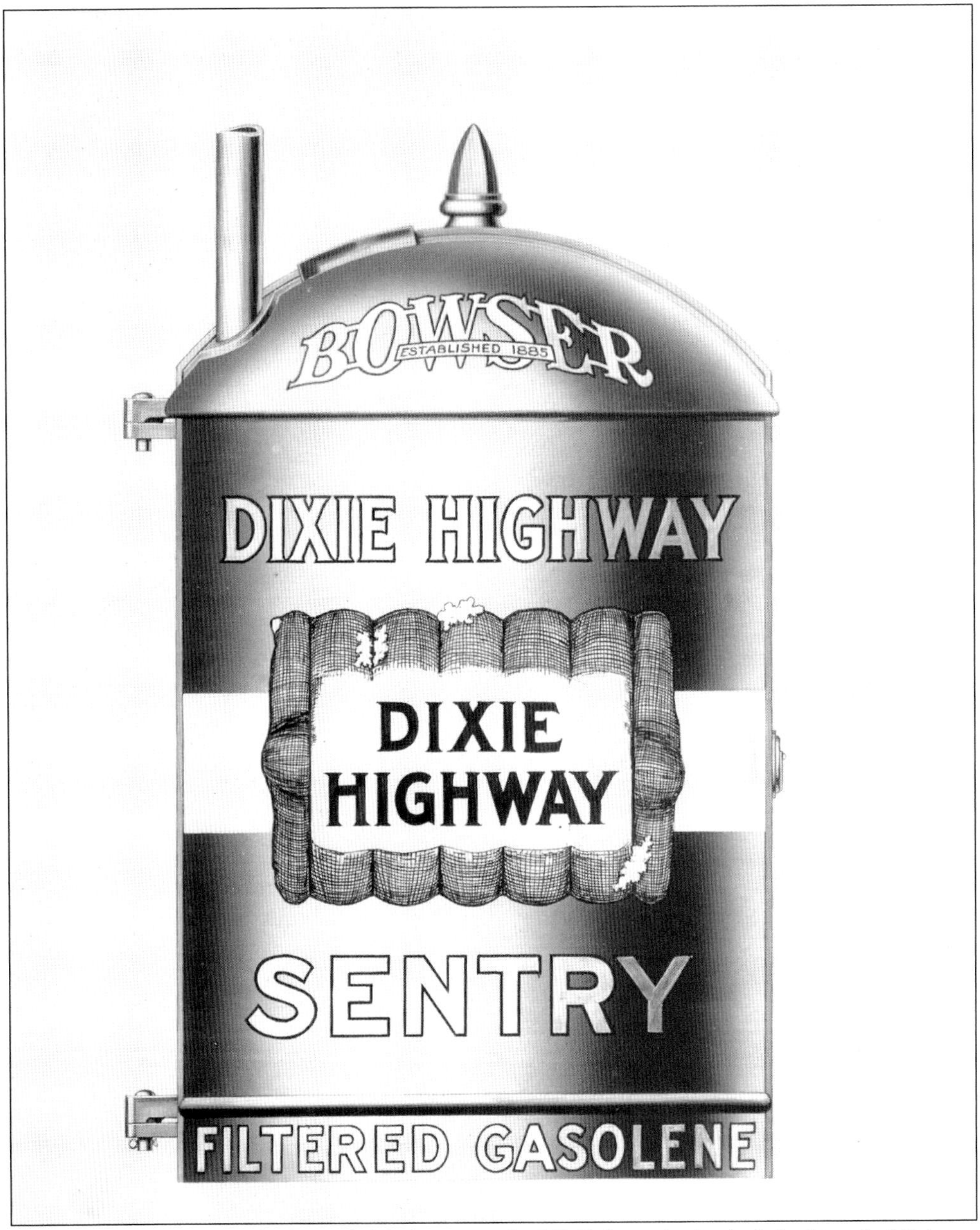

The Dixie Highway was the brainchild of Hoosier Carl G. Fisher, who backed the Lincoln Highway and the Indianapolis Motor Speedway. The Dixie stretched as far north as Ontario, Canada, and reached as far south as Florida City, Florida, which was south of Miami. S.F. Bowser and Company, located in Fort Wayne, Indiana, sold stylized gas pumps to gas stations along the Dixie and Lincoln Highways. This pump was designed with the original Dixie Highway logo that depicts a bale of cotton. Tourists followed the signs along the route that opened up the South to tourists from the North. The retirees who left the north for warmer winter climates such as Miami Beach became known as snowbirds, and their seasonal migration continues today. (Courtesy Allen County-Fort Wayne Historical Society.)

INDEX